Louise Pound

THE 19TH CENTURY ICONOCLAST
WHO FOREVER CHANGED
AMERICA'S VIEWS ABOUT
WOMEN, ACADEMICS AND SPORTS

Louise Pound
(circa 1891)

Louise Pound

The 19th Century Iconoclast
Who Forever Changed
America's Views About
Women, Academics and Sports

By Marie Krohn

ISBN-10: 09796896-2-7
ISBN-13: 978-09796896-2-8

Library of Congress Cataloging in Publication Data
Krohn, Marie, 1938-
Louise Pound : the 19th century iconoclast who forever changed America's views on women, academics, and sports / Marie Krohn.
p. cm.
Includes bibliographical references and index.
ISBN 978-0-9796896-2-8 (trade paper)
1. Pound, Louise, 1872-1958. 2. College teachers--Nebraska--Biography. 3. Athletes--Nebraska--Biography. 4. Women athletes--Nebraska--Biography. 5. Folklorists--United States--Biography. 6. Women's rights--United States. 7. Nebraska--Biography. I. Title.
CT275.P7525K76 2007
978.2'01092--dc22
[B]
2007029200

Questions regarding content of this book should be addressed to:
American Legacy Historical Press, Clearfield, Utah
A Division of American Legacy Media

Printed in the United States of America

To Alison and Kristin

Contents

By Robert Cochran

LOUISE POUND HAS waited nearly half a century, since her death in 1958, for the appearance of her first substantial biography. But now it's here, and it is most welcome.

Marie Krohn, retired from teaching school herself (an experience which no doubt made her more capable of empathy with Pound's lifelong commitment to teaching) and determined to make herself anew as a free-lance journalist, was initially inspired to focus on Pound by a family connection. For seven years she worked, reading and writing. The reading included Louise Pound's two University of Nebraska Press books, but Krohn concentrated her research most of all in the large collection of Pound's papers at the Nebraska State Historical Society and the University of Nebraska.

Prior to this period of intensive research, Krohn was already pursuing what she calls her "writing apprenticeship"—enrolling regularly in summer workshops at the University of Iowa. In 2000, preparing for a workshop devoted specifically to "Writing Lives," she connected her interest in family history and ties to Nebraska to Louise Pound—her husband had attended the University in Lincoln, and when their younger daughter followed in his footsteps she was assigned a room in Cather-Pound Hall.

Further inspired by Anne Cognard's 1984 essay, "Louise Pound: Renaissance Woman," Krohn set diligently to work. The result is *Louise Pound: The 19th Century Iconoclast Who Forever Changed America's Views About Women, Academics and Sports*. That's a mouthful of a title, and Krohn's initial preference for the much shorter and more lyric The Flame of Learning: The Life of Louise Pound is understandable. But the replacement has the compensating virtue of indicating right from the beginning the central concerns of her study. In labeling Pound an "iconoclast," and backing up the assertion with careful attention to (among other things) the surprising "oration" she delivered at her 1892 graduation ceremonies, a piece Pound titled "The Apotheosis of the Common," Krohn focuses upon one of several paradoxes in Pound's makeup.

For Louise Pound was both a staunch conservative and almost a radical, an unapologetic elitist (even a snob) and a thoroughgoing egalitarian, a renowned humanities scholar who recognized in herself a fundamental attraction to the observational and taxonomical emphases of the sciences. If she worked all her life for causes that would today be recognized as feminist, if the Title IX legislation that created greatly enlarged opportunities for women in intercollegiate athletics would have been music to her ears, something she was already advocating in 1900, she was also (and at the same time) a fervent admirer and defender of attitudes deprecated even in her own day as "Victorian." She was to the manor born, insofar as the manor existed in Lincoln, Nebraska in the 1870s, but she ends up championing the academic respectability of studying various dialects, argots, and slangs customarily viewed with horror and distaste by those trained to "correct" standards.

Krohn's work will be especially appreciated for its careful attention to Pound's family background. Stephen B. Pound and Laura Biddlecome Pound, as the title of Krohn's first section—"The Pounds of Lincoln: An Unconventional Pioneer Family"—makes clear, were spectacularly gifted parents. If their coming to Nebraska in the 1860s demonstrated both ambition and fortitude, they raised their three children (Louise as the middle child) with a strikingly fervent commitment to education. Krohn's chronicle of the parents themselves, as well as their innovative educational methods, is one of the highlights of her study. She also has a very strong sense of the road not taken in Pound's career, of conscious, deliberate choices that steered her away from music, art, and fiction and into the world of teaching and scholarship. Krohn's detailed attention to Pound's youthful achievements in all three areas—she received a diploma in music, published fiction, and made a number of still-extant drawings—highlights by contrast her decision for an academic career. Krohn's sense of significant parallels in both the attitudes and career paths of the Pound children is another strength—all three became teachers; Louise and her younger sister Olivia devoted themselves to advancing opportunities for women.

I am especially pleased to note in Krohn's study a finely articulated appreciation of Pound's long friendship with Ani Königsberger. For at least two decades now, scholars interested not in Pound but in Willa Cather have turned again and again to their undergraduate relationship, infatuated and passionate on Cather's part, decidedly cooler on Pound's. They've been barking, all this time, up the wrong tree. Pound and Königsberger met in Heidelberg in 1899, while Pound was in Germany studying for her Ph.D. In less than a year, they formed a friendship that lasted the rest of their lives, and Krohn's study, based on a careful reading of Königsberger's many letters, makes its importance clear. If her sister Olivia, with whom she shared their childhood home for more than fifty years, was clearly Pound's closest companion, Ani Königsberger, no less clearly, was her most intimate and most enduring friend.

Biography is a strange endeavor—an attempt to make a person who started as a stranger come alive as a coherent personality upon a page. Marie Krohn and I, unknown to each other and approaching by very different paths, spent the early years of the 21st century immersed in the life and work of Louise Pound. My own study was complete and submitted to the University of Nebraska Press before I knew of hers; hers was likewise finished before she learned of mine. They are in some ways very different books—I am a folklorist and scholar with no family connection to the Pounds or to Nebraska. No child of mine has yet enrolled in Lincoln. Pound's role in the study of folksongs in America, her leadership in the struggle to promote and encourage the study of American English in universities—these get more sustained attention in my study, just as the family history of the Pounds and the Lincoln life of Louise and Olivia are more fully described in Krohn's. Louise Pound was a complex woman who was many things to many people. Her story is big enough for both of us.

Let me close by saying that I understand Marie Krohn's invitation to write this "Foreword" as an act of generosity—I've already asked the editors at Nebraska to allow my biography to be updated by inclusion of a brief account of hers. On the other hand, I was in many ways the best prepared reader of her book, just as she will be (with Robert Knoll, historian of the University of Nebraska and former student of Louise Pound) the most knowing reader of mine. We are, by the parallel enterprise we each entered alone, secret sharers, possessors of a common ground. Louise Pound captured both of us, and I am grateful to be one of the first to enjoy Krohn's work. I am sure there will be many others.

Robert Cochran Ph. D.
University of Arkansas

Preface

DURING MY RESEARCH of Louise Pound's life, I wondered why no one had written her biography. Many articles about this exceptional woman appeared in past issues of Lincoln, Nebraska, newspapers and in scholarly journals. Summaries of her life were included in biographical dictionaries, but an official biography had never been published.

The articles and profiles referred to Louise Pound as a "Renaissance Woman" and a scholar of "eclectic" interests. She also was "enigmatic" and "brilliant," yet she possessed common sense and had a practical nature. She was a complex and fascinating woman, but the scarcity of her personal letters, and her refusal to keep a journal or write her memoir cloaked the real Louise Pound in mystery. Nevertheless, I decided to piece together a picture of Louise from the letters that others wrote to her, from her writings, and from the many articles written about her.

When weaving together the fabric of Louise Pound's life, I listened to music-usually recordings of pianists playing Bach or jazz, and the music reminded me that Louise Pound might have become a concert pianist. In 1892 she earned a Bachelor of Letters degree and a degree in Piano from the University of Nebraska.

I also discovered her sketch book in a box of her papers and wondered if she had possessed the talent to become an artist of Mary Cassatt's caliber. She wrote a story that was published in a University of Nebraska literary journal, and she might have written fiction equal to that of her friends, Dorothy Canfield Fisher, Willa Cather, and Mari Sandoz, but she chose a more structured career path.

In addition to these accomplishments, all publications featuring Louise mention her phenomenal athletic ability. Louise might have won Olympic medals after the games began in 1896. Fortunately for her future pupils, she directed her tremendous drive and energy to teaching and research, although she always gave her best whether on the playing field or in the classroom.

Those who studied under her direction remember Louise Pound as a great person as well as a great teacher. Her graduate students, especially, treasured her guidance and friendship. She encouraged them to stay in touch with her and with each other after they earned their degrees, and those who did referred to themselves as the "Louise Pound Alumni Association." B.A. Botkin wrote that "the devotion and loyalty of the Louise Pound Alumni Association meant more to Louise than all her academic achievements and accolades."

I first noticed the Pound family name in a booklet, "The Kester Family," which traced the genealogy of my father's ancestors. One of the sources listed was a book published in 1906 titled, *The Pound and Kester Families*. The author, John Hunt, stated that his incentive for writing the book was the close and novel union between the Pound and Kester families. Hunt was intrigued by the fact that in the 1700s three Kester brothers married three Pound sisters.

When I was researching my father's ancestors, my husband and I were living in Illinois, our home for 28 years. We had raised our two daughters in Rockford, but we always maintained close ties with our families in Neligh, Nebraska. Our youngest daughter, Kristin, attended the University of Nebraska, her father's alma mater, and she was assigned a dormitory room in Cather-Pound Hall.

I knew the reason the dormitory bore Cather's name and had read in Cather biographies about the friendship that briefly existed between Willa Cather and Louise Pound when they were University of Nebraska students. Seeing the name, Pound, on my daughter's dormitory reminded me of reading about the Kester and Pound family association, and I became curious about Louise Pound.

My desire to learn more about Louise increased after Kristin, an English major, loaned me a textbook, *Perspectives: Women in Nebraska History*, containing an article by Anne Cognard, "Louise Pound: Renaissance Woman." Cognard maintained that Pound's personality was evident from her eclectic choice of subject-matter and her writing style. Reading that piece and another article, "Louise Pound," in Donald R. Hickey's book, *Nebraska Moments: Glimpses of Nebraska's Past,* gave Louise Pound a permanent place in my mind, but the profiles didn't satisfy my growing interest in her life.

At the time I began researching family history, I had resigned from teaching middle school English to concentrate on my writing apprenticeship. As often as possible, I attended summer workshops at the University of Iowa. For the July 2000 workshop, "Writing Lives," I needed a subject to research. That's when my associations with Louise Pound connected, and I began reading Pound family papers located in the University of Nebraska's archival library and in the Nebraska State Historical Society Archives. I also bought and read two books that Louise had written.

After reading Louise Pound's *Selected Writings,* and *Nebraska Folklore,* I agreed with Anne Cognard's assessment of Pound's writing as "eminently readable." Her strong prose held my attention. In sentences of reasonable length and understandable words, Louise Pound educated her readers. Using a direct and objective approach, she also presented her material in a broad rather than a narrow historical context. This was a writing style that I respected, one that was ahead of its time.

As an English professor at the University of Nebraska for over fifty years, Louise passed to her students the flame of learning that her parents, Laura and Stephen Pound, had given her. I agreed with Botkin's statement in "First Lady of Letters" that Laura and Stephen Pound also "instilled in their children a way of life that stressed integrity, truth, service, and sociability." Roscoe, Louise, and Olivia passed those values, along with a respect for learning, on to their pupils and reflected them in their personal friendships and professional relationships.

Prologue

Although Louise Pound was a popular speaker at Folklore Festivals, she experienced her "most embarrassing moment" at a 1936 meeting of the American Folk Festival Society held in Dallas Texas. Recalling the event during an interview with *Omaha World-Herald* reporter, Evelyn Simpson, Louise admitted that she had made false assumptions about her audience when preparing a paper to read before the Texas group.

She accepted the invitation to speak at the folklore meeting instead of attending Heidelberg University's 550th anniversary celebration. The University invited her because she had taken her doctorate at Heidelberg in 1900, and officials considered her a "distinguished foreign scholar." But the unstable German political situation caused Louise to send the officials her regrets, and she attended the folklore festival instead.

Since she would be speaking before a Texas folklore group for the second time, Louise relied on her first experience when choosing her topic. She prepared a speech for an audience "who would look for a fairly learned, fairly popular lecture." Assuming that such a group would expect her to appear well-dressed, Louise bought a wide-brimmed picture hat and a white silk suit for the occasion.

When the hour of her speech arrived, Louise was so confident of her listeners' interests that she marched to the lectern without looking at the audience. After arranging her material on the podium, she gave the room an appraising glance and was shocked to see only a few white faces. A tribe of Cherokee Indians, wrapped in blankets and holding papooses in their laps, along with African Americans had been invited to attend the festival. As the audience gazed solemnly at Louise, she realized that her picture hat and white silk suit were out-of-place and that the paper she planned to read would be meaningless for the listeners.

Scanning the sea of red and brown faces again, she recognized Jean Thomas of Ashland, Kentucky, and called her to speak. Thomas, an author, lecturer, and folk festival promoter was used to speaking to mixed racial groups. Her extemporaneous address pleased the audience and saved them from a boring experience. Louise's tactful handling of the Dallas episode reflected her integrity and practicality—qualities that she had absorbed from her parents' teaching and example.

PART ONE:
AN UNCONVENTIONAL PIONEER FAMILY
1869–1886

Chapter One

The Achievers

WHEN LOUISE POUND'S mother, Laura Biddlecombe, was a child, she preferred tramping through the woods on her father's farm over sitting indoors doing needlework. In her memoir, *My Childhood*, she wrote, "My sister was famous for her needlework and fancy knitting and crocheting, but I never did any more than was required of me."

Exploring the woods in rural New York was "a source of delight" for Laura. During one of her explorations she "found a pair of curious insects on a log . . . They were such awkward things and so nearly the color of the wood that I stopped to see if they were really alive. The other girls shrieked and cried, 'They're poisonous' and ran away." But Laura never forgot those insects and learned their identity 20 years later when her son, Roscoe, included them in his insect collection.

Laura's curiosity and love of adventure served her well after she married Stephen Pound. Writing about her wedding journey in "A Wedding Trip in February 1869," Laura recalled traveling from Rochester, New York, to Lincoln, Nebraska. On the Friday evening of the couple's arrival in Lincoln, she wondered how she looked. "The mud had spattered me all the way from Plattsmouth; I had eaten nothing since the 3:00 dinner at Nine-Mile-Grove, Thursday, and there had been no chance to mend my toilet."

When she and her husband reached their lodgings, she didn't stop to look at herself. After changing their muddy clothes they went to the large dining room. It was crowded because the legislature was in session. "I was surprised to find that I was the only woman there," Laura wrote. "I was too hungry, however, to permit this fact to spoil a good dinner for me."

A sense of adventure fueled by the pioneering spirit that characterized late nineteenth-century America inspired newly married Stephen and Laura Biddlecombe Pound to leave their families in upstate New York and build a new life on the frontier. After their wedding in February 1869, they boarded a train for Nebraska. Laura had always wanted to go West, and Stephen was looking for a town in which to establish a law practice. By 1877 they had settled in Lincoln and were the parents of three children: Roscoe (1870), Louise (1872), and Olivia (1874).

The Pounds differed from most Lincoln-area settlers, who tended farms or managed businesses. In addition to fulfilling legal duties, Stephen Pound helped Laura home-school their children. He read the classics to Roscoe, Louise, and Olivia and instructed them in Greek. Energetic Laura Pound not only taught her children, she also attended language and literature classes at the University and pursued her interest in botany.

Their unique lifestyle didn't harm the family's local reputation. In *The Life of Roscoe Pound*, Paul Sayre wrote that "Judge Pound's high character and social position as well as Mrs. Pound's unusual (intellectual) abilities were recognized and accepted." In spite of their home-schooling, Roscoe, Louise, and Olivia enjoyed an easy-going association with neighborhood playmates.

Isolated from their New York relatives, the Pound family resembled later-day nuclear families, who lived far from loved ones. Such families often formed a self-contained unit that fostered loyalty between parents and siblings. But the Pounds also welcomed like-minded Lincolnites into their home to share their appreciation of knowledge and culture. As Bernice Slote stated in *The Kingdom of Art*, educated families who settled in Lincoln "tried to keep life very much as it had been in Ohio, New York, Virginia, or Illinois."

In addition to educating their children, Stephen and Laura Pound contributed to Lincoln's growing reputation as the intellectual and cultural center of the state. Stephen Pound established a law practice in 1869 then left it for the post of probate judge in 1870. In 1872-73, he served in the Nebraska legislature and was a member of the 1875 constitutional convention. In 1876 he was elected district judge, a post he held for twelve years before returning to the practice of law. Laura Pound was instrumental in founding the Lincoln Public Library and was a charter member of the Women's Club and the Hayden Art Society which became the Nebraska Art Association.

Roscoe, Louise, and Olivia, became educators of influence. The reputations of Roscoe and Louise reached national and international levels, while Olivia achieved prominence on the local scene. Of the three, Louise was the most versatile. Born on June 30, 1872, her accomplishments reflected her parents' pioneering spirits. As an English professor at the University of Nebraska, she broke new ground in the study of American literature, speech, and folklore. A natural athlete, she ignored the physical constraints placed upon women during the Victorian era and competed against men in tennis. Making a name for herself in the male-dominated fields of sports and scholarship, Louise joined the ranks of the "New Women" who ignored gender restrictions.

The New Women emerged in the 1890s and sparked controversy throughout the 1920s. They came from both the working class and elite society. Shunning the home-centered roles of their mothers, they were sometimes aggressive in their quest for self-fulfillment through education and careers. Often, their chosen occupations invaded fields dominated by men.

They picked up tennis rackets, hopped on bicycles, and at the same time, changed their clothing style to accommodate their athletic pursuits. Rejecting corsets, petticoats, and frills, they donned shirtwaists (blouses) and long skirts which eased the acts of running across tennis courts and peddling bicycles.

As a typical New Woman, Louise won tennis and golf championships and bicycling medals. She excelled at ice-skating, held the Lincoln record for diving, displayed expertise in horse-riding, and, with a friend, introduced downhill skiing to Lincoln. In *Nebraska Moments: Glimpses of Nebraska's Past*, David Hickey praised Louise Pound's accomplishments. "Of all Nebraskans who have achieved excellence in a chosen field, the one who has probably done the most to advance the cause of women in academia and sports is Louise Pound."

As the middle child, separated by two years from Roscoe and Olivia, Louise competed with her older brother. Although she challenged him in sports and intellectual pursuits, their rivalry was friendly, and Roscoe allowed Louise to participate in the games that he and his pals organized. Because Olivia had a gentle disposition, she and Louise enjoyed a companionable relationship. During their University years they were known as "the sisters." Later, Louise was referred to as "Miss Pound," and Olivia was called "Miss Olivia."

Laura Pound encouraged the cooperative spirit between her children as she supervised their play and educated them at home. Her reasons for educating her children were based on her past experiences as a teacher in New York and a realistic understanding of her offsprings' intellect. After she and her husband settled in Lincoln, Laura taught in a local school. Observing the lack of supplies and the inadequate classroom, she decided to teach Roscoe, Louise, and Olivia herself.

Under the guidance of their mother during their formative years, the minds of the Pound children flourished like the prairie grasses and wild flowers near their Lincoln home. Laura Pound had the wisdom and courage to tailor the education of her children to fit their individual needs. Confident of her opinions and unafraid to act on them, Mrs. Pound inspired the same self-assurance in her children. She was a trend-setter, a New Woman before the term was coined.

Sayre wrote that Roscoe and Louise resembled their mother in their "aggressive thirst for knowledge as well as in their forthright determination to reach the truth of the matter for its own sake." Quiet-natured Olivia was similar to her father in character. Writing to Sayre, Roscoe stated that his father was deliberate, reserved, and self-contained and lacked the nervous energy that Roscoe inherited from his mother. "But he has a vast amount of quiet determination which my oldest sister (Louise) has inherited."

When choosing careers, the Pound children followed in their parents' footsteps. After earning a Ph.D. in botany, Roscoe entered the law profession. He served as dean of the University of Nebraska law school before leaving the state to teach at Northwestern and the University of Chicago. After three years in Illinois, he accepted a teaching offer at Harvard and eventually became dean of the law school. Roscoe had hesitated before deciding on law rather than botany, but Louise and Olivia didn't vacillate when choosing their careers. They followed their mother's example and became teachers.

Channeling their yen for adventure into scholastic avenues, the three Pound siblings challenged the status quo. As a practicing lawyer and a professor of law, Roscoe shocked the legal world by advocating a revision of existing laws to reflect social changes. Louise questioned the prevailing belief in the supremacy of British English over American English, and her common sense examples of individual ballad origins upset academic pundits who believed that ballads had communal beginnings. As dean of girls and assistant principal at Lincoln High School, Olivia developed a vocational counseling department for students and found homes for needy female pupils, often inviting them to share the Pound home while they completed their educations.

Performing a valuable service as family historian, Olivia corresponded with Paul Sayre (Roscoe Pound's biographer) giving glimpses of life in the Pound household. From her letters and essays readers learn of the children's daily routines and interests and gain insights into the personalities of Stephen and Laura Pound.

CHAPTER TWO

The Exceptional Parents

IN 1866, THREE years before he married Laura Biddlecombe, Stephen Pound had become part of the Westward migration that occurred during the restless years following the Civil War. Nebraska territory earned statehood in 1867, and Stephen chose to settle in Lancaster, a tiny place of a few dozen people. Before the century ended, Lancaster was renamed Lincoln and became the Nebraska state capital.

The turn-of-the century was an energetic era, and Victorian Americans believed in working and striving. The "Great West" offered an opportunity to struggle, to contend, and ultimately to fulfill one's dreams. Stephen Pound had already turned his back on farming to achieve his ambition of becoming a lawyer. He traveled to Nebraska territory to establish his law practice as well as to participate in settling and civilizing the frontier. When he married Laura Biddlecombe, he found an enthusiastic partner in his desire to take part in building a new city and state.

The first ancestor of Stephen Pound to immigrate to America was John Pound, a Quaker. He left his home in England and settled in New Jersey in 1663. Early in the nineteenth century, Hugh Pound, a fifth generation descendent of John Pound and the grandfather of Stephen Pound moved his family in a covered wagon to Farmington,

New York. They settled on land adjoining the farm of Joab Stafford Biddlecombe, the father of Laura Biddlecombe Pound.

In her memoir, Laura Pound recalled her future husband's grandfather: "Hugh Pound was a man of whom no one ever spoke an unkind word and was beloved and respected by all. He was a Hicksite Quaker." The Hicksite Quakers differed from the Orthodox Friends whose creed was strictly evangelical. In 1826 the Hicksite Friends—led by Elias Hicks—separated from the orthodox branch. Hicks emphasized the principle of the light within as did the Orthodox Friends, but he opposed the adoption of a set creed. In 1850, the orthodox branch made the following distinction: they were Friends, and the Hicksites were Quakers.

Hugh Pound's wife, Sarah King Pound, was clerk of the monthly meeting of the Farmington Quakers for many years. Both Hugh Pound and his wife were active in the anti-slave movement, Sayre stated, and their farm was an important station on the underground railroad as slaves made their way to Canada. When warning his family that slaves were on their property, Sayre reported Hugh Pound as saying, "I would that thee did not go into the barn tonight."

Nathan Pound, son of Hugh and Sarah, moved with his wife to a farm near Ontario, New York, where Stephen Bosworth Pound was born in 1833. Nathan Pound, in the words of his grandson, Roscoe, was a "dogmatic, obstinate man, quite inclined to be violent in his opinions." In spite of his forceful personality, Nathan Pound dealt realistically with his son, Stephen's, dislike of farming. His brothers claimed that whenever there was extra work to do, Stephen disappeared. Later, he would be found tucked away somewhere reading a book. Yielding to his son's thirst for learning, Nathan sent him to an academy in Macedon, New York, and then to Union College in Schenectady, New York, where Stephen graduated as Valedictorian of his class in 1859.

Roscoe wrote that his father was "one of the mildest and least violent of men—ordinarily." But on rare occasions he showed the dogmatism of his father, Nathan Pound. Stephen Pound was deliberate, reserved, and self-contained. Lacking this wife's nervous energy, Stephen worked at a comparatively slower pace. His father, Roscoe continued, was one of the most scrupulously truthful men and "wouldn't say knowingly what he didn't believe, for anyone or of anyone."

In 1863, Stephen Pound had been admitted to the New York bar and had formed a law partnership with Judge Lyman Sherwood of Lyons, New York. After Judge Sherwood's death, Stephen traveled to Platteville, Wisconsin. An acquaintance described Nebraska to him in glowing terms, and Stephen went to Omaha in the summer of 1866. There, a prominent attorney told him that young lawyers had trouble getting a "foothold" in the city and advised him to travel on to Nebraska City.

At that time Nebraska City was an active trading center on the Missouri River. In a 1900 *State Journal* article, Judge Pound recalled that he didn't stay in Nebraska City long because "a great many people had their eyes turned toward Lancaster, later called Lincoln. Though the capital had not been located there at this time, it was confidently expected that it would be, and I decided to cast my fortune there. I have never been sorry, either."

Although the town wasn't inviting, it had "an air of push and hope that was infectious." Lancaster was located on the east bank of Salt Creek, and had been designated Lancaster County seat in 1859. Newcomers expected to make an industry of the salt that crusted the ground in sunny weather. Pumping brine from the creek into vats, then boiling away the water produced the precious commodity that was used in preserving meat. Unfortunately, the commercial salt venture died when J. Sterling Morton of Nebraska City transferred his salt mining efforts to Kansas City.

Nevertheless the potential for future wealth from the salt mines still existed in 1867, and Lancaster was chosen as the site for the Nebraska state capital. Politicians who considered the town too remote from the rest of the state (it was located on the eastern boundary) attempted to block the selection by renaming the future capital Lincoln, knowing that many in the area opposed the politics of Abraham Lincoln. When a Lincoln opponent seconded the motion to rename the community, the site and the capital city's name were settled.

To support himself while studying Nebraska law, Stephen Pound opened a small merchandise store. Sayre wrote that "as a merchant, he was noted for his application to law studies." He also found time to follow the winning or losing of his favorite athletic teams in football, baseball, and boxing. He joined a Lincoln-based literary society in 1868 and wrote to his future bride that he was reading Bulwer's *Rise and Fall of Athens* and trying to find a copy of Hallam's *History of the Middle Ages*.

After passing the Nebraska Bar and entering a law partnership with Seth Robinson, he returned to Macedon, New York, in January 1869, to marry Laura Biddlecombe. The circumstances of their meeting and courtship aren't recorded, but Laura was well-acquainted with relatives of Stephen. She and her future husband attended an academy in Macedon, New York, and part of their mutual attraction probably was based on matters of the mind. Sayre stated that Stephen and Laura Pound were both strong and independent persons, yet they found friendly companionship and intellectual stimulation in each other's company.

Stephen Pound became a probate judge in 1869, and subsequently, was elected a district court judge on the Republican ticket, a post he held for twelve years. He also served as state senator from 1872 to 1874. As a delegate to the Nebraska Constitutional Convention in 1875, he was influential in keeping the state capital in Lincoln and for the insertion of the provision that "the property of no person shall be damaged for public use without just compensation." (Section 21, article I.)

Pound's reputation for personal and professional integrity prompted a jury to find in favor of his client accused of a crime, because they believed that Stephen Pound never would have defended a guilty man. Another example of his high ethical standards occurred when he voluntarily retired as district judge. He thought that his "incumbency had been as long as due regard for propriety permitted and that he ought to step aside and give the waiting list a chance." The newspaper article reporting the incident was published as a memorial after Stephen Pound's death and also praised his "fine judicial temperament" and his "unusual gift of logical perception and analysis."

It's not surprising that Laura Biddlecombe, Stephen Pound's future wife, would have innovative ideas for educating their children, since she had always thirsted for knowledge and had taught school before her marriage. Born on a farm in New York near the hamlet of Plainsville, on May 15, 1841, Laura was the daughter of Olivia (Mathewson) Biddlecombe and Joab Biddlecombe. Joab Biddlecombe's Quaker ancestors had immigrated from England to America in 1630. Joab's mother was Sarah Read, a great granddaughter of Daniell Southwick who with his sister, Provided, became Quaker martyrs. After entering Massachusetts illegally and failing to attend divine service, Daniell and Provided were sold into slavery.

The first ancestor to leave England on Laura's maternal side was Thomas Angell, who sailed from Bristol to Boston in 1630. In 1636 Angell traveled to Salem and joined Roger Williams and his followers in establishing Rhode Island. Sayre claimed that Laura and her son, Roscoe, inherited their excellent memories and writing ability from the Angell/Mathewson branch of the family.

Before Laura reached adulthood, Joab Biddlecombe and his family moved several times. The first relocation occurred in 1846 when Laura was five. In her memoir, she wrote that her mother didn't like the environment of Plainsville and felt that "it was not a good place to raise a family." They moved to a farm in Deerfield, Oneida County, New York, where they lived until 1847. Joab Biddlecombe then purchased a farm in Ontario County, about 115 miles west of Deerfield. "It was going west in the forties if you went one hundred miles in that direction," Laura wrote, "and this is when I began going west." The new farm was located near the small village of Brownsville that bordered the larger Quaker settlement of Farmington.

Laura attended her favorite school while living near Brownsville on property that she referred to as the "old farm." She described the school as a "neat little white one, tucked into the corner of (a farmer's) woods. A more attractive site for a country school could not be found today." In addition to a sloping road that was suitable for sledding, a creek ran through the property and provided a skating surface for boys in the winter.

Laura explained that girls weren't allowed to sled. "They could ride downhill in front of a boy who steered the sled if popular enough to be invited. The little girls could wear out their thick calfskin shoes sliding on the ice—there was always plenty of that in the hollows near the schoolhouse—providing their parents didn't forbid it which sometimes happened."

For Laura, the woods were more than just a playground. She viewed the outdoors with an intellectual curiosity that sparked her lifelong interest in plants and encouraged her to explore the Nebraska prairie with her children. Writing in 1920, she stated that she hadn't been in those woods since the summer of 1852, but she could remember almost every flower that grew there. "Hepaticas, acutiloba and triloba bloomed before the snow was gone. Next came spring beauty, the trilliums, and the yellow dog tooth violet . . . Later came the mandrake, the crane's bill, and herb Robert, ferns of all varieties, squirrel corn, dutchmen's breeches, and violets without end." Recalling her delight in the old farm which her father sold in 1853, Laura wrote:

> *Had there been nature books for children then, I shouldn't have had to wait until I was middle-aged to know the names of things I found on the old farm. For example, one day I found a pair of curious insects on a log in the woods . . . It was not until Roscoe began to study insects that I learned their real name, Walking Stick or Aplopus Mayeri. Another time I was playing in the orchard when I saw a curious stone with something on it that resembled a shell. I wondered how it got on the stone. I had to wait until I was twenty years old before I knew.*

When Laura scouted the woods on pleasant summer days she wore calico or gingham dresses. "Mine, I think, were mostly pink gingham . . . Usually our dresses were covered by a gingham or white apron, according to the occasion," Laura wrote, "and we all wore gingham or calico sunbonnets. This was our school dress." Laura's description of herself at age twelve suggested that she, as well as her husband, possessed the athletic skill that their daughter, Louise, inherited.

I was small for my age, not at all good looking, had very light, almost white hair and very little of it, which was always worn in two small braids. I was very active and could outrun almost all the small boys my age, and slapped them if I thought it necessary. As I have said, from the age of seven I recited in school with boys and girls much older than myself and if they made any grave mistake in recitation I could generally correct them, if asked, but I always stayed down where I belonged. I could climb the hickory tree in the orchard and outlast all the other girls when it came to a contest in jumping the rope.

Olivia Biddlecombe assumed an active role in educating her three children, Laura, Sarah, and Charley, just as Laura would take charge of her children's future education. Mrs. Pound encouraged Roscoe, Louise, and Olivia to view learning as part of their daily lives. Laura wrote that she didn't remember much of what she learned at school, but she was always learning at home. Like her mother, Laura guided her children's reading choices and gave them opportunities to create their own games.

Although Laura couldn't remember when she "learned her letters," her mother said she began to read at age three. Laura recalled that her mother had given the children an atlas to use in entertaining themselves. Laura, Sarah, and Charley invented a game "in which a place would be given for us to find . . . It was by playing this game that I learned to read."

Mrs. Biddlecombe "kept watch" of the books her children read.

When Laura borrowed a book from school or from a friend, her mother read it first. "If she did not approve of it, I had to return it." When visiting a friend's home, Laura noticed books that had come from a former school library and borrowed one that pleased her mother. Continuing to read the loaned books, she especially enjoyed Heightley's *Mythology*, a selection that she had expected her mother to reject. "So when I began my study of ancient history, I had by reading mythology, a background and knew about the Argonauts, the labors of Hercules, and the siege of Troy."

Because the Biddlecombes lived in an area inhabited by Quakers, Laura often attended Quaker select schools. Quakers had brought with them to America the tradition of educating girls as well as boys. Soon after William Penn established Philadelphia, he granted a charter to the Philadelphia Monthly Meeting allowing them to run schools for Quakers and for non-Quakers as well as blacks and whites of both sexes. As the religious group immigrated to other locations, they tended to live near each other, and they established grammar schools in which children of the area learned to read and write.

While living on the "old farm" near Farmington, Laura recalled that her favorite instructor during this period was Edwin Pound. He was the grandson of Hugh Pound whose land adjoined her father's property. Twenty-one-year-old Edwin Pound had interrupted his studies at Oberlin College to teach in the school that Laura attended. She stated:

> *He was a much higher type than any of my previous teachers ... He became my ideal of everything a young man should be ... In fine weather he generally walked to and from school, about two miles, and very often it happened that I walked with him. If his father came for him I was asked to ride with them, so I came to know him the best of all my early teachers. To me he was perfect both as to looks, and manly qualities.*

Because of her admiration and respect for Edwin Pound, Laura may have been predisposed to fall in love with Stephen Bosworth Pound, Edwin's cousin.

Although the ancestors of Olivia Mathewson and Joab Biddlecombe had been Quakers, the couple and their near relatives were Universalists. Universalism, founded in 1779, emphasized the universal Fatherhood of God and the final salvation of all souls, rejecting the concept of hell. Universalists were liberal-thinkers, who aimed to loosen rigid Puritan beliefs. In 1961, the Universalists joined the Unitarians. Laura recalled that "In every Universalist Church ... you would see in some conspicuous place the words, 'God is love.'" Decades later, Laura and her children reclaimed their Quaker heritage.

In the spring of 1853, after Laura's father sold the "old farm," he accepted the job of overseeing the building of a steam dredge at Erie Pennsylvania. Laura and her mother spent the summer in "a pretty little cottage" in New York, while her brother, Charley, went to Pennsylvania to help her father. Her sister, Sarah, taught school. After the dredge was completed, the family was reunited except for Sarah, who returned to Clover Street Academy, a Girls Finishing School.

When the owner of the cottage sold it in 1855, Joab Biddlecombe looked for a home near a good school which Laura could attend. They settled in Macedon Locks, and Laura completed her secondary schooling at the academy. Most middle-class young women at this time attended finishing schools after completing their basic education, but Laura turned down her father's offer to send her to Clover Street Academy. She considered the subject offerings of finishing schools boring and the teaching superficial. Displaying traits of the future New Women, she took control of her education by asking to attend Lombard College in Galesburg, Illinois, a Universalist institution and one of the few colleges to admit women. A cousin had written tantalizing accounts of the co-educational school, and Laura convinced her father to send her there.

Founded in 1851, Lombard College provided a liberal alternative to the narrow sectarianism of neighboring Knox College. A hotbed of abolition, Lombard College hosted the fifth Lincoln-Douglas debate.

By the outbreak of the Civil War several Negro students had earned degrees from the college. The school thrived until male students joined the Union Army, an event that lowered the enrollment and brought unsettled times to the college.

Laura enjoyed traveling "West" to Galesburg and was delighted with her instructors and her studies. She was an exceptional student, and the college arranged a course of study that would allow her to earn a degree in two years. Unfortunately, the outbreak of the Civil War worried her father, who felt that conditions in the country were too unstable to allow Laura to complete her second year of study. She returned to New York and taught school until her marriage to Stephen Pound in 1869, an event that took her further west.

Writing about her wedding journey of February, 1869, Laura Pound stated that she and her husband had traveled to Rochester, New York, from a nearby village to take the westbound express train. After reaching Chicago, they spent two "delightful" days with friends before continuing their trip. They intended to take the noon express train from Chicago to Council Bluffs, but their luggage "went astray," and Stephen Pound spent the afternoon locating their trunks.

Missing the express forced Laura and Stephen to take the mail train which left at midnight and stopped at every station between Chicago and Council Bluffs. For Laura, riding on the "slippery, black hair cloth seats" was an uncomfortable experience. "I did not weigh very much and my feet hardly touched the floor, so I had to hold onto the arm of the seat . . . to keep from falling off. It was only when the train stopped that I could get any rest."

Physically, Laura Pound always appeared to be a "frail little woman." Olivia wrote that her mother never weighed more than one hundred pounds. She had large, dark eyes, and thick brown hair that never turned gray. She compensated for her delicate appearance with unusual energy, persistence, and resourcefulness. She refused to be discouraged by the obstacles she encountered during the westward journey or by the inconveniences of frontier life.

As they rode through Iowa, Stephen Pound asked his bride,

"Have you any idea what sort of a place you are going to?" When she replied that she did, he said, "Show me a place you think something like Lincoln." Laura chose Tama, Iowa, "where there were a few dingy shops with the regulation low, square fronts." Stephen Pound cheerfully assured his bride that she had chosen a suitable comparison "only it is better than Lincoln."

After they arrived in Council Bluffs, the couple changed trains to reach Pacific Junction where they expected to meet a stage coach that would take them across the ice-covered Missouri River. But the stage coach had a broken wheel and couldn't make the trip until the next day. A family consisting of a man, his teen-age son, and ten-year-old daughter, also wanted to cross the Missouri. After the man hired a wagon, Laura wrote, "We decided to go with him since he was the type that inspires confidence."

When the hired wagon reached the Missouri, the driver refused to cross the thin ice and left his passengers and their baggage on a sandbar. Determined to cross the river, the man who had hired the wagon directed his son to walk on the ice to Portsmouth and bring back a rope and bob sled. Laura Pound and the ten-year-old girl accompanied the teenager, walking in single-file. "In many places," Laura wrote, "the water stood in pools, and I would step aside only to be told peremptorily by my guide to 'get back in line.'" When they reached the Nebraska side, mud on the bank was "almost impassable." The boy carried his sister up the bank, but Laura "stuck fast and had to be pulled out."

Laura and the young girl were led to the Plattsmouth Valley House and told to wait for the rest of the party to arrive. For the first time since leaving New York, Laura began to worry about her future. "Would I be left a widow on the west bank of the Missouri! Finally there came the rumble of a wagon. I looked out and there was the rest of our party with my dignified husband perched on top of a trunk."

Platte Valley House provided the Pounds with "a good dinner and a night's sleep that would have been restful but for the bits of corncob left in the husks that filled our mattress." The next day, Stephen Pound introduced his bride to a lawyer who had graduated from Cornell University in New York. The gentleman said, "Mrs. Pound, you won't like Nebraska."

Intent on adjusting to her new home, Laura said, "I have burned my bridges behind me and there will be no going back to New York to stay." She learned later that the lawyer returned to New York "when the grasshoppers came." But Stephen and Laura Pound "were content to stay." Writing about the grasshopper invasions during the dry summers of 1873 and 1874, Laura Pound recalled that crops spared by the drought and hail were eaten by the grasshoppers. Fortunately, the summer of 1875 was rainy and by July 1, the grasshoppers had flown.

Laura Pound never regretted being transplanted to Nebraska. Unlike many frontier wives whose solemn faces gazing from photographs hinted at their unhappiness over being uprooted, Laura looked forward to the challenge of building a life with her husband in a new city and state. Overcoming the obstacles that faced her in the small frontier town called into play her storehouse of intellectual interests and her teaching talent.

The stage coach journey to Lincoln at first passed through "thrifty farms that had a homelike look," wrote Laura, "but on the last stretch of the trip "there was nothing to be seen but the bare brown prairie, not a tree nor shrub, not a human being, nor bird nor animal of any kind." When they reached Lincoln, the couple stayed at Atwood House located on the corner of 9th and P Streets.

The recently settled community that Laura and Stephen Pound were determined to call home was described by Elizabeth Little Admanson in a newspaper article. Admanson recalled vacant town lots covered with yellow honeysuckle that children gathered. "Occasionally an Indian was seen begging at the door, and night after night we watched the prairie fires racing far into the distance." Because of the fires many houses were built of native sandstone.

Watching a prairie fire come sweeping down from the south consuming everything before it caused Laura Pound, for the first and only time, to wish she were back in New York. The night of the fire she was alone with Roscoe in the first house she and Stephen owned, and the house wasn't built of sandstone. Later, Laura confessed that prairie fires were the only thing she disliked about Nebraska. "I liked the altitude, the dry climate, the blue skies, the sunny days and gorgeous sunsets, the strange, new flora and the song of the prairie lark."

Laura and Stephen Pound's first home was a poorly built structure located near the salt marshes. Like most of the early buildings erected in town, the small house had been put up quickly. All materials arrived by freight train, and builders used whatever quality wood the train delivered. Laura's resolve to adjust to life on the frontier was tested during a windy day in that first home. Olivia, described the incident in a letter to Paul Sayre.

As Laura went about her household chores on that blustery day, she noticed smoke rolling from the stove, creating a gray cloud that hung in the room. To keep soot from dropping over floors, walls, and furniture, she poked the fire and shook the stove. When these efforts failed to stop the billowing smoke, she climbed onto a chair and took the stovepipe apart. Noticing that bricks had blown down the chimney into the stovepipe, she took them out, then she replaced the pipe and rekindled the fire. Everything was back in place when her husband came home.

Feeling proud of herself for solving the problem, she related the incident to Stephen, and said, "Now Stephen Pound if that chimney isn't fixed right away, the house is likely to burn down."

Murmuring his agreement, Stephen continued to pace up and down the room, a habit he had developed when analyzing a troublesome case. Several hours later when they were closing up the house for the night, he turned to Laura and asked, "Just what was that you said about the house burning down?" After that Laura never told her husband anything important when he was working on a difficult case.

In 1874 Judge Pound bought the family's second home with a large backyard and stretches of prairie nearby. An episode that probably occurred in this house revealed Laura Pound's ability to cope with unusual circumstances. On a day when her children were young and Judge Pound was away at court, Laura felt ill and was resting while a sewing woman worked in the living room. Suddenly the outside door to the living room opened and "a tall Indian dressed in full trappings walked in." While the family dog barked furiously, the sewing woman tried to shut the door on the Indian.

The commotion roused Mrs. Pound, and she walked to the living room. As soon as she saw the Indian, she extended her hand in friendship. He gave her a petition from his tribe requesting that Judge Pound intercede on behalf of a fellow tribesman imprisoned in the state penitentiary. Using sign language, Mrs. Pound made the Indian understand that her husband wasn't home and that she would give Judge Pound the petition when he returned. When asked later why she immediately offered her hand to the Indian, she said it was an "instinctive" reaction.

For Laura and Stephen Pound, "there was something inspiring in having a share in the building of a new state." They both were active in civic affairs. Because of her interest in education, Laura Pound helped establish the first Lincoln public library and served on the board for ten years (1880-1890). After she left the board, she remained interested in the library and played an active role in preserving it during an 1891 crisis. An 19 April 1920, newspaper article among her papers related Laura's role in preventing a Lincoln reform mayor, A.H. Weir, from repealing an 1891 law which provided a small tax (half a mil) to support the public library.

Just before the mayor repealed the mil levy, Stephen and Laura Pound had taken their first trip together without the children since their 1869 wedding journey. Less than a week into their vacation Laura read a copy of the Lincoln newspaper reporting Mayor Weir's intent to end support of the library. Turning to her husband, she said, "We must go home." He agreed, and the couple returned to Lincoln.

Laura called on the mayor, the city council members, and several prominent community leaders. Nearly all the men she called on supported the library board's positive stand on the mil levy. Although she succeeded in saving the library, Laura wasn't able to help the board members retain their positions. One by one, when their terms expired, Mayor Weir dropped the members who had protested his cancellation of the tax.

Laura Pound was instrumental in establishing the Deborah Avery Chapter of the Daughters of the American Revolution in Lincoln in May 1896. She served as the organization's first state regent that year, and she held the post again in 1901. Because of her initiative, the group maintained the Antelope Park Botanical Garden and erected a memorial fountain and bench in the park. The fountain now stands outside a fence surrounding the Children's Zoo.

The Hayden Art Club (which became the Nebraska Art Association) and the Lincoln Woman's Club list Laura Pound as a charter member. Because of her interest in botany, she headed the Woman's Club Science Department. The Nebraska State Historical Society also benefitted from her membership.

Along with furthering the cultural growth of Lincoln and teaching her own children, Laura also continued her education by enrolling in language classes at the university. A classmate wrote to her fifty years later after reading the account of her wedding journey in the newspaper. The unnamed student stated: "I well remember the years 1885-1886 when I was a lonely student attending the state university. You probably never realized how much your kindness meant to me then, beginning with the day you spoke to me as we were leaving Dr. Edgren's French class, and including many pleasant hours I spent in your delightful home."

Her encouragement of the shy, young student demonstrated Laura's concern for others, an inborn characteristic inherited from Quaker ancestors. She passed this trait to her children as she prepared them for future academic careers. In teaching her offspring, she used methods that her contemporaries considered unorthodox.

CHAPTER THREE

The Living Room Education

"THE POWER TO make a decision is most important to every person," Laura Pound informed a *Lincoln Journal Star* reporter in 1922. In a letter to Paul Sayre, Olivia confirmed her mother's belief in the importance of decision-making. She described two rules the children had to follow: "We had to do without argument what we were told to do. If we wanted to undertake something that might prove too much for us, we had to consider the pros and cons carefully, then if we went ahead, we had to stay by the undertaking till it was done." Following this rule the Pound youngsters learned to become responsible for their choices.

Laura Pound shared additional teaching advice with the reporter, stating that she believed in "beginning the training and teaching" as soon as children were born. "Their inquiries should be answered intelligently; if a parent does not know the correct answer let him find out what it is." To insure that she would be the best possible teacher for her children, Laura Pound continued her own education at the fledgling University of Nebraska, an institution which allowed women to take classes along with men.

When deciding how to educate their children, Stephen and Laura Pound disregarded prevailing beliefs. They ignored educational tracts advising parents to avoid taxing their daughters' brains with masculine subjects such as science and mathematics. Other advice they refused to follow came from physicians, who warned that playing sports might damage girls' reproductive organs. Both parents considered their daughters capable of learning the same subjects as Roscoe, and they never discouraged Louise and Olivia from playing outdoor games.

Continuing to step across boundaries, Laura installed a blackboard on her living room wall, an action that shocked her neighbors. Hanging a blackboard in the room reserved for entertaining guests was a daring act for a woman of Laura's time and place. As the wife of a lawyer, who aimed to establish a trustworthy and respected practice, she was expected to create a formal home atmosphere, one that banished children and their belongings to unseen parts of the house. Instead of following customs of the day, Laura decided to carry out her own ideas about raising and educating children. She turned the family home into a learning center—not just for Roscoe, Louise, and Olivia, but for neighborhood youngsters as well.

Learning was woven into the fabric of the children's day and became an integral part of their lives. After the ritual of their mother's formal instruction in the mornings, Louise, Roscoe, and Olivia entertained themselves the rest of the day. Their recreation profited from their lessons and independent reading.

Weather allowing, the Pound backyard served as a gathering place for neighborhood youngsters and provided the setting for games that the children invented. Recalling happy times inside and outside the Pound home, a boyhood chum of Roscoe's thanked Laura for her lasting influence. "I have never forgotten your kindness to me when I was a boy, and your high ideals did not fail to make a lasting impression on me, though harum-scarum as I was."

The youngsters' day often began with a cheerful summons from their father. Standing at the foot of the stairs, he called, "Hurrah. The Generals." Roscoe, Louise, and Olivia dressed quickly, Olivia recalled, rushed into the hall, and slid down the "banister of the curved stairway ready to start a new day." Judge Pound referred to his offspring as "the generals" after hearing a foreigner testifying in court call his children the 'genrans,' a term that amused the judge.

Olivia wrote that her father had a "whimsical sense of humor and it was well that he did for otherwise he might not have been able to stand for so many years the long and tedious grind of the courtroom." He often regaled the children at mealtimes with courtroom stories, recounting the mannerisms, odd remarks, or pronunciations of lawyers and witnesses. One colorful lawyer trying a case that involved missing check stubs referred to the stubs as "the bust of Brutus." Thereafter, whenever Judge Pound was missing anything around the house, he would "call out, where is the 'bust of Brutus?"

Laura prepared a family breakfast of applesauce, oatmeal, or cracked wheat mush and graham gems. After the meal ended, she left the clean-up and other household duties in the hands of a maid, while she tutored Roscoe, Louise, and Olivia. According to Olivia, Mrs. Pound had trouble finding competent 'hired girls.' "Most of them were untrained and undependable." However, when Roscoe entered the preparatory school of the University, a rather well-educated German girl applied for work with the family, and she was hired. "She proved to be a jewel and stayed with us four or five years. Since she could take over managing the home, Mother was left free to teach us children."

Mrs. Pound taught Roscoe arithmetic each weekday morning at 9:00, Olivia stated. Often the lessons were stormy because he disliked the "hum-drum work." In the middle of the morning, he went to the University for classes in German and beginning Latin. Laura Pound had begun to teach Roscoe German while she was studying the subject at the University. Sayre reported that when Roscoe was ten, she asked her professor, Harrington Emerson, if Roscoe could take the beginning German class. In a letter to a friend, she recorded the professor's answer. "He said, 'Yes, Mrs. Pound, but you know he will have to pass his examinations." Not wanting her son to receive special treatment, Laura replied that she, too, expected Roscoe to pass the tests:

Louise Pound

While Roscoe was at the university, Mother taught Louise and me reading, spelling, arithmetic, and later, geography, grammar, and United States history," Olivia remembered. Louise recalled that her mother taught each child for one hour a day
We learned and believe me we studied. I remember one summer when Mother tired of her teaching duties (and) enrolled us in a 'select school.' After three days, we begged her to take us back. The routine was too slow. Moreover having to stay in school several hours out of each day instead of but one seemed to be a great waste of time.

Describing her teaching methods to the *Journal Star* reporter, Laura said that her children "had a great deal of time because their studying covered but one hour of the day." This hour, however, was required, so that they learned "regularity and system." The phrase "not prepared" was unknown to Louise and Olivia until they became teachers. Following the rule to do as they were told without argument, Louise, Olivia, and Roscoe learned more than "regularity and system." They also developed self-discipline, a trait that contributed to their future successes.

After the morning lessons, Laura allowed the children to pursue their own interests, although she often took them with her on expeditions to the nearby prairie. Her continued study of botany resulted in her discovery of several new plant specimens as she explored the fields near their Lincoln home. Roscoe shared his mother's interest in plants and earned a Ph.D. in botany. Louise, too, profited from the prairie excursions, developing a respect for scientific research methods which she used in her language studies.

Weather allowing, the Pound backyard often served as the setting for imaginative games in the afternoons. Entertaining neighborhood playmates, the Pound children turned the large area into little cities, "complete with public buildings and street rail, or a robber's cave, or in the sunflower patch next door, 'Leatherstockings' went seeking adventure," Olivia explained. Mrs. Pound dressed her children appropriately for outdoor play, and she never scolded them for tearing or soiling their clothes.

During pleasant winter afternoons Louise taught herself to ice-skate. In her scrapbook, she wrote that her happiest Christmas occurred when she received a pair of skates from relatives in Rochester, N.Y. "Real boys skates of fine steel fastening with the 'heel plates' then popular and having clamps at both toe and heel." In and around Lincoln, the icy ponds were too small to allow distance skating, so Louise taught herself to figure skate. In a summary of her sports achievements Louise wrote: "I bought myself a ten-cent book and from it practiced figure skating to my heart's content." She learned to do the Maltese Cross backwards, the double-two-steps, and the 'on-to-Richmond.'

She also credited the "example and encouragement" of college football player, Orley Thorp, and Lincoln resident, J.D. Lau, for her figure-skating progress. Lincoln ball club manager, Thomas Hickey, an expert roller skater, taught Louise dance steps on the ice. "I was told that I had a "monopoly" in Nebraska for figure skating on ice. Louise admitted that there were no competitors in 19th century Nebraska, and the "title, if I had it, (was) by default." To reporter, Evelyn Simpson, Louise said, "Of course, I wasn't a Sonja Henie; my skirts were too long and cumbersome. But I had fun even though I was the only girl figure-skater." Practicing and perfecting the art of figure skating foretold her future creed of individual excellence.

During spells of bad weather, the controversial blackboard on the living room wall provided space on which the Pound youngsters and their pals wrote stories and drew pictures. They also devised games to play indoors. Like most children of mid-to-late Victorian upbringing, Louise, Olivia, and Roscoe read *Pilgrim's Progress*, the tale of a traveler named Christian who encountered many obstacles on his way to salvation. The Pound offspring designed a Pilgrim's Progress board game in which the traveler, (Christian) endured endless perils. "He was beset by robbers, fell into swamps, battled hurricanes, and struggled with wild beasts," Olivia wrote, "only to be sent back to start over again when he was just in sight of his goal."

Another indoor occupation the children created used two sets of wooden soldiers. Louise whittled the soldiers, Olivia dressed them, and Roscoe assigned their military rankings. Louise and Roscoe wrote histories and designed geographies of the warring countries as well as the full peerage. In this learning-centered home, the war games probably took place on the dining room table with no objection from Laura Pound. She only interfered, Olivia recalled, when the battles between opposing armies became too fierce. Then Mrs. Pound imprisoned both armies until a truce was declared.

Insisting that Roscoe, Louise, and Olivia agree on a truce taught them to cooperate with each other and gave them experience in dealing with conflict in a positive manner. It also strengthened their decision-making skills. A woman of many interests, Laura Pound was too busy to be a domineering mother. Allowed to use their imaginations in entertaining themselves and in finding solutions to their quarrels, the minds of the three Pound youngsters thrived.

If the children tired of board games on bleak afternoons, they turned to their collections, a pastime that their mother encouraged, saying, "Every child should have a fad." On 20 August, 1881, Louise wrote to a cousin thanking her for stamps:

> *I thank you for the stamps you sent me. Three of them I did not have, the envelope stamp is very old and hard to get, and I would like to have more of them. Tude (Olivia) is collecting coins and has 26; she has one English coin of the reign of Charles II ... Can you send her an old-fashioned big copper cent or a 3 cent nickel. We don't have them here in Neb ... Ross (Roscoe) has a collection of butterflies and bugs, and some geological specimens.*

Roscoe probably developed his hobby of collecting insects while tramping on the prairies with his mother and sisters. His parents encouraged this pastime and bought him "an expensive article," (probably a cabinet or cutting board) to use in his studies. Laura told the *Journal Star* reporter that a wealthy neighbor criticized the purchase. An able woman in defending her actions, Laura said to the neighbor, "You would think it all right for me to spend ten dollars on a hat."

When buying toys for the children, Laura stated that she and the judge "paid enough to get a good article for we did not buy many and the children valued them for that reason." J. R. Johnson wrote in *Representative Nebraskans* that Roscoe "had been supplied with cabinets, cutting boards, and other paraphernalia and had a large collection of insects properly mounted and classified."

Like other children of middle-class parents in the late 1800s, the Pound youngsters were avid readers. Laura Pound taught her children to read at an early age. Sayre reported that she began teaching Roscoe at age three. In a 1922 letter to a friend, she wrote that Roscoe had a "wonderful memory," but he didn't learn to read very quickly. Nevertheless, she had him try to read for a few minutes every day "just as I had him wash his hands and face." Laura wrote that Roscoe could read "quite well" by age six, and she then began teaching him German. One can admire her matter-of-fact and successful means of teaching her willful son.

Louise also began learning to read at age three, but not from her mother. Corresponding with reading specialist, Grace Munson, Olivia wrote that Louise began teaching herself to read from listening to Roscoe and from newspapers that a maid tacked above the kitchen sink. As the maid washed dishes, she would point to words in the newspaper, pronounce them, and encourage Louise to repeat them. Overhearing the unique reading lesson, Mrs. Pound realized that Louise was echoing the maid's rural pronunciations and began teaching her daughter to read by more traditional methods.

According to Olivia, Louise's competitive spirit motivated her desire to read. She wanted to do what Roscoe did and "was always quick and accurate with her eyes so it was easy for her to read rapidly." Soon, she was able to read Roscoe's material. When Roscoe was twelve and Louise ten, their parents encouraged their good-natured competition, offering them a dollar each to read Macauley's *History of England*. Reading the book together, they raced to the end of each page. To prevent cheating they asked each other questions before turning the page. Roscoe remembered more, but Louise read faster.

When teaching her children to read, Laura Pound laid the foundation for their future achievements. Her husband helped build that foundation by sharing his love of literature with them. If he was holding court in Lincoln, Judge Pound read selections from Dickens, Thackeray, or Shakespeare to the children at noon while Laura prepared their meal. Olivia stated that they weren't forced to listen to their father read as they waited for their mother to place the beef or ham, potatoes, another vegetable, and fruit on the table. "Louise never cared much about listening. She would rather have the book to herself and read it at her own lightening speed." Although she was impatient, Louise spent an hour practicing the piano after dinner, playing selections from Chopin, Beethoven, Schubert, or Mendelssohn.

Reading took place again after the evening meal of oyster soup, creamed dried beef, cod fish, or fried mush with baked apples, cheese, or cookies for dessert. Settled in the living room after the dishes were washed, Judge Pound read while Mrs. Pound did the family's mending. Often Louise would play the piano again, then she joined Roscoe and Olivia in reading, or in playing other games they had created.

Olivia wrote that her father helped her mother select books for the children. They were of such interest that the three offspring couldn't resist reading them. They were fond of the 'Alice' books, Kingsley's *Greek Heroes*, and *Water Babies*. They also liked Grimm's and Laboulaye's fairy tales, Hawthorne's *Wonder Book* and *Tanglewood Tales*, *Froissart's Chronicles*, *Zig Zag's Journeys in Classic Lands*, *A Child's Book of Nature*, and Charlotte M. Young's histories for children. "Louise and I found the 'Elsie' books and Louisa Alcott's too slow," Olivia declared.

In addition to reading the books their parents had chosen, the Pound youngsters browsed among the books in their father's extensive library. Borrowing books from their father's library was a privilege they shared with other children who achieved fame—the novelists, Virginia Woolf and Edith Wharton, and the future United States president, Theodore Roosevelt. Woolf, Wharton, and Roosevelt also received their early educations at home.

Like his wife, who shared her love of botany with the children, Stephen Pound, a Greek scholar, taught them to read and write Greek. On Sunday afternoons the family demonstrated their proficiency in the language by reading the Greek scriptures. Any visitors present on those afternoons acted as audience. Exposure to German, Greek, and Latin at an early age must have influenced Louise Pound's future interest in language.

Regardless of their unorthodox child-training practices, Stephen and Laura Pound were a prominent and influential Lincoln couple, who frequently entertained University faculty members and state officials in their home. During these visits the children weren't barricaded in the nursery. Instead they listened to their parents and guests discuss a broad range of topics. Mingling with influential Lincolnites allowed the children to develop a confident ease of manner in official situations. Louise and Roscoe, especially, never hesitated to question authority.

The Sunday afternoon Greek-reading sessions probably took place in the second of three homes in which the family lived. Each house had been an improvement on the previous one. Their first, badly built, home with the faulty chimney was located near the salt marshes in the vicinity of the city park and close to land designated for the county court house.

After Olivia's birth in 1874, the family moved to an area on the eastern edge of Lincoln (at that time,) 1542 P Street. Because the tract of land on which it stood was in litigation, it was referred to as "the disputed 80," Olivia reported. By 1892, businesses had begun to spread into the neighborhood, and the Pounds moved to a large Victorian home with a tower that eventually housed Louise's library-study. This home, 1632 L Street, was located near the present state capital and no longer exists.

Louise Pound

The picture of young Louise Pound growing up in the rich learning environment of the P Street home is that of a lively, determined child both intellectually and physically. She doesn't tag along behind her brother, but races beside him as they run across fields or read books together. Her toy soldiers engage in battle with those of Roscoe, neither of them yielding until their mother forces them to make a truce. As her mind races to match that of her brother, her body exudes energy that she controls to her advantage, teaching herself to figure skate and bicycle and play tennis to name just a few of the sports in which Louise Pound excelled.

Part Two:
Emerging Scholars and the Emerging University
1871–1889

CHAPTER FOUR

Shaping The Golden Era

Before Nebraska towns established high schools, students desiring a University of Nebraska education enrolled in a two-year preparatory school affiliated with the University. First year subjects included mathematics, English grammar, history, geography, and physiology. During the second and final year, pupils studied Latin, mathematics, Greek or German, along with ancient history and rhetoric.

After passing the entrance exam in 1886 at age 14, Louise Pound's fast-paced mind allowed her an easy mastery of the preparatory school curriculum. The regularity and system she developed under her mother's direction was an additional advantage.

Young Louise Pound and the growing University ran a parallel course during the early years of her association with the institution. Both bloomed. As the University followed an innovative path leading to its Golden Era (1891-1900), Louise Pound's adult personality took shape. With her quick mind and her zeal on the playing fields, she was destined to become a New Woman.

The New Woman emerged between the 1880s and 1890s, at the time when Louise Pound was shaping her identity. She was undoubtedly drawn to the New Women's goals of fighting "stagnation" and gaining independence. Carroll Smith-Rosenberg asserted in

Disorderly Conduct that this generation of young women had been influenced by their mothers. They were "the daughters of the new bourgeois matrons" and benefitted from "bourgeois affluence" which allowed them to attend college and train for professions. Their mothers had organized women's clubs and attended lyceum talks, promoting their daughters' "consciousness of women's new role possibilities almost as their birthright."

In addition to setting an example for her daughters to follow in pursuing college degrees, Laura Pound was instrumental in establishing women's organizations in the city and state. Her activities encouraged Louise and Olivia's rejection of "conventional female roles" and their pursuit of careers as well as their desire to enjoy the rights and privileges usually "accorded to bourgeois men."

When Louise entered the University in 1888 at age 16, she was an attractive young woman with a slender build and medium height. Her red hair and the intense expression in her dark eyes drew the attention of others. Her classmates, especially those from rural areas and small communities, probably envied the poise and confidence— both intellectual and physical—that flowed from Louise.

In her novel, *My Antonia*, Willa Cather described the unsophisticated, but sincere, rural students who were Louise Pound's and Cather's University classmates in the early 1890s.

> *In those days there were many serious young men and women among the students who had come up to the University from farms and the little towns scattered over the thinly settled state. Some of those boys came straight from the cornfields with only a summer's wage in their pockets, hung on through the four years, shabby and underfed and completed the course by really heroic self-sacrifice . . . There was an atmosphere of expectancy and bright hopefulness about the young college that had lifted its head from the prairie only a few years before.*

The University of Nebraska was established under the provisions of the Morrill Act which Congress had passed in 1862. Robert Knoll reported in *prairie university* that the Morrill Act provided lands for public universities and stipulated the study of the useful arts and sciences. Many institutions founded under the Morrill Act ignored the land-grant college concept of providing students with training in agricultural and mechanical arts. The University of Nebraska charter broadened the provisions of the Morrill Act stating that the institution should "reach out to all the people."

Section 18 of the original charter states: "No person shall, because of age, sex, color, or nationality, be deprived of the privileges of this institution." Providing for the education of women, the charter further stated, "Provisions shall be made for the education of females apart from male students in separate apartments or buildings; provided that persons of different sexes of the same proficiency of study may attend regular college lectures together." From the beginning, women were enrolled with men. Laura Pound was one of those females, who, though married and a mother, attended the University.

In its infancy, the University simply blended into the prairie that surrounded it. Knoll wrote that "Citizens tethered family cows on it. Children picked violets and buffalo beans there." Lincoln was a village of 2,000 people in 1871, and only 130 students matriculated when the school opened its doors. 110 of those students enrolled in the preparatory school. Knoll wrote that "five, including one woman, were collegiate freshmen; two were sophomores; and one was a junior. Twelve, including six women, were irregular students."

The University was located on four square blocks from 10th to 12th Streets. The planning commissioners hadn't considered the school's potential growth when laying out the grounds, an oversight that Stephen Pound predicted they would regret. His forecast proved accurate when University officials began buying back land that should have been part of the original purchase.

The main building on campus, University Hall, was a more imposing structure than the state capitol which lay half a mile to the south. Viewing the building from 11th and S Streets, an incoming student compared it to the palaces of Rome. The structure sat behind a high iron fence that enclosed the University grounds. Describing his first view of University Hall, in 1892, Alvin Johnson wrote in *Pioneer's Progress*: "The building before me seemed huge and majestic. It had four strata of windows, some of them lighted, under a mansard roof. A square tower topped the building." Three other structures of varying architectural style stood to the right of University Hall, and they, too, impressed Johnson's "country eyes."

University Hall was three stories high without the basement and mansard, according to Robert Manley's *Centennial History of the University of Nebraska*. The building included a chapel with a 42 by 60 foot gallery. Twenty rooms were used for class recitations, and others served as music and painting areas. The third floor provided space for literary society meetings. A cabinet room housed a collection of geographical, botanical, and biological specimens that formed the nucleus of the future natural history museum. An armory, a ladies reception room, and a printing office also were housed in the building.

Unfortunately, University Hall was unstable from its first days. Locally manufactured bricks used in the construction were soft. The roof leaked. The furnace failed to heat classrooms adequately, and warmth never reached the corridors. Knoll stated that extensive graft had been involved in contracting the work, and the building had to be repaired several times before the Nebraska legislature agreed in 1945 to replace it.

It's not surprising that graft and corruption marked the early days of Nebraska's statehood and the building of Lincoln. While many settlers, like the Pounds, came to improve their own prospects, they also helped the city and state grow and develop in positive ways. Others came for only one reason: to gain a personal fortune using any means. The first two state capitol buildings erected in 1867 and 1880 were also victims of unscrupulous contractors and suffered from shoddy construction.

The first University chancellor, Allen R. Benton, left his post as president of Mount Union College in Ohio for a higher paid position in Nebraska. A student of ancient languages and an ordained minister of the Christian Church, Benton embraced a classical but nonsectarian course of study, agreeing with board of regents' president, W.H. James, on subject matter. Knoll wrote that James believed a sectarian education bound "the infant mind with an iron cord." When conflict erupted between newly elected fundamentalist Christians and the humanists serving on the 1875 board of regents, Benton resigned rather than take a stand on the issue. He left Nebraska after the University's 1876 commencement.

The quarrel between the uncompromising fundamentalists and modernists also hounded newly elected chancellor, Edmund B. Fairfield. He was a religious and educational conservative, but supported continuing the classical curriculum. Nevertheless three young teachers, Latin professor, George Church; modern language professor, Harrington Emerson; and comparative literature professor, George Edward Woodberry, spoke out in favor of raising teaching standards. They recommended teaching with "scientific impartiality," Knoll reported, allowing students to select their own course of study and encouraging both students and professors to engage in independent investigations. The three professors won their point, and the board of regents asked for Fairfield's resignation on September 30, 1882.

From 1882 until 1884, Henry E. Hitchcock, mathematics professor and Presbyterian minister, who sympathized with the liberal thinkers, served as temporary chancellor. In 1884, J. Irving Manatt accepted the chancellorship, leaving his position as professor of Greek at Marietta College in Ohio. Although he possessed impressive credentials—a Ph.D. from Yale and a doctorate from Leipzig University—Manatt's term of office was doomed from the beginning. Immediately after he arrived, conflict erupted between Manatt and the faculty.

He dismissed Rachel Lloyd, a chemistry professor who was instrumental in developing Nebraska's sugar beet industry, because he questioned the sincerity of her religious beliefs.

He also failed to prevent physics professor, D.B. Brace from resigning. Brace was doing important research on the nature of light.

Incensed by Manatt's highhanded treatment of Lloyd and his indifference to Brace's threatened departure, the faculty took matters into their own hands, bypassing Manatt and appealing to the regents to make changes that would keep Brace on the faculty. To satisfy the protesting faculty and Brace, the regents financed a physics laboratory and requested Manatt's resignation. Knoll stated that Manatt's arrogance and sarcasm combined with his uncompromising and authoritarian ways had alienated the men and women of the University's student body and staff.

The school's growing pains eased when Charles Bessey reluctantly assumed the chancellorship after Manatt's departure. Refusing to accept the office permanently because he was more interested in plant research and teaching, Bessy, nonetheless, healed the wound growing between faculty, students, and administration. In contrast to Manatt's dictatorial leadership, Knoll wrote that Bessey applied his scientific beliefs to University management, claiming that the "The proper pursuit of science should develop a judicial state of mind toward all problems."

Bessey's qualifications were less prestigious than those of previous chancellors. After a "spotty elementary and secondary education," Knoll reported that Bessey graduated "brilliantly" from Michigan Agricultural College in 1869. He also studied with Asa Gray at Harvard, who influenced Bessey's acceptance of Darwinian thinking.

After teaching botany and horticulture at Iowa State College of Agriculture, Bessey eventually became that school's president. In 1884 he accepted a position at the University of Nebraska. During his years of teaching and his temporary chancellorship, Knoll wrote that Bessey influenced the University to become a research center "devoted to the discovery and dissemination of new knowledge, not just to the transmission of received lore."

Laura and Stephen Pound probably were relieved when Bessey assumed the chancellorship. Since they welcomed many of the professors into their home, they would have been aware of the controversy over the academic course the University followed. Because of their Quaker and Universalist backgrounds stressing more liberal religious views, they probably lacked sympathy for dogmatic fundamentalists, nor would they have endorsed a sectarian course of study.

During the summer of 1891, Bessey handed over leadership of the University to James Hulme Canfield. Canfield had come "West with the youthful vigor of a hopeful time," Knoll stated, and the University radiated an atmosphere of "bright hopefulness" under his leadership. Canfield had graduated from Williams College in Williamstown, Massachusetts, in 1868. After studying and practicing law in St. Joseph, Michigan, he decided that he preferred teaching and through an influential friend obtained a position teaching history at the University of Kansas.

After his arrival in Lincoln, Canfield set to work beautifying the campus with stone walks and an iron fence.

Within a year he had charmed students, professors, and state residents with his egalitarian idealism. He believed the University belonged to Nebraska citizens and encouraged the children of all classes to view the school as an extension of the education they were entitled to receive. Even though the economy was depressed, Canfield traveled throughout the state, advising audiences, "If you cannot earn, you can at least learn." Under his leadership the University entered a period that Knoll and Manley referred to as the "Golden Era." During this phase it joined Michigan, Wisconsin, and California as one of the nation's big four universities.

Outstanding professors were a factor in the school's reputation as a leading center of learning. Many of them had come west to take advantage of opportunities that existed in undeveloped states such as Nebraska. Charles Bessey had been attracted to the possibility of studying Nebraska's unexplored plant life.

Reporting Roscoe Pound's description of Bessey's teaching style, Manley wrote that the professor often sat on the corner of a laboratory table and asked a student what he was doing and why he was doing it. After hearing the answer, he would stroll to the botanical library, pull out a book and open it to a page that held important information for the pupil's use. Roscoe claimed that Bessey made laboratory work one of the great experiences of college life.

Bessey taught Roscoe and Louise Pound. Both claimed that his teachings influenced their scientific approach to their studies in law and language. Embracing Darwin's belief in natural selection, (survival of the fittest), Bessey stressed studying more than just plant structure. Believing that living plants had a capacity for growth and development, he explored the uncharted fields of plant pathology and physiological botany. Wigdor wrote that "botanists inspired by (Darwin's) theory of evolution could hardly be content with gathering, mounting, and classifying." In addition to laboratory work, Bessey's students participated in fieldwork, exploring problems that had formerly been considered unworthy of scientific inquiry.

English professor, Lucius Sherman, who became dean of the College of Arts and Sciences, did not perch on the edge of a table and visit with his students. Displaying a stern demeanor in his photograph, Sherman's down-turned mouth beneath a white mustache matched the severity of his direct and uncompromising gaze. He probably stood ramrod straight in front of a classroom as he lectured students on analyzing words and phrases according to his scientific method. Sherman stressed that students should find the elements composing excellence and beauty in literature through numbering and diagraming words and sentences in the same way that elements were identified in chemistry laboratories.

Although Louise Pound considered Sherman's analytic approach to determining excellence in literature to be "silly," she wisely refrained from challenging the professor. Reflecting her practical nature, she realized that his opinion of her work would impact her future, a realization that reaped career benefits. He offered her a position as theme reader in the English department while she studied for her Master's degree in 1893-94. After she completed her degree, he employed her as an instructor in the English department. He also encouraged her to get her doctorate, assuring her of continued employment at the University after she had finished her studies at Heidelberg in 1900.

Another important professor during Louise Pound's college years was August Hjalmer Edgren, who came to the University as a professor of comparative philology, modern languages, and Sanskrit. Edgren, a friend of Sherman's, also recommended using the scientific method of inquiry when analyzing literary works. Along with Bessey, Sherman, and history professor, George Howard, Edgren helped shape the graduate program at the University. As dean of the graduate school, Edgren encouraged his colleagues to judge student performance on the quality of work rather than on class attendance. Nevertheless, advanced degrees were granted only after stated requirements had been fulfilled and candidates had passed a written and oral examination and written a thesis.

Louise, Roscoe, and Olivia earned their M.A. degrees during the programs's formative years. By 1896, it was the first graduate program west of the Mississippi. In 1898, only three state universities and approximately twelve other colleges had larger graduate attendance than the University of Nebraska. In 27 years, the University in Lincoln had risen from the surrounding prairie attracting remarkable students. Many of them gained national fame. Among those students were Louise and Roscoe Pound.

The city grew and prospered alongside the University. From a town of 2,000 in 1871, Lincoln's population had reached 20,000 by 1885. When Canfield arrived in 1891, 35,000 people lived in the city. Becoming a boom town during the 1880s and early 1890s, Lincoln's progress was reported in Robert Olson and Ronald Naugle's *History of Nebraska*. "New additions were laid out, and the city began to assume a metropolitan air with an electric light plant, a water system, street railways, and a few blocks of paved streets. Its citizens, however, still used the University of Nebraska's campus as a pasture for their livestock."

In 1893 a severe depression aggravated by drought and grasshoppers blighted the state. In spite of the depression and the changing political atmosphere created by populists who insisted on bringing economic reform to Nebraska, the University continued to grow, and Lincoln boasted of its culture. Bernice Slote described Lincoln in the early 1890s in her book, *The Kingdom of Art*:

> *In Lincoln there were opera cloaks and oysters in ice, but always in spring came the smell of burning prairie grass, for this was still the edge of the frontier, and the frontier still had teeth. Some summers, grasshoppers stripped the newly planted trees; and one winter after a blizzard, just outside town a man was found sitting straight up in the middle of the road frozen to death. And yet in 1893, after bank failures, panic and drouth, a pre-theatre reception on the night Clara Morris played in Camille had a menu of twenty-four items, from "Blue Points on Shell" through "Fillet of Beef aux Truffles" to "Charlotte Russe" and "Cafe Noir."*

Faith in the power of learning was a strong tenet of Victorian America, and a college education was one way of getting ahead in life. Demonstrating these values, an eclectic population came to the University. Students from families of varying economic and social status arrived. Many professors who had studied at prestigious universities in the east settled in Lincoln to teach those students.

Recalling her student days at the University, Louise Pound wrote in the May, 1942, *Nebraska Alumnus* magazine that "Campus life, though somewhat Spartan, was stimulating ... There was a fine faculty and a tonic atmosphere ... 'Victorian' was not yet a term of disparagement, and in the long run it will not be; for it was perhaps the most highly civilized period that the world has known."

CHAPTER FIVE

Scholar and Athlete

A s Louise raced across the University campus, mastering studies and sports without effort, she perplexed her fellow students. They wondered how one young woman could accomplish so much. She wrote stories, plays and poems, and contributed articles to the *Lincoln Journal*. With Willa Cather, another fascinating coed, Louise edited a short-lived literary journal, *The Lasso*. She led the women's military drill team and took an active role in a literary society. Yet she managed to study for a degree in harmony, piano, and sight-reading along with a diploma in English philology.

After classes ended for the day, Louise was a familiar sight riding her bicycle to tennis courts where she played and won matches with men. In winter she laced up her skates and cut complicated figures on icy ponds. In addition to taking part in sports and studying, Louise was a campus leader. The Pound home was a hive of activity, providing space for clubs to meet, for parties to take place, and for students to discuss campus politics. It wasn't surprising that less ambitious and talented classmates viewed Louise Pound with awe. She amazed them.

When her University class prepared for graduation, a student publication, *The Hesperion*, wrote a brief summary of each member of the 1892 class. The journal gave Louise a mixed review:

Miss Louise Pound, a favorite in society and in the classroom, is next to engage our attention. She has been thought by many to be cold-hearted. This is due, perhaps, to the fact that many have not become well-acquainted with her. She has many admirable traits of character and will be successful in anything she undertakes.

Without doubt, Louise belonged to an elite group on campus. Her familiarity with the University and with many of the professors, as well as her family's leading role in Lincoln's cultural and political matters gave her an advantage over those students who struggled to improve themselves and their future through education. Those who were less gifted, who lacked social connections, or who weren't interested in mingling with a socially prominent group would have viewed Louise as a cold-hearted snob. Certainly, she had an aloof demeanor and considered herself above average.

Students who admired, and possibly, envied Louise's accomplishments had adopted the competitive spirit that characterized turn-of-the-century America. Darwin's study of natural selection had encouraged the widespread belief that only the fittest contender survived, a belief that fostered competition especially in ambitious individuals such as Louise.

Another achiever in the 1890s, Thomas Edison, voiced a commonly held opinion about career advancement. In *1898: The Birth of the American Century*, David Traxel reported Edison's philosophy: "I don't care so much for a great fortune, as I do for getting ahead of the other fellow." In her campus activities Louise appeared to agree with Edison's doctrine. She played games to win, and she studied to excel. Another motivation for her excellence was her continued desire to keep pace with Roscoe.

Keeping up with her brother was quite a challenge for Louise. Knoll wrote that she and Roscoe were "exceedingly jolly," and both loved jokes, pranks, and parties. Described by Knoll as "perhaps the most brilliant" among the remarkable student population during Canfield's reign as chancellor, Roscoe made a name for himself in botany and law. Louise outdistanced her brother only in athletics. A bout of German measles in childhood weakened Roscoe's eyesight and kept him from playing college sports. He led the cheers or acted as umpire for University teams but substituted rapid, long-distance walking for game-playing.

When Bessey took over the chancellorship in 1888, Louise was a freshman, Olivia a preparatory school student, and Roscoe had begun work toward his master's degree in botany. He also served as Bessey's laboratory assistant. After earning his master's degree in 1889, Roscoe spent a year studying law at Harvard. Perhaps he couldn't decide which career to pursue, law or science, or he may have studied law to please his father. Whatever motivated him to go to Harvard, he combined his interests in law and botany when he returned to Nebraska in 1890, working in his father's law firm during the day and studying botany at night.

Roscoe and Frederick Clements studied the relationship of plants to the environment. Their research, published as *The Phytogeography of Nebraska*, resulted in their Ph.D. degrees in botany. Roscoe received his degree in 1897, and Clements earned his in 1898. Knoll stated that in applying Darwin's continuum for biology to plants, Pound and Clements earned permanent places in American science. Knoll also contended that the study of modern ecology began in Bessey's laboratory.

Roscoe maintained an interest in military drill throughout his student years at the University. Prescribed by the Morrill Act, military tactics were included in the curriculum of land grant universities. From age ten, when he was a student in Professor Emerson's German class, Roscoe faithfully observed the cadet battalion. Using the toy soldiers he and his sisters had made, he plotted movements for the battalion. He was drum major for the military band in 1889. Manley wrote that he was "the smallest drum major in the nation."

Inspired by Roscoe's military endeavors, Louise helped organize a women's military drill team in the spring of 1888. Company D with Louise as second sergeant used the same heavy rifles that were issued to men. The girls wore dark blue uniforms trimmed with white braid, and their caps had two buttons and a gilt cord. According to Manley, Louise believed the girls joined the team because they wanted to wear the impressive uniform.

Unfortunately, pandemonium broke loose during the first competitive drill with men. The nervous young women became confused, and the men's team was distracted by the sight of uniformed females marching down the field. After disbanding in the fall of 1888, Company D was replaced with Company Q, a women's drill team which outdid the men's team. But Louise realized that she lacked the desire to lead a drill team and wisely ended her association with military endeavors.

Her description of the experience published in an 1895 *Sombrero* article is an example of her practical nature and her realistic approach in choosing her specialties:

> *Over the first dress parade I ought perhaps to draw the curtain of charity. To say that our appearance created a sensation would be doing scant justice. I recall vividly my extreme trepidation of finding myself, in my capacity of second sergeant, the end "man" of the whole battalion, with several new duties to perform of which I had not the faintest idea and all of which I got wrong. Indeed, I believe that the whole company felt greatly confused, if not pathetically rattled. There was an unusually large number of spectators present, the guns seemed unusually heavy, and the other companies seemed to take dreadfully long steps. No wonder our fours all turned different ways or that our gun movements were executed a varying number of seconds too late. The other companies too became so interested in us as not to drill with their usual precision.*

Although she abandoned her efforts at military leadership, Louise maintained her interest in a University Literary Society, the Union. Roscoe and Olivia also belonged to the Union which had been established in 1876. Preceding the Union, the Palladian had been founded in 1871, and the Adelphian had been established in 1873. A fourth society, the Delian, was organized in 1899. Louise and Willa Cather acted as "sergeants at arms" in the Union, and Louise served as its president in 1892.

In *Professing Literature: An Institutional History*, Gerald Graff emphasized the importance of literary societies in offsetting the "aridity" of college classrooms where teaching emphasized "textbook learning and forced recitations." Since the society's libraries were larger, more accessible, and contained books with a broader range of interest such as American fiction and English literature the literary societies gained readers among members. Nineteenth century American writers, Emerson, Hawthorne, Dana, Holmes, Lowell, and Henry Adams received their formative literary education through literary societies.

University of Nebraska literary societies introduced students from farms and small towns to the arts of socializing and speaking in public. Both skills were useful in "getting ahead." The 15 December, 1888, *Hesperion* stated: "Students are beginning to learn that the work afforded them by literary societies is worth more to them than any other study in the university curriculum." The article contended that public speaking was not an inherent ability but could be learned through training.

As etiquette demanded, women attending meetings usually were accompanied by men. To insure that girls were escorted to the meetings, the literary societies used a 'slate'—a small book containing the names of female members. Manley reported Louise Pound's description of the system. The slate circulated among the young men who would scratch the name of a girl they wanted to accompany to the meeting. During leap years the women carried and scratched the slate.

Was Louise courted by any of the young men belonging to the Union literary society or by other male acquaintances? These questions can be answered only through assumptions, since her papers lack references to relationships with the opposite sex. Although sl̶ ...as popular as a dance partner at the parties she enjoyed attending, her aloof manner combined with her athletic feats and academic excellence may have kept possible suitors at arm's length.

Men were not immune to her beauty, nor was Willa Cather.

Louise's comeliness and popularity aroused Cather's jealousy when both women attended the same party in 1892. In Heidelberg, Louise talked with male students and danced with a Russian gentleman. Knoll stated that Louise had always enjoyed the company of young men.

Knoll also recalled a conversation with a colleague, Orin Stepanek, about Louise Pound's reply to a comment Stepanek had made about young women's responses to masculinity—"referring of course to the sexual attraction between the sexes." Stepanek reported that Louise had looked him up the next day and said, "I've never felt anything like what you were talking about. And I went home and asked Olivia, and she hasn't either." Perhaps Louise and Olivia sublimated sexual impulses in their concentration on studies, and in Louise's case, on sports. Later, they devoted their energies to their careers.

Since they lacked interest in attracting men and possessed independent spirits, Louise and Olivia probably belonged to the group of female students who rebelled against the need for male escorts. These young women formed the order of Go Out Independents (GOI) and attended college sporting events and meetings on their own. Louise stated that after Chancellor Canfield arrived, he supported the GOI and in general was solicitous of women students. Perhaps GOI members refused to subject themselves to the slate system of having male escorts when attending literary society meetings.

Along with other female members, Louise and Olivia wore the current fashion as they climbed the stairs to the meeting room. Long-skirted gowns accented tiny waists and featured balloon sleeves and high necks. Their long hair was combed into buns or braids that wound around their heads. The young men probably wore close-cut suits of dark colors. Their hair was often parted in the middle, and some sported curving mustaches. A watch chain often dangled from vests.

Located on the third floor of University Hall, the drafty meeting rooms were heated by a wood-burning stove. In the University's *Semi-Centennial Anniversary Book*, Louise described the evening's agenda. The program always included orations and essays alternating with musical numbers. Usually the sessions ended with a debate followed by a social hour that included refreshments such as doughnuts, popcorn, and occasionally, ice cream. Meetings ended with a promenade through the building's long corridors.

Literary societies poked fun at one another in a good-natured way. Louise wrote a satire in five acts titled "The Perjured Palladian." Staged at the University chapel on December 10, 1892, the play featured Louise as co-ed, Sophmorista Saltonstall; Olivia Pound played Prepletta Higby, and Willa Cather appeared as Diamond Witherspoon. The brief synopsis emphasized the foremost position of the Palladian Literary Society amidst its rivals and the steadfast loyalty of Miss Saltonstall. Reviewing the play favorably, the *Hesperion* declared Louise's creation "artistic and unique."

At the turn-of-the-century, entertainment revolved around groups of friends who shared common interests. No matter what set one belonged to, Traxel wrote, activities took place in parlors during winter, on porches in spring and fall, and in yards during summer hot spells. Because Louise, Roscoe, and Olivia, had many of the same friends, student meetings often took place in the Pound home. Olivia described a variety of gatherings. "They might be taking an active part in school politics, getting up programs, having an evening of music, taking off the bombastic in some write-up for the school paper, or holding an impromptu dance."

In 1892, friends of the Pound siblings met in their new home on 1632 L Street. Front and side porches and a second floor balcony provided a choice of gathering places during hot weather. Inside the house, fireplaces, carved dark woodwork, stained glass, and oriental rugs created an elegant atmosphere. The connecting rooms on the main floor were often cleared for dancing. Olivia wrote that Judge Pound was a beautiful dancer and was in great demand as a partner.

Perhaps by 1898 the Pounds had purchased a mass-produced version of Edison's improved Gramophone that sold for twenty dollars.

More at ease on literary terrain than she had been on a military parade ground, Louise, along with Roscoe and Olivia, organized the Carroll Club for the purpose of examining the works of Lewis Carroll in a light-hearted way. Designing the Carroll Club as a parody of the Browning Clubs popular at that time, honoring British poets Robert Browning and his wife, Elizabeth, allowed Louise and Roscoe to indulge their fun-loving natures. Combining learning with entertainment just as they had when they were children, the three welcomed their friends to 1632 L Street for the first Carroll Club meeting in January, 1892.

That evening a young woman recited "The Walrus and the Carpenter" accenting the poem's pathos in the style of a nineteenth century elocutionist. When Louise stood before her friends at a later meeting, she regaled them with a paper on Lewis Carroll's theory of portmanteau words. Her presentation was useful in her future studies. Using examples from Carroll, Louise wrote an article titled, "On Indefinite Composites and Word-Coinage." Her paper emphasized the telescoping of words into one— such as dumbfound from dumb and confound, electrocute from electric and execute, etc.

Another Carroll Club member, Dick Lehmer, used meetings to try out his musical compositions. He arranged "Jabberwocky" to music and sang the tune at club gatherings while Louise accompanied him on the piano. He set other Carroll poems to music as well, but "Jabberwocky" became Judge Pound's favorite. During future meetings whenever Lehmer started the opening recitative, "Twas a brillig," Judge Pound's chuckles could be heard coming from his study. "By the time the cadenzas of burbling reached their full fortissimo," Olivia wrote, "Judge Pound's hearty laugh would ring out as a resounding accompaniment."

Although Lehmer became a professor of mathematics at the University of California, he continued pursuing his musical and literary interests, composing poems, songs, and two operas. Staying in touch with the Pound family after he left Nebraska, Lehmer was one of several students who thanked Mrs. Pound for her positive influence. After receiving a copy of Laura's article about her wedding journey, he expressed his appreciation in a letter: "I am glad you have not entirely forgotten me. You were very good to me as a crude, raw young student and if I am not quite such idiot as I was then much of its credit is due to you."

Lehmer was one of several outstanding young people attending the University with Roscoe, Louise, and Olivia. Other remarkable individuals included Samuel Avery, a future University chancellor and George Sheldon, who would become a distinguished Nebraska governor. Frederic Clements continued his botanical studies and founded plant ecology. Two women writers, Willa Cather and Dorothy Canfield Fisher (daughter of Chancellor James Canfield), achieved national recognition for their novels. Alvin Johnson, the student who gazed at University Hall with awe, eventually became one of the founders of the New School for Social Research in New York. Hartley Burr Alexander mastered several fields including philosophy and anthropology, but he made a lasting mark in the architectural profession. Of course, Louise, Roscoe, and Olivia Pound were among the outstanding students attending the University in its early decades.

A passage in Johnson's autobiography, relating an incident during Louise Pound's undergraduate years foretold the path that her career would follow. Although getting ahead in life was a primary goal, Johnson stated that a skeptical attitude existed toward having scholastic aspirations beyond an undergraduate degree. "A declaration that you meant to devote your life to scholarship would have been regarded by most of our students as arrogance," Johnson wrote. It was fine to say that you were becoming a teacher because "teachers were made, not born, often out of coarse-grained, resistant material, and in current folklore, all the better teachers for that."

When a classmate asked Louise Pound whether or not he should devote his life to scholarship, she encouraged him. "Scholarship is a mission," she said. "It needs many workers. If you can add just one cubic centimeter to the mass achievement of scholarship, you have not lived in vain." Her brown eyes probably darkened with intensity as she advised her friend. There is no doubt that beneath the jolly, fun-loving surface of Louise Pound there lived a serious scholar, one who believed in individual excellence.

Nurtured by her parents who had planted within their children a respect for scholarship, Louise would follow the advice she gave her classmate. Staying on at the University to continue her quest for learning, Louise added to the institution's prestige. Through her scholarship and teaching she also added to the world's store of knowledge.

CHAPTER SIX

A Versatile Graduate

THE UNIVERSITY OF Nebraska class of 1892 was the "brightest that ever mashed peanut shells into a Brussels carpet," the group's historian, J.L. Porterfield, said when he related the class history during the commencement ceremony. As the one of those bright individuals, Louise gave the class oration. Her speech, on Tuesday, June 14, 1892, shocked the audience with controversial views on the elevation of the common man and the resulting disregard for individual achievement of excellence.

As the top student in her class, Louise stood before the crowd on that fine May day, her rust-colored hair shining and her slim figure clad in a dress with a nineteen-inch waist. The dress proved that she was more than a talented athlete and a top scholar, she also was a competent seamstress; she had sewed her own graduation gown.

Fifty years later, Louise claimed that she had forgotten the topic of the talk she gave as class poet and orator. Disregarding her denial, reading the speech in the light of her accomplishments reveals values that influenced her decisions and actions throughout her life. Louise Pound believed in and aimed for individual excellence in every endeavor. She placed individualism above commonality, and she rated personal excellence above mediocrity.

Her speech, "Apotheosis of the Common," stated a concern that she shared with the British writer, Matthew Arnold, about the general sterility of mind and thought that threatened the minds of Americans. Louise believed that the British began the exaltation of the common man, but the idea grew most rapidly in America. "Here the commonplace is a god. The average man and his average performance are the measure of all things. Everything must be common to be of value—thus glory and loveliness have passed away because they are not common."

What caused this bright young woman, a magna cum laude graduate with a degree in literary studies and music to give a lengthy speech denouncing the glorification of the common man?

Perhaps her family's stand against the Populism that ran rampant throughout the state during the 1890s influenced her thinking. Nebraska Populists devoted a large portion of their legislative programs to educational matters and campaigned for the election of Populist University regents who would overturn the traditional curriculum in favor of training young people in the trades and professions needed in the state.

Sayre wrote that "the horrors of a Populist landslide were not only possible, but a very real specter in the (Pound) home." The professional and financial people in Lincoln felt that William Jennings Bryan and other Democrats, many of whom agreed with the Populists, were "essentially demagogues." Their demand that silver be coined at the rate of 16 to 1 for gold could have ruined rich and poor alike.

Louise had no fear of taking on the populists and their followers who exalted the common and devalued excellence in individuals. Like her mother's challenge of the Lincoln mayor's plan to paralyze the city library, Louise's speech questioned the wisdom of ignoring the contributions of achieving individuals.

Praising individualism, Louise referred to the "general sterility of heart and mind" that would characterize the country's population if "the average man and his average performance (continued) to be the measure of all things." The commonplace, according to Louise, was sweeping the country in three ways: In thought as sentimentality; in art and literature as realism; in society as democracy. The newspaper was the "oracle" of the common man, but the chief manifestation of the common in thought was sentimentality—a refusal to recognize that "there is such a thing as force in this world, an inability to see that there are stern and harsh things in existence which sentiment and the commonplace cannot meet."

Confirming her stance as an elitist, Louise believed that people who achieved excellence earned the right to an elevated status. Emphasizing the common in outstanding individuals damages the integrity of their contributions to society. As an example she cited biographers' emphasis of George Washington's false teeth and of the gossip "floating through great men's kitchens." She advocated noting their accomplishments rather than the ordinary aspects of their everyday lives.

Louise believed that when "our forefathers wrote that all men are created free and equal, they laid down a principle of good government—that before the law all citizens should have equal rights." She argued against the common interpretation which emphasized that all men were intrinsically equal. An outcome of this belief was the lack of respect for public office. The concept of "majesty of state" had become obsolete and had caused patriotism to disappear. Indifference to the nation and the national honor were the natural results.

In conclusion, she placed her faith for the future on individualism. As a motivating power and force in civilization for over a thousand years, she reasoned that individualism may yet override the descent of humanity to a common level. "For individualism means equality of individuals only in the sense of freedom of thought and action on the part of each individual rather than the pulling down of excellence to its level." Her concluding sentence restated her belief in individual excellence, a stance that she maintained throughout her life. "Where the individual must be common, he loses that identity which makes him an individual. All is one dead-level—a lifeless average."

The *Lincoln Journal* reported that Louise Pound's speech was a "most scholarly oration. Whether or not the audience agreed with her assertions none could question the strength of her argument... it appealed to that feeling possessed by so many that they are endowed with certain qualities entitling them to a place higher than that deserved by their fellow man."

An article in *The Hesperian* summarized Louise's speech but gave no opinion of the content. It stated that Louise delivered her oration in a "clear and forcible manner," but she "showed nervousness." Perhaps she was uneasy because she understood the controversial nature of her speech. Even though she felt entitled to an elevated status because of her family's position in the community and her own demonstrations of excellence, she must have known that those with average grades and a lack of athletic skill, along with those lacking social status, probably disagreed with her opinions.

Challenging the elevation of the common in life and art was a daring act for twenty-year-old Louise. Making such a speech implied that she placed herself among extraordinary individuals. Thus far she had succeeded in her drive to excel, but the rest of her life lay before her. Perhaps she was anxious about continuing to earn the superior banner that marked her achievements. In every respect, the remainder of her years would be devoted to reaching and maintaining excellence in sports and in her profession.

Her oration climaxed Louise's graduation activities. The night before she stood behind the podium praising excellence, she had received a diploma in piano as well as in music theory and harmony. Displaying her skill at the keyboard, Louise participated in the commencement concert and the music department's graduating exercises at the University chapel. The June 13, 8:00 P.M. program featured several soloists including Louise Pound and Carrie Melville McClurkin. Miss Pound and Miss McClurkin were the first to receive music diplomas from the University.

Louise played all movements of Beethoven's "Sonata Pathetique," Opus 13, No. 8; Chopin's polonaise, Opus 26, No. 2; and Rubenstein's "Le Bal." Carrie M. McClurken performed the presto movement of Mendelssohn's G Minor Concerto, Op. 25 on the violin with orchestral accompaniment. The University orchestra as well as the chorus in which Olivia Pound sang alto performed several numbers. When Chancellor Canfield presented diplomas to Louise and Carrie McClurken, he remarked that "one with harmony flowing from the ends of his fingers or from the tip of his tongue possessed a power rarely excelled."

No record exists of Louise maintaining her interest in piano performance or in using her knowledge of harmony and theory to compose music. She probably mastered the piano because it was easy for her, and at the turn-of-the-century girls were expected to learn to play an instrument, just as they learned to draw and paint. No doubt Louise outperformed other girls her age, and for that reason continued her piano training throughout college.

Her fingers may have skipped across the keyboard with the same agility of her feet as they tripped across tennis courts, but a musician's most important attribute is interpreting the composition and developing an individual style. The speedy comprehension which allowed Louise to play with technical accuracy may not have encouraged personal empathy with the spirit of the music. Slowing her mind enough to reflect on the composition and express her feelings about it through her performance may not have appealed to Louise. She kept a tight rein on her emotions.

It's also important to understand that Louise was a practical person. Making a name for herself as a musician would be a greater challenge than winning athletic championships or researching literary facts. Especially at the turn-of-the-century, the most likely future she could expect as a pianist would be to teach others, or to become a church pianist and organist. It's not surprising that she gave up performing and favored attending concerts and operas.

LIKE OTHER YOUNG women of upper-middle-class families, Louise had learned to draw and paint. Artistic skills served a useful purpose. When vacationing, one could sketch scenic views. At home, drawing portraits of family members and friends in domestic settings substituted for the more expensive use of a camera.

By 1888 George Eastman had developed the first hand-held Kodak camera. Although operating the camera was a simple process of pulling a string, turning a key, and pressing a button, producing photographs was a complicated procedure. The camera which contained 100 exposure film had to be returned to the factory to have the pictures developed. After the photographs were processed and mounted, the camera was reloaded with film and sent back to the owner.

Although the Pounds were well-to-do, they practiced economy and probably had not invested in a camera. Louise would have considered it more convenient and cheaper to sketch the scenes she wished to record. One can imagine her riding a bicycle around Lincoln and the surrounding countryside with a sketch book and charcoal pencil in her pocket. Her papers include three sketch books filled with drawings of Lincoln and European scenes as well as portraits of family members.

In July 1889, Louise drew the "old" Baptist Church, and in July 1891, she sketched the Church of the Holy Trinity. Country scenes included a bridge over a stream, barns, and horses. A log building labeled, "Indian Cabin," appeared in the 1894 sketchbook. That same year she also drew a cook wearing a chef's hat, a woman reading (perhaps her mother) and portraits of her father, Roscoe, and Olivia. A drawing of a hammock on a porch depicted the Pound home at 1632 L Street.

European scenes, possibly drawn when she studied in Heidelberg, included a view of the Rhine riverbank, a house in Frankfurt, and a church in Strasbourg. She also sketched a waterfront view of St. Petersburg.

Apparently, sketching was a hobby for Louise. She simply enjoyed filling her sketchbooks with scenes of people, buildings, and the countryside. Not all of the drawings contained in the existing sketchbooks are dated, but many were drawn in July over a period of several years. Her earliest effort, drawn in July, 1886, was of Lincoln's Grace Methodist Church.

Perhaps drawing was a vacation pleasure that gave Louise freedom from competing for prizes or gaining personal recognition.

As her sketches reveal, Louise appreciated beauty and had an artist's eye. She exercised her grasp of a scene's details not just in her drawings, but also in her stories. "By Homeopathic Treatment," published in a University literary journal that preceded *The Prairie Schooner*, and "The Passenger from Metropolis," an unpublished story among her papers, have descriptions that form a picture in the reader's mind. A third story, "Miss Adelaide and Miss Amy," lacks descriptive scenes but concentrates on language.

Louise wrote these tales while studying for her master's degree and working as a theme reader in the English department. In 1894, the year that "By Homeopathic Treatment" was published, she earned her MA in philology. Then she stayed on as an instructor in the English department. Family connections in addition to her scholarship influenced Lucius A. Sherman, head of the department, to keep Louise on the faculty.

"By Homeopathic Treatment" was shaped around the attempt of a group of women to cure a friend (Matilda) of her radical stance on women's suffrage. Louise opened the story with a descriptive paragraph that engaged the readers attention in 1894 and does the same today:

> *We had to face a dreadful wind to carry out our plan of meeting, a wind of that gusty, (——) kind that lures you on gently for a square or two, then pounces on you from around a corner tugging fitfully at your hat, burrowing into your dress and twisting it about you in impelling spirals, making the houses blink at you dizzily and the trees spin like tee-totums as you pass along. We had to face it, and we did face it, hesitating, but determined. The case was too urgent to admit of delay. Something had to be done about Matilda, and at once. The trouble was to decide what.*

Matilda talks of nothing but getting the vote for women, and her friends find her boring. Her refusal to discuss anything ordinary—such as the current fashions—inspires the women to invite Matilda to an afternoon tea where they plan to introduce her to Clementine, a woman obsessed with social issues. "She doesn't care two pins about the ballot or woman's sphere but she is all wrapped up in slumming and that sort of thing."

When Mathilda and Clementine meet at the tea, Clementine asks Mathilda if she would "exalt" getting the vote for women over "remedying social disorder." The two disagree over the importance of their causes, and the afternoon passes "painfully." The arranged meeting of Mathilda and Clementine did not "cure" Mathilda of her obsession with women's suffrage; it only reinforced her devotion to the cause. Nevertheless, "in spite of the failure of the cure, we could not help feeling that that afternoon had been its own reward."

While Louise, like her characters, Mathilda and Clementine, was a typical New Woman, she maintained an impartial tone in this story, not revealing support for women's suffrage or for righting social injustice. She must have favored women getting the vote because her mother had supported the cause since childhood. An anecdote from Laura Pound's memoirs recorded her mother's (Olivia Biddlecombe's) inability to vote. Laura had asked her father why her mother hadn't gone with him when he voted in a school election. Her father answered that women weren't allowed to vote. From that time on, Laura Pound wrote, she favored women's suffrage.

Two other unpublished stories among Louise Pound's papers reflect her interest in language. "Miss Adelaide and Miss Amy" is set in an English village and is written in dialect. The tale reveals Louise's knowledge of British customs and her familiarity with speech patterns of the common people–one of whom narrates the story. Unfortunately, the dialect confuses the reader, and the plot is hard to follow.

Adelaide and Amy are squire's daughters who have no brother to inherit their father's property. After Adelaide becomes engaged to a gentleman from a nearby shire, Amy becomes ill and never fully recovers—until she replaces Adelaide as the bride-to-be. Three years after the wedding in which Adelaide serves as maid of honor, Amy dies. Adelaide doesn't marry Amy's widower because that practice is forbidden. Instead, the manor house becomes a school, and Adelaide lives out her days in a nearby farmhouse.

Because Louise used archaic spelling and dialect, the story is difficult to read. An unidentified critic declared the tale "overdone," "too hard to read," and requested that Louise "simplify" the text. No revisions exist among her papers. Only "By Homeopathic Treatment," the unrevised "Adelaide and Amy," and a third story, "The Passenger from Metropolis" demonstrate Louise Pound's attempts to write fiction.

"The Passenger from Metropolis" is an example of Louise's fascination with names. The story is about a young woman, Mary Barton, who, as a girl, reads a news item in the personal column of a daily paper stating that "Miss Ingalletta Prichard went to Hockersville last Thursday." Thereafter, whenever she reads news items about Ingalletta Prichard, Mary Barton cuts them out and pastes them in a scrapbook.

Several years later Mary notices a newspaper announcement of the forthcoming marriage of Miss Etta Prichard to Phillips Baxter, and she wonders if Engalletta has shortened her first name to Etta. Not long after reading the wedding announcement, Mary reads another article stating that Mrs. Etta Baxter is visiting Metropolis and will give an elocutionary recital at the Methodist Church on Friday afternoon. Wanting to discover whether or not Ingalletta Prichard is Etta Baxter, Mary takes the morning train to Metropolis and attends the lecture.

On her return journey from Metropolis, Mary encounters a friend who asks why she is on the train. Mary tells her friend about her attempt to discover the identity of Ingalletta Prichard. The narrator of the story, also a passenger on the train, eavesdrops on the conversation between Mary Barton and her friend as does a female passenger sitting beside the narrator.

When Mary admits that she hasn't discovered whether or not the speaker had been the Ingalletta Prichard whose social activities she has followed for years, the narrator's seat partner (the former Ingalletta Prichard) taps Mary Barton on the shoulder and says, "If the information will afford you relief, Mrs. John Phillips Baxter's first name was once Ingalletta.

The beginning of this story reveals the same descriptive ability that Louise displays in her published story, "By Homeopathic Treatment." Readers see the thriving village of Metropolis from the view of passengers just before the train leaves the station: "All that can be seen of Metropolis from the car windows is the inevitable low red 'depot' of western stations, a three-story frame structure just across the street labeled in large letters, The Cosmopolitan Hotel, and several brick store buildings that catch and reflect the rays of the afternoon sun. The main business and residence parts of the village straggle away out of view behind hills and clumps of trees."

"The Passenger From Metropolis" and "Miss Adelaide and Miss Amy," especially, have flat characters. Louise fails to reveal their personalities. Instead, these stories explore language. While she could play the piano with technical skill and sketch scenes with above average talent, Louise shied away from emotional involvement with her music, her drawings, and her story characters. She had a technical mind, a mind attuned to the scientific method she had learned under Charles Bessey's direction.

Interpreting music, evoking the mood of a scene, or portraying a fictional character's personality are abstract and intuitive endeavors requiring personal reflection and emotional involvement. Nevertheless, Louise was capable of emotional involvement during athletic competitions. She gave her whole self to winning—her mind and her body worked together, propelling her across tennis courts and inspiring her to pedal her bicycle mile after mile.

DURING THE EARLY 1890s, Louise had become one of the first Lincoln residents to own a bicycle. Cycling had been gaining popularity since 1885 when the British introduced a low-wheeled safety bicycle that balanced easily on two smaller, equal-sized wheels.

This Fabulous Century: 1870-1900, reported that "Americans took to the wheel, from clergymen on their rounds to young ladies clad in skirts that rose scandalously above the ankles to make pedaling easier."

A photograph of Louise standing beside her bicycle shows her wearing an ankle-length skirt and a print shirtwaist with white cuffs and collar. A ribbon, tied into a bow, circles the shirtwaist collar. Her upswept hair is topped with a man's billed riding cap, and her feet are shod in black, low-heeled Oxfords. Although Louise is petite, her oval face reveals her characteristic intense expression. This is a portrait of a young woman who is sure of herself, one who intends to win races.

For the late Victorian era, Louise was wearing comfortable clothing. She joined other New Women who freed themselves from the customary heavy, clinging skirts and stout boots. Her simplified dress style encouraged physical movement and allowed her to control her bicycle as it bounced over the deep ruts that often cut into the dirt roads in and around Lincoln. During a few of these jaunts, she must have paused beside picturesque scenes and recorded them in her sketchbook. During other excursions she was intent only on building a mileage record.

Meeting the challenge of keeping her wheel on the road regardless of conditions spurred Louise's competitive spirit, and she completed 100 miles in a day, a feat that entitled her to a Century Road Club Bar in 1895 and 1896. She also earned a Rambler Gold Medal for riding 5,000 miles in one year, an accomplishment that gave her a membership in the Century Road Club of America.

Bicycling, more than any other sport, furthered the end-of-century women's movement in a radical manner, observed Patricia Marks in *Bicycles, Bangs, and Bloomers*. It was inexpensive and available to almost everyone. "It could be ladylike or daring depending on whether its rider pedaled demurely, petticoats and all, on a tricycle or donned bloomers, tie, and waistcoat and 'scorched' down the streets on a two-wheeler." Dressed comfortably, Louise enjoyed the freedom of riding a bicycle rapidly through the countryside when road conditions allowed.

In addition to changing women's clothing styles, the bicycle changed women's lifestyles. Caring for their own bicycles—inflating tires and fastening and oiling chains–increased their range of labor. "The woman who traveled on her own wheels, whether she did so for a lark or for serious transportation, expanded her boundaries well beyond the home circle. She became a citizen of the world," Marks wrote.

The bicycle, popular with both men and women, helped break down the old-fashioned image of women as being weak and helpless. In both tennis and cycling, Louise broke boundaries for her sex, and it wasn't surprising that she attracted another young woman intent on breaking sexual boundaries, Willa Cather.

CHAPTER SEVEN

An Ill-fated Friendship

RUSSET HAIR PUSHED under her flat billed cap, skirts moving
with the circular motion of her legs, Louise rode to the
University's Main Hall, dismounted, and parked her bike before
going to class. Willa Cather, a University Preparatory student, must
have witnessed Louise Pound's self-assured movements and been
impressed.

Circumstances of the meeting of Willa Cather and Louise Pound
remain unknown, but their acquaintance would have been inevitable
on such a small campus. Sharing characteristics of the New Woman
as well as an interest in literary matters, the two were close friends
for three years (1891-1894). Cather biographers always mention the
Cather/Pound relationship as an important chapter in Cather's life.
Whether or not the friendship occupied an equally noteworthy place
in Louise Pound's life is questionable.

Nine-year-old Willa Cather moved with her family from Virginia
to Nebraska in 1883. After his four-story sheep barn burned down,
Willa's father, Charles Cather, sold his property and joined his father,
brother, and other Virginians in Nebraska. The death of relatives from
tuberculosis while living in the Shenandoah Valley also motivated
Charles Cather to leave Virginia. James Woodress wrote, in Willa
Cather: Her Life, that rumors of top-soil twelve inches deep as well

as "the general westering spirit of Americans" provided another reason for Charles Cather to uproot his young family.

After 18 months of farming, Cather moved with his wife, mother-in-law, and children into Red Cloud, a town of 2,500 people. A division point on the Burlington Railroad, Red Cloud was a bustling community, and Willa's father set up a business making farm loans, selling insurance, and writing title abstracts. The Cathers may have left the farm because Willa's mother was more of a town woman than a farm wife, and Charles Cather probably realized that he, too, was more inclined toward business than farming. Better schooling for Willa was another reason for relocating. The rural school that she would have attended was in session only three months a year.

During her first months in Nebraska, Willa didn't like the rolling prairies that formed the landscape of her new home. Woodress recorded Cather's early opinion of Nebraska that she shared with a reporter in 1913. "The land seemed as bare as a piece of sheet iron," she said.

In 1921, she told another reporter of her initial estrangement from her new surroundings. "I was little and homesick and lonely and my mother was homesick and nobody paid any attention to us. So the country and I had it out together." By the end of her year on the farm, she had fallen under the spell of the imposing prairie that waved beneath a vast sky. "It has been the happiness and the curse of my life," she said.

Willa attended Red Cloud public schools and benefitted from the instruction of a few outstanding teachers. In addition to her formal education, Woodress noted that Willa's intellectual development profited from extra-curricular reading during her adolescence. Mr. and Mrs. Charles Weiner, who lived near the Cathers, welcomed Willa into their home and allowed her to use their extensive library. Weiner, a local merchant, and his wife, an educated French woman, also introduced Willa to French and German literature in translation and encouraged her to go to college.

According to Woodress, William Drucker was the most influential of Willa's friends. Drucker clerked in his brother's store and had a passion for Latin and Greek literature. Willa had already learned Latin and had begun to learn Greek. With Drucker, she read the classics: Virgil, Ovid, the Iliad, and the Odes of Anacreon. She continued her studies and discussions with Drucker during the summer vacations of her college years.

While young Willa cultivated Red Cloud inhabitants with scholarly minds, the Pound youngsters found intellectual stimulation at home. Willa went to Will Drucker's residence to read the classics, but the Pound children absorbed literature under their parent's guidance. Louise, Roscoe, and Olivia played with neighbors in their own backyard, and Willa spent hours at the home of her girlfriends, Carrie, Irene, and Mary Miner.

Their peers accepted Louise, Roscoe, and Olivia, even though they were home-schooled and intellectually gifted, but many of Willa's contemporaries considered her a conspicuous show-off. Gregarious and outgoing as an adolescent, she also was a non-conformist. Openly expressing her desire to be a boy, Willa cut her hair even shorter than boys her age wore their hair and signed her name William Cather Jr. or Wm. Cather M.D. If Louise or Olivia had assumed a male persona it's likely that Mrs. Pound would have warned them to consider the consequences of their actions. Although she allowed her children to make their own decisions, Laura Pound never hesitated to voice her opinions.

Unlike Laura Pound who had refused to attend finishing school because she wanted a broad education, Willa Cather's mother studied music, sketching, elocution, and French at a Baltimore finishing school. A few female academies also introduced their students to mathematics, geography, grammar, and rhetoric. Perhaps Virginia Boak's exposure to these subjects prompted her to encourage Willa's desire for higher education. But Virginia Boak Cather hadn't been trained in the homemaking skills that Laura Pound learned from her mother: gardening, sewing, cooking, and preserving foods. She was unprepared for pioneer life.

Refusing to appear in public until she had spent at least an hour getting dressed, Mrs. Cather was known to change costumes several times a day. She also loved jewelry and perfume. The practical-minded residents of Red Cloud viewed Virginia Cather as a woman who gave herself airs, although, in their eyes, she had nothing to be haughty about. Her husband had trouble making ends meet. She may have relied on family name and background to establish a superior attitude in Virginia, but folks in Red Cloud had no interest in lineage. They focused on coping in the present, and Virginia Cather held herself above mundane daily cares.

Nevertheless, Mrs. Cather was a woman to be reckoned with. Woodress noted that she provided the "spark that drove her household and more than made up for Charles Cather's easy manner." A tyrannical ruler, she "exacted a strict adherence to discipline and punished disobedience with a rawhide whip." Many of Willa Cather's biographers refer to her mother as "imperious."

Yet Mrs. Cather allowed her children enough freedom to develop their own personalities. It was remarkable that a woman who maintained a meticulous and stylish appearance permitted her daughter to wear male clothing and have her hair cut in a boyish style. One could argue that she was so preoccupied with herself and with her current infant that she was indifferent to Willa's assumption of a masculine identity, or perhaps she realized that objecting to Willa's behavior would only encourage it.

Cather biographer, Mildred Bennett, suggested that "Willa's rebellion against fashion was perhaps as much a revolt against maternal influence as it was an intense dislike of the "corseted discomfort" that fashions of the time demanded. When visiting the homes of other Red Cloud residents, Willa must have noticed the more informal style of dress and household management that other women employed, and she may have wished that her mother were more like them.

During the first two years of her sojourn in Lincoln, Willa maintained her masculine persona, dressing in boyish outfits, signing her name as Willie or William Cather, and hanging her coat in the boys coatroom. In *Willa Cather: The Writer and Her World*, Janis P. Stout reasoned that Cather may have been "defining herself from an early age" as a New Woman by dressing in a mannish style. Later, she took up bicycling and smoking—other "defining behaviors of the New Woman." Knoll wrote that Louise Pound also smoked, but "very little," and, as he remembered, "she did not inhale."

A picture of Willa Cather and Louise Pound attired in boyish clothing emphasized their masculine-styled hats. Louise wore a billed cap, and Willa sported a hat with a full brim. They wore broad knotted ties and jackets with wide collars. Such masculine attire, softened with feminine accents, was fashionable for all women during the 1890s.

The photograph probably was taken when their friendship reached its peak. During this period Louise and Willa shared the editorship of a literary journal, *The Lasso*. Reflecting the editors' enthusiastic natures, The Lasso was designed to foster school spirit. The two friends also acted together in the University's drama society, and both had important roles in the five-act play, "The Perjured Palladian," that Louise had written.

Resuming her tendency to befriend influential people, as she had in Red Cloud, Willa gravitated to the important residents of Lincoln. In addition to being attracted to Louise, Willa cultivated the Pound family because they were prominent in University and community affairs. Cather also established a friendship with the Charles H. Gere family. Gere published the *State Journal,* and his two daughters, Mariel and Frances, remained Willa's close friends even after she left Lincoln.

Louise was a year older than Willa and was a University sophomore when Willa entered preparatory school. Their friendship began the following year when Willa matriculated as a University freshman. In Louise, Cather discovered the tough competitiveness that she admired in men counter-balanced by female beauty. Louise might clap a boy's hat atop her burnished red hair when riding her bicycle, but she also struck a feminine pose when attending University dances or sitting for a class photograph. One picture revealed the delicate-featured Louise with her long hair styled in the conventional upswept fashion and wearing a high-necked dress with leg-of-mutton sleeves. A pendant necklace enhanced the bodice.

Fitting the New Woman category as defined by Smith-Rosenberg, Willa and Louise had been born between the late 1800s and 1900 and came from upper or middle-class families. In their rejection of traditional female roles, Louise and Willa had been influenced by their mothers' examples. Virginia Cather and Laura Pound were strong-minded individuals who adjusted to frontier life in unique ways: Virginia Cather assumed the privileged role of a grand lady while holding herself aloof from the community, but Laura Pound took an active role in furthering Lincoln's cultural development while home-schooling her children.

Cather biographers agree that her years at the University were emotionally stormy. Sharon O'Brien wrote, in *Willa Cather: The Emerging Voice*, that the storm center of Cather's world in the early 1890s was Louise Pound. Combining athleticism and scholarship, Louise fit the image of the emancipated New Woman that Willa admired. Although Cather cultivated an image of herself as lonely and rebellious, she was infatuated with Louise and desperately yearned for a return of her affection.

In June 1892, before Willa left Lincoln for Red Cloud after her freshman year, she wrote to Louise telling her that she'd seen her at a party. The letter as paraphrased by O'Brien included praise for the color, the neck, and the train of the new gown Louise had worn. Willa also complimented her friend's beauty. Then she wrote about the care she had taken to choose a parting gift for Louise. Willa had presented her friend with an edition of Fitzgerald's *Rubiyat of Omar Khayyam*. Giving one's friend or lover a copy of Fitzgerald's masterpiece was a popular expression of affection during the 1890s.

Continuing to reveal her feelings in her letter, Cather mentioned that it would be strange not to see Louise for a while, and that she was jealous of Louise's other friends. She admitted that she hadn't realized the depth of her feelings and knew that she shouldn't have them. It didn't seem fair to Willa that feminine friendships should be unnatural. She signed the letter, William.

The following summer, Louise accepted an invitation to visit Willa in Red Cloud. According to a letter in the University of Nebraska Archives that Cather had written to her friend, Mariel Gere, the visit wasn't a success. Knowing that Louise wasn't comfortable around children, Willa had bribed her young brother, James, with two nickels and a bottle of pop to go into the country where their father was working. Unfortunately James returned sooner than Willa expected and made a nuisance of himself by caressing Louise and asking her to buy him chocolate.

Cather claimed that James liked Louise but struck the same ice that Willa had been trying to break through for three years. For Willa, her friend's visit seemed too short, just long enough to reawaken her need for affection from Louise. Nevertheless Louise earned Willa's praise by remaining calm when Willa used only one hand to steer the car in which they were riding over banks and haystacks. Apologizing for the melancholy letter, Cather admitted that Louise had broken her of writing in a sentimental style, but on this occasion her bad habits had crept back.

Although there was no mention in Willa's letter to Mariel Gere of the illness Louise experienced after her one and only visit to Red Cloud, a letter that Mamie Meredith wrote to Mari Sandoz in 1958 revealed that Louise contracted malarial fever from the "swarms of mosquitoes" that plagued her during the sojourn in Red Cloud. The consequences of that illness, Meredith contended, contributed to the heart attack that ended Louise's life in June 1958. Meredith wrote that Olivia had told her of Louise's unfortunate visit to Willa's home. After returning to Lincoln, Louise "characteristically tried to cure the fever by exercise--riding her bicycle back in Lincoln," Meredith wrote. "Olivia thinks that the several heart lesions that puzzled the Lincoln doctors in June when they X-rayed L.P.'s heart date from that period."

Another Cather letter that O'Brien summarized was penned over a year later. Willa again expressed her desire to have Louise visit her in Red Cloud. She described her depressed spirits, attributing them to her doubts about Louise's love and commitment toward her. Giving Louise responsibility for curing her sense of worthlessness, Willa informed her friend that if she did come to Red Cloud, she should bring a pistol and deliver Willa from torment. If Louise did not come, their relationship was over.

Louise did not go to Red Cloud a second time. In addition to becoming ill after her first visit, Louise probably was appalled at Willa's melodramatic statements. If Louise had been tempted to behave in such an overwrought manner, she would have released her emotions through aggressive tennis playing or bicycle riding. As a practical and emotionally reserved person, she wouldn't have responded to the ultimatum that Willa demanded: (Visit me or the friendship is over.) She probably became wary of continuing a close relationship with a woman of impulsive action and effusive affection.

Willa's frank expression of her feelings in a letter to Louise wasn't unusual for that era. Smith-Rosenberg observed that "an abundance of manuscript evidence (letters and diaries) suggested that eighteenth and nineteenth century women routinely formed emotional ties with other women." Female relationships "ranged through the supportive love of sisters, through the enthusiasm of adolescent girls, to the sensual avowals of love by mature women." Nevertheless, Louise Pound's sensible nature resisted a close relationship with Cather.

It's possible that Louise, like Roscoe, had many acquaintances and friends but avoided personal intimacy with them. Sayre quoted a letter from an unidentified contemporary of Roscoe Pound concerning Pound's character: "There was nothing companionable about the man in the sense that you wanted to call him Roscoe within a few minutes of meeting him . . . There simply was no vulgarity to the man and for all his boisterous manner, I think he had a strange and deep shyness beneath . . . I was no closer to him after our two years of constant discussions than I was at the end of the first week."

Although Louise relished having fun and breaking down barriers for women in sports and academia, she might have been shy beneath her confident surface—not hesitant or fearful, simply shy. No wonder she refused to visit Cather a second time. Willa confided in a letter to Mariel Gere that Louise wouldn't call her "Love" the term Cather had chosen as a middle name. Such behavior would have embarrassed Louise. As a woman who enjoyed freedom of movement and independence of thought, Louise would have felt emotionally suffocated by Cather's advances.

While O'Brien stressed the impact on Willa Cather of her friendship with Louise Pound, Phyllis Robinson, in *Willa: The Life of Willa Cather*, emphasized the role that Roscoe may have played in ending the friendship of the two young women. Roscoe had just returned from a year at Harvard Law School when Willa Cather entered the University as a freshman in 1891. Before going to Harvard, Roscoe had taken a degree in botany at the University in 1888 at age 18.

At that time, he had been a member of the Botanical Seminar, a group of Charles Bessey's students who wrote and read serious scientific papers to one another. The group enjoyed a sense of fun and referred to themselves as the "Sem Bots." They made life miserable for the students of letters on campus, a group that included Louise and Willa Cather. The Sem Bots were known to cry out, "Show me a lit," Knoll wrote. Those shouts probably irritated Willa's sensitive and egotistical nature. The jeers undoubtedly increased the competition existing between Louise and Roscoe.

When Roscoe returned from Harvard in 1891, he again assumed leadership of the Botanical Seminar and also joined his father's law firm. Quickly becoming successful in law, Roscoe was named to a state bar examination board by the state supreme court in 1896. He also served as first secretary of the Nebraska State Bar Association and managed all association business. At the same time he continued his botanical studies with fellow student, Frederic Clements, during evenings and weekends.

Roscoe would have known Willa Cather through Louise, and he

undoubtedly encountered her on the University campus and in the Pound home. Willa would have been among the groups of students who met at 1632 L Street to plan campus events or to simply enjoy each other's company. Robinson speculated that Roscoe had been attracted to the outspoken and bright young Willa and that she possibly rejected him. While this speculation seems improbable, it is a consideration, and Robinson wrote that Roscoe may have lashed out at Willa in retaliation for her rejection.

A more realistic assessment could be that Roscoe wasn't attracted to Willa but noticed her attachment to his sister and referred to their friendship as unnatural. Robinson also stated that the episode with Louise, though painful, forced Willa to become aware of her sexual nature. "If Roscoe Pound saw through her and charged her with loving his sister like a man, it would have been enough to make Willa fear and hate him, and being Willa, she would have punished him with her pen."

If Roscoe also commented to Louise about Willa's excessive affection, he may have jolted Louise into an awareness of the impropriety of her relationship with Willa. If the experience was painful for Willa, was it also painful for Louise? As a sensible person, Louise would have been embarrassed to learn that others noticed the excessive closeness of her friendship with Willa Cather. She may not have taken Willa's overtures seriously until Roscoe remarked about the relationship. While she adhered to the New Women's stance on fighting for equality with men, she did not embrace breaking the prevailing standards of sexual conduct toward her own sex.

April 1894 marked the end of Louise and Willa's friendship and with Willa's relationship with the Pound family. Probably due to a remark or an action on Roscoe's part, perhaps criticizing Willa's displays of affection toward his sister, Willa wrote a blistering attack on him in her column, "Pastels in Prose," that appeared in the March 10 edition of *The Hesperian.* Cather referred to Roscoe's appearance among the University students during a Charter Day celebration: He appeared "in his own mind, at least, one of the heroes of yore days."

Roscoe escorted "old acquaintances" around the University with an air of ownership and "pleased condescension." As a member of the botanical seminar, "He called everything by its longest and most Latin name . . ."

Continuing her scornful remarks, Cather referred to Roscoe as a "notorious bully" in his youth, who now bullies mentally just as he used to physically. "He loves to take rather weak-minded persons and browbeat them, argue them down, Latin them into a corner, and botany them into a shapeless mass." She accused him of perpetuating "his own name and fame among students." He hung around the University only to brag about himself. "He is a University graduate, and that's all he ever will be in this world or that to come." Willa's predictions did not come true. Roscoe became the Dean of Harvard Law School and wrote many respected books on the philosophy of law.

The vindictive column could be read as the raging of a jealous young woman, one who envied Roscoe's achievements. By 1894, he had passed the Nebraska Bar and was practicing law with his father. He also taught law at the University while working on his doctorate in botany. Willa probably felt that gender played a role in Roscoe's ease of scholastic accomplishment—that because he was a man he received more attention than she.

Whatever the reasons for Willa Cather's criticism of Roscoe Pound, her "Pastels in Prose" column brought a dramatic end to her friendship with the Pound family. Robinson reported that Mrs. Pound considered Willa's behavior "an unforgivable breach of etiquette" and no longer welcomed her into the Pound home. Both Louise and Olivia ended their association with her. According to Robinson, Dorothy Canfield Fisher knew about the Pound/Cather conflict, but she considered it too painful to discuss. Because she considered the elder Pounds cold and self-important, Willa had never liked them. But she gave no reasons for her hatred of Roscoe.

Secretly and perhaps even unknown to herself, Willa possibly envied the Pound family's position in the community and wished that her parents had given her the same background and advantages that

Roscoe, Louise, and Olivia enjoyed. She considered them cold, because they seemed to form a cohesive world of their own, a world that excluded her. Willa craved attention, and from her letters to Louise, one can see that she also demanded it. The end of the friendship probably was inevitable. It would have been impossible to give Willa the affection she demanded.

Whatever caused the breach between the Pounds and Willa Cather, the incident demonstrated the cohesiveness within the Pound family. Given a choice between Roscoe's respect and Willa's love, Louise chose Roscoe's respect. She may not have been an introspective individual, but she was proud. The Cather chapter in her life was an embarrassing event that she kept to herself, and pride prevented her from showing charity toward Willa.

Nevertheless, the Pound family didn't hold Willa's behavior against her sister, Elsie. Elsie Cather always was welcome at 1632 L Street, and she did graduate work under Louise before teaching English at Lincoln High School where she remained a friend and colleague of Olivia Pound. As in many conflicts, the situation eased with the passage of time. Willa and Louise corresponded after Willa left Nebraska, although Louise never again trusted Cather. Willa "always addressed Louise warmly" in her letters, reported Robinson, but Louise was "less charitable" and when referring to Willa "often spoke in a mocking tone."

Chapter Eight

Collecting Trophies

While Willa Cather longed for a return of affection from Louise, Louise was channeling her passion into winning athletic competitions. As Knoll wrote, "Clearly what Miss Pound liked was competition and *winning*, (Knoll's emphasis) prominence and success, what she wanted was to head the parade, any parade."

Her favorite sport was tennis, a game she taught herself to play at age fourteen after she had mastered and become bored with lawn croquet, the favored game for Victorian women. Even though ankle-length skirts hampered movement, Louise began to win tennis championships. She only entered tournaments when they were held at a time and place convenient for her, placing greater weight on learning and teaching when balancing her interests.

When Louise began playing tennis in the late 1880s, the game was a recent addition to the sports genre and had been played in the United States only since 1874. From the beginning of the game's introduction to the United States women participated in the sport. Louise Pound broke no gender barriers in playing tennis, but she did become a local celebrity as the first female member of the Lincoln Tennis Club. She was awarded an honorary membership because she was such a good player.

Louise recalled Lincoln's first tennis clubs when interviewed by *Lincoln Journal & Star* reporter, Jean Millane. The early courts were marked out in the city in the 1880s. The first court, laid out on the state capitol grounds, was grass and had no backstops. After objections to the location, private courts sprang up. The first tennis club, organized in 1890, consisted of three dirt courts and a clubhouse on the northwest corner of 6th and G Streets.

At age 18, in 1890, Louise was the city of Lincoln's tennis champion, Simpson reported. During the 1890s, she remained the only female member of the tennis club and was unbeatable in the singles. The club's best player, S.L. Geisthardt became nervous whenever he played against Louise and hit most of his shots into the net. But Louise didn't have the same success playing against the Cornhusker football coach, "Jumbo" Stiehm. He was too large. She couldn't hit the ball over his head or avoid his long reach.

As an avid tennis player, Louise probably campaigned for the installation of tennis courts at the University. When co-editing *The Lasso* she may have composed the February, 1892, announcement stating that Chancellor Canfield and Lt. Pershing ordered a tennis court to be marked out in the armory "which will be available to members of the Tennis Association when the floor is not occupied by gymnasium classes."

Lt. John J. Pershing, who helped Chancellor Canfield lay out the tennis courts, became commander-in-chief of the U.S. Expeditionary Force in Europe in 1917 and later became Chief-of-Staff of the U.S. Army (1921-24.) He served as commandant of cadets at the University from 1891 until 1895, a position he had wanted since 1888. His parents and a brother lived in Lincoln, and Pershing received the University teaching appointment through his brother's influence.

During his years at the University, Chancellor Canfield encouraged Pershing to study law and assigned him the task of teaching geometry in the preparatory school. Pershing taught math "rather badly," according to Knoll. "But he never forgot his students and called them by their names when they met many years later," Knoll stated.

In 1891 and 1892, Louise won the Nebraska Women's State Singles Championships, but she never entered that competition again. During those same years, she was the University Men's Singles and Doubles Champion. Simpson reported that "As runner-up in the Intercollegiate Championships representing Nebraska, Miss Pound won a men's 'N'." She also played by invitation in three men's state tournaments and was runner-up each time. In 1894, she won an intercollegiate championship in mixed doubles with the professor of religion at Yale University, Charles Foster Kent.

But her greatest tennis triumphs took place in Chicago during the summers of 1897-98. While attending summer school sessions at the University of Chicago, she won the Western Women's championship in 1897, and in 1898 she won the University of Chicago's Women's singles and mixed doubles championships. She also claimed the Women's Tennis prize at Kenwood Country Club in Chicago.

In a letter to her parents, Louise summarized her difficult 1897 win:

> *There were but two matches this afternoon, and those were intense... Miss Wimer, a large tall muscular girl, with a powerful backhand stroke, exasperating success in getting back the ball, playing for times as good a game as she has yet played in the tournament was making me run frantically from one end of the court to the other, up and back, and working me to death. So I hoped to have an easy time the second set, but gracious. She won from me six-one (Louise had won the first set.) Remember I was playing just as hard as I know how. Every single game ran to deuce. Then back and forth. Every single game, every single point was fought for for minutes. Time after time I would get "advantage" and lose the game. That girl got absolutely everything, and played a swifter game than any I have run across since I have been in Chicago. I was playing as hard as I could (and) never even served a double. Served to one side, then the other, down the middle line and she whacked everything back. I tried tricks. I tried everything. I was cool. I fought— and she beat me 6-1. I know I never worked so*

hard in my life at a set. . . All this time that she got me three love the deciding set, I was trying to follow Mr. Gardner's advice, and place, not send them swift, which suits her. She's swifter.

On the fourth game, I succeeded, I placed down the side lines, and managed to get to the net. I won. Score 1–3. Then the girl gave out, while I was fresher and fresher. She served doubles and grew wild. I persisted and took the net. Soon 3–all. Then we fought and I got the game. We fought again harder, and she won. Score 4–all. Was there suspense?

The match hung on the next two games, and the crowd stopped cheering us and was breathless. I never played such tennis as these last two games in my life. Luck was with me! And helped me down the side lines, on the base line. I don't know just how I got these two games, but I did. And the match was mine.

And I was given a regular ovation . . . I've made a name for myself now and have won a prize and am content. Who could do better—do so well—with my experience?

In *Tennis: Game of Motion*, Eugene Scott comments that "competitiveness combines many elusive elements, some of which are distinct frames of mind." Those mind sets consist of "the understanding that no matter how far you may be ahead in a match you can't afford to let up; the understanding that even when a situation is hopeless, when defeat is imminent, you must fight down to the last point." Scott also notes that every professional is a "top competitor." Regardless of a player's particular physical attributes or drawbacks, an unknown element causes them to "emerge as winners."

Demonstrating the qualities of a "top competitor," Louise never "let up," during her match with the larger girl who had the advantage of a powerful backhand. When she was losing points to her opponent, Louise stayed "cool," and devised a strategy to confuse her challenger. Placing her shots instead of sending fast returns, Louise gained the advantage and won the game.

The next year, 1898, The *Nebraska State Journal* informed

their readers of Louise's tennis victories during the Round-robin women's singles and mixed doubles tournament at the University of Chicago.

An 11 August, 1898, article with the headline "Miss Pound Wins," quoted the *Chicago Tribune*: "the chief interest centered in the match between Miss Pound of Nebraska, the Western Women's Champion and Miss Neely, one of the strongest local players . . . Miss Pound had no difficulty with the Chicagoan, defeating her in straight sets, 6-1; 6-3.'"

On August 12, the Lincoln paper quoted *The Chicago Record* stating that "Miss Pound's smashing and net playing were too strong" for her opponent, Miss Tilton. By August 13, a newspaper headline proclaimed, "Miss Pound Wins Out." Louise had won four matches and lost none to win the Women's Invitation Tournament at the University of Chicago. "The most interesting match of the day was that between Miss Cloes and Miss Pound. Winning that match forced "Miss Pound to fight for every point she won."

The following week, Louise competed in the Kenwood Country Club tennis championship for women. One of her opponents was Juliette Atkinson, the national women's champion. Louise had defeated Atkinson to win the 1897 Western Women's Championship.

Quoting the *Chicago Tribune*, a Lincoln newspaper stated, "The tennis tournament that begins on the courts of the Kenwood Country Club next Saturday to determine the woman champion of the west promises to be not only the best women's tournament that has ever been held in the west, but in the country."

The article reported that the contest was notable because it attracted the "largest number of eastern women players that has ever been seen in the west." They were eager to "vanquish" Louise. (Julliette Atkinson was from the east.) Because she had been playing on the clay courts at the University of Chicago, Louise's critics hoped the turf courts of the Kenwood Country Club would slow her down.

Always a formidable competitor, Louise allowed neither the clay courts or the elitist attitude of eastern players to intimidate her. A sports writer conceded that Louise "never gives up, and while her strokes may not be as pretty as those of Miss Atkinson, they are stronger and harder to return. Both cover the court well, but Miss Pound cannot be tired out …" Louise triumphed once again, winning the Kenwood Country Club women's title.

When reporters asked Louise to pose for a photograph after winning the tournament, she refused. But one reporter persisted in searching for a photo. A handwritten note found among Louise Pound's papers stated that the newspaper had published a picture of Lydia Pinkham, identifying her as Louise Pound. Pinkham's face was familiar to many women of the late 1800s because it graced the bottles of her popular vegetable extract. They credited the concoction with easing "female complaints"—ailments they didn't care to discuss with their doctors. After this incident, Louise posed more willingly for reporters.

She developed a friendship with Carrie Neely, one of her opponents on Chicago's tennis courts. According to society column clippings found among the her papers, whenever Louise traveled to Chicago, she contacted Neely, and they attended plays and concerts together. In 1915, the two women combined their tennis skills and won two doubles championships: The Women's Western Championship in Chicago, and the Central Western Women's Doubles in Kansas City.

A letter to Louise from a former classmate at the University of Chicago, Robert Cecil MacMahon, who became a New York City rare book dealer contains a colorful description of Louise as she whirled across the University of Chicago campus during the summers of 1897-98:

> *Having become a partner in this firm dealing in rare and foreign books, I have stumbled upon your name in a college catalog. I can hardly think of you as a sedate and learned professor as my memory of you at the "U of C" is chiefly of a slender, red-headed, young sprite with one foot in the air, playing tennis like the seven devils. I believe I do remember that you did do some studying late*

at night, when it was too dark to play games out-of-doors, so you evidently absorbed enough dry learning between tennis matches to hold down a university chair. Here's to you!

Although tennis was her favorite game, Louise also played basketball during her Chicago summers, a sport she had helped establish at the University of Nebraska in 1895 at the request of Anne Barr, head of Women's Athletics. Barr had been teaching University girls to swing Indian clubs until Chancellor Canfield asked her to act as head of physical education for men and women in 1894. In 1902, she relinquished the position to R.C. Clapp, a medical doctor. Barr married Clapp in 1903, and Knoll stated that the couple "dominated physical education in Nebraska for the next twenty years."

When basketball was first introduced at the University in 1896-97, the girls took more interest in it than the boys, and the Nebraska women's basketball teams earned a winning reputation in the late 1890s and early 1900s—the years that Louise coached, played with, and managed teams. Players took the game seriously. Manley reported a recollection from a student of that era: "It was not an unheard of thing to meet at a promenade a proud coed blushing behind a black eye received in the afternoon's practice."

Louise Pound's energy impressed Chicago sports fans. A *Chicago Sun-Times* August 14, 1898, clipping displayed the headline, "Athletic Young Women Indulge in a Rough Game No Weaklings Are Allowed." A sketch of Louise accompanied the article, showing her wearing a flat-topped straw hat with a ribbon circling the crown. "She is forward and captain of the basketball team composed of coeds from the University of Chicago and she captains basketball teams from other Western Colleges," the article stated.

A description of the lively game followed: "The big ball would purl through the air like a cannon ball and with a swirling impetus half a dozen bloomered forms would shoot after it. Once the elusive sphere struck a bench and one girl flung herself full length and astride across the seat to grab for it while another girl rolled underneath with the lightening like rapidity and agility of a kitten. The contestants fell over one another and they rolled as they fell."

In an interview, Louise commented on the games, saying, "Oh nothing much happens as a rule. Sometimes there's a dislocated wrist or collar-bone, a black eye, a cut on the lip, a broken finger or some little thing like that but I never saw anything serious happen. Oh yes, I know one girl was killed in Minnesota last year—fractured her heart, I believe—but then, she ought never to have been playing. Defective hearts will not do in basketball." This remark was typical of Louise and revealed her forthright way of stating facts.

Louise was a memorable character as she dashed across tennis courts and rode her bicycle through the streets of Chicago in 1897-98. In a letter informing Olivia that her prize for winning a tennis match was "a cut glass smelling salt bottle with [a] gold top," Louise reported that she hadn't received her bicycle saddle (seat) with the rest of her "wheel." She had traipsed all over the region until she found "a bicycle man who was trusting and safe" and talked him into loaning her "a saddle for a few days for ten cents."

Although tennis was her game of choice, she continued to enjoy ice-skating during winter months. With the young Dorothy Canfield, daughter of Chancellor James H. Canfield, Louise skated on Lincoln's small ponds. In 1932 Louise told *The Daily Nebraskan,* reporter, Gretchen Schrag, "I have never held a prize for or a title for figure skating, but I was supposed to be the only woman in the state who could make the Maltese Cross backward, the double grapevine, and many waltz figures."

With her friend, Verna Edgren, a daughter of Hjalmer Edgren, dean of the University's graduate school, Louise had imported skis from Sweden and introduced the sport to Lincoln. "There were a few hills in the city," Louise said to reporter Shrag, "and we tried them all." She admitted that she had less experience with skiing "than with tennis, golf, cycling, and skating."

Having proved her excellence as an athlete, Louise faced an academic hurdle, becoming the first female graduate of the University of Nebraska to earn a Ph.D. Although she claimed that her supervising professor, Lucius Sherman, encouraged her to study for the higher degree, it would have been characteristic of Louise to seek a Ph.D. from a prestigious university. In Knoll's words, Louise wanted to "win," and she wanted to "lead the parade."

PART THREE:
CAREER AND LIFESTYLE CHANGES
1899-1920

.

CHAPTER NINE

The Heidelberg Challenge

I N THE MIDST of her friendship with Willa Cather, Louise began her Master's Degree studies. At the same time, she served as an assistant in the English department, an appointment that Lucius Sherman, Dean of the College of Arts & Sciences, granted her. By 1894, the year that her association with Cather ended, Louise earned her second degree and had been promoted to assistant instructor. Cather had also applied for an assistantship in 1896, the year after her graduation from the University, but Sherman denied Cather's request.

Possibly, Sherman refused to grant Cather a position because she openly ridiculed his literary theory. In her *Lincoln Journal* book review column, Willa penned antagonizing comments about Sherman's method of evaluating excellence and beauty in literature through numbering and diagraming words and sentences.

His method seemed absurd to both Willa and Louise, but Louise was more respectful of Sherman, perhaps because he was a family friend. Cather biographer, Robinson, speculated that if Cather had been hired by the University she might have stayed there all her life, "like her friend, Louise Pound."

At age 26, Louise was still an instructor and may have felt frozen in place, a feeling that lured her competitive nature into action. Although she had been taking classes at the University of Chicago during the summers of 1897-98, Louise may have become discouraged about the possibility of getting her Ph.D. from Chicago. Women weren't encouraged to pursue doctorates at the turn-of-the-century when the majority of college professors were men. Only those females, like Louise, who were classified as New Women, dared to join predominantly male professions.

Louise had an influential supporter in her desire to advance professionally. Lucius Sherman encouraged her to complete her doctorate and assured her of continued work (and probably a promotion as well) on completion of her Ph.D. Because two of the male English professors at the University had received their doctorates from German universities, Louise, in her decisive and competitive way, was determined to try for a degree from Germany. In the words of her former classmate, Alvin Johnson, "A degree from a German university was considered the ultimate in higher education so Pound decided to reach for the highest credentials."

During the nineteenth century, German universities set the standard for scholarship in the Western world and attracted at least 10,000 American students. The only female pupils German universities admitted were those training to be teachers. Perhaps Louise gained entrance to Heidelberg because of her teaching experience and her plan to remain in the profession. In addition, her excellent academic record allowed professors with whom she had studied to recommend her as a doctoral candidate.

In her 1955 acceptance speech as president of the Modern Language Association–the only document in which Louise discussed her past–she explained why she pursued her doctorate in Germany. She stated that philology was "in the ascendent" at the turn-of-the-century, and that "ambitious students were supposed to study linguistics in Germany" under distinguished professors. Then she mentioned Professor Sherman's encouragement of her continued study.

When Louise applied to Leipzig University where the two former University of Nebraska professors had studied, the school replied, "Nien, nien, NEIN!!!' with exclamation points." Louise was not deterred from her decision to study in Germany and considered Leipzig's refusal "fortunate." Her practical nature prevented her from applying to Berlin because she felt that she would be "lost in numbers at so large an institution." She then presented an application to Dr. Johannes Hoops of Heidelberg, editor of *Englishe Studien*. In Dr. Hoops, she met an enlightened gentleman who became a lasting friend.

> *He was not dismayed at the thought of a feminine candidate but had had able and successful women students, and he proved to be one of the friendliest and most helpful of men. I had a beautiful year. I did not have . . . to listen to the professors from behind a curtain. But had I wished to hear the lectures on Goethe by a celebrated professor at Heidelberg or to those by him on art, I would have been cautioned to watch my mode of dress carefully, 'Too elaborate feminine dress was barred,' I was told, 'lest it distract the attention of the Herren.'*

Before Louise left for Heidelberg in the summer of 1899, Roscoe and his fiance, Grace Gerrard, married. Roscoe and Grace had been dating since 1895, but their formal engagement took place two years later. They were married June 17, 1899. According to Sayre, Grace had been a classmate of Olivia and was a "fast friend of Louise." Laura Pound also approved of Roscoe's future wife and referred to her as "a little ray of sunshine.'"

A month before Roscoe and Grace married, Louise received her passport. At that time detailed physical descriptions of the traveler were used rather than photographs. Louise was issued Passport 7231 on May 29, 1899. She was 26 years old, five feet four inches tall with a high forehead, brown eyes, straight nose, small mouth, red-brown hair, and an oval face. *Lincoln Journal Star* reporter, Simpson, speculated that "Heidelberg must have shaked (sic) its head at this attractive

American woman. She was but twenty-seven. (Louise turned 27 on June 30, 1899.) Her trim red pompadour, fair skin, and delicately sculpted nose made her something to look at."

Heidelberg provided a picturesque setting for Louise's year of study. The city was surrounded by mountains, forests, vineyards, and the Neckar River. Crowned by a ruined castle, Heidelberg had always appealed to Romantic writers and composers. Carl Maria von Weber wrote his Romantic opera, *Der Freischütz* (The Marksman) in Heidelberg. Other famous individuals associated with the city were the German writer, Goethe; the American author, Mark Twain, and the German composers, Robert and Clara Schumann and Johannes Brahms. The University of Heidelberg was the setting for the popular Sigmund Romberg operetta, *The Student Prince.*

The city that Louise encountered in 1899 was best described by Mark Twain. He wrote about Heidelberg in 1878, twenty-one years before Louise arrived, yet his description bears consideration since changes occurred at a slower pace in the nineteenth century. In *A Tramp Abroad,* Twain stated that Heidelberg lay at the mouth of a narrow gorge shaped like a "shepherd's crook." At the bottom of this gorge flowed the "swift Neckar" confined between densely wooded steep ridges. Two picturesque bridges spanned the river. Rising out of a "billowy upheaval of vivid green foliage," a ruined castle looked down on the "compact brown-roofed town."

Twain arrived in Heidelberg when the summer semester was in "full tide." Although most students were German, other nationalities were represented. He stated that "instruction is cheap in Heidelberg, and so is living, too." Student routine was one of individual choice. "One sees so many students abroad at all hours, that he presently begins to wonder if they have any working hours." Unrestrained, the students found their own lodgings wherever they desired and kept hours that suited them. Referring to a male student, Twain wrote:

> *He is not entered at the university for any particular length of time; so he is likely to change about. He passes no examination upon*

entering college. He merely pays a trifling fee of five or ten dollars, receives a card entitling him to the privileges of the university, and that is the end of it.

He is now ready for business,—or play, as he shall prefer. If he elects to work, he finds a large list of lectures to chose from. He selects the subjects which he shall study, and enters his name for these studies, but he can skip attendance.

Lectures were the main avenue of learning, and one followed on "the heels of another," Twain observed. Students ran from lecture to lecture, and professors appeared promptly "in their little boxed-up pulpits" when the hours struck. A lecture hall that Twain visited had "simple, unpainted pine desks and benches for about 200 persons."

Thirty years after Louise studied in Heidelberg, travel writer, Clara Laughlin, recommended visiting the city for its "youth, love, and fellowship." It enshrined "youth in its last period of care-freeness and comradeship and romance before taking up the serious business of life." Louise could be counted among those students who celebrated the end of their youth while in Heidelberg. With her Ph.D. in hand, Louise left the city well-prepared for adulthood.

Perhaps Louise viewed her year in Germany as a sporting event—a competition she needed to win, one that would insure her future at the University of Nebraska or any other college or university. She overcame three obstacles before winning her degree: an illness after her arrival in Heidelberg, a need to master the German language, and a social life that threatened to distract her from her studies.

A record of Louise's year of study exists in the letters she wrote to her family. Because many of the letters aren't dated, they lack chronological order. Her handwriting is difficult to read, and she wrote on both sides of very thin paper. Her correspondence contains few descriptions of her daily routines, nor does it give a picture of student life such as Twain's work described. But her letters do reflect her concern about completing work for her Ph.D. in one year. She had set a goal that would prove her excellence—if she achieved it.

Never one to falter when faced with a challenge in sports or scholarship, Louise faced the most critical hurdle thus far in her life when she decided to complete her philological studies in one year instead of the customary two. Perhaps money was a factor in her decision. She may have estimated that she had saved enough for one year of foreign study. Or, she might have been worried about losing her University position if she stayed in Heidelberg longer than one year. It's also important to remember that Louise did everything quickly. She was not a patient or long-suffering person, and she intended to finish her studies as fast as possible.

When Louise arrived in Heidelberg, she impressed her professors by playing in the local tennis match—1899—and winning it. She also met Johannes Hoops, the professor with whom she would do most of her work. She wrote that it was "fine good fortune that I struck a man like Professor Hoops . . . Dr. Hoops is young . . . He covers a lot of ground quickly and well . . ." It's not surprising that Louise admired Dr. Hoops' speedy teaching method, because it matched her own fast pace.

Relieved that Hoops wasn't going to slow her down, Louise began a campaign to take her final examination after two semesters of study. She also began writing her dissertation. A letter to her family stated, "They would be making an exception for me-letting me off with two semesters instead of the required three. And this would be justified only by a better examination that I could pass, working awfully hard by next July."

In September 1899, Louise wrote to her mother that she had been ill but had recovered and resumed her studies. "I'm only waiting till Dr. Hoops comes back to Heidelberg to show him my dissertation. I want to see whether I'll have to do it all over." She thought it would be fine to have the dissertation rest before the semester began: "to have done the whole thing in August and September with weeks of sickness thrown in . . . If it is accepted, my outlook for a degree ought to be pretty good." She explained that her friends, concerned for her health and warmth, had kept the fire burning in her room as she worked.

A month later, October 1899, Louise explained that she usually felt cold. "I don't think much of German stoves. They aren't base burners. Fires are built everyday." Since there was no way of heating water on the stoves, Louise hadn't washed in warm water. "Everybody washes in ice cold water," she wrote. "However it's good for me—cold water."

In this letter she also reported a conversation with a German woman: "Her father is a professor but is paid nothing. He is one of the richest men in Heidelberg, and is a sort of volunteer professor—for the honor. Although Americans were allowed to come up for examination after two semesters, the woman informed Louise that "all possible obstacles were thrown in the way of a woman's taking a degree." This remark merely caused Louise to work harder. She reveled in challenges, especially those that allowed her to best the men.

Although she was confident that she was prepared for the test, Louise worried that she wouldn't be allowed to take it and informed her family of her concern: "The professors are nice to me and I'll be ready all right—but I'm much afraid about getting permission" (to take the exam after two semesters.)

Because of her illness, Louise had sacrificed exercise to make up for lost study time. She regretted her absence from the playing fields and from walking in the hills. Complaining to her family, she wrote, "If I get hard up for exercise in the winter I shall go snow-shoeing in the hills with the girls. It's the rage here in winter, with the skating." She and her friends also considered the possibility of playing basketball on Saturday afternoons, but doubted they could find an indoor space in which to play. She wrote that she had to "exercise—to learn more quickly . . . I'll not try to do without it anymore." Taking part in sports had helped her a lot, "in making friends and having a pleasant time . . ."

When family friends from Lincoln visited Louise she ferried with them over the Neckar River and climbed the surrounding hills. After their departure, she settled in and concentrated on Old French and

German. "It's time I was taking a few German lessons. I suppose I've had six or eight in all," she wrote. She reassured her family that she now felt well and was "much encouraged," although her letters would be "scarce for a while." She planned to withdraw from the world, except for occasional games of tennis, "but I'll like that." Looking forward to a visit from Olivia, she observed, "My, I want to see her."

> *I'm not looking forward with much pleasure to these months between now and the end of July. There is too much to do. I do hope I can take the examination but they may not let me just at the last moment—and then again they may make it so hard I can't get through. There is no telling.*

Another letter from Louise to her family mentioned that she had moved and was living with an American friend, Adele Lathrop.

> *Adele isn't so well nor strong as Nellie— but it's great to have her here just the same. Our breakfasts and dinner are served up in our rooms but at noon we eat below so that I can hear and talk a little German. I have little more chance to hear it or speak it than I did last semester.*

Again expressing her concern about having to take the examination in German and hoping she wouldn't fail, Louise informed her family: "Heidelberg is the worst place in the world to learn German in . . . I had to move away from Landhaus-strasse because there wasn't room enough for two, and especially because there was nothing but Americans there . . . We spoke only English."

Adele Lathrop and Louise had probably become friends through their membership in the Nebraska chapter of Kappa Kappa Gamma Sorority. After her stay in Heidelberg, Adele earned her degree from the University of Nebraska in 1904. Then she became the first principal of Pine Manor Junior College in Wellesley, Massachusetts, a position she held for the rest of her life. Continuing their friendship, Louise and

Adele met again in London when Louise was the American delegate to the International Council of English in June, 1927. Probably, Louise visited Adele whenever she had speaking engagements or vacationed in the eastern U.S.

The rooms that Louise and Adele shared were in the vicinity of the Neckar River and the castle ruins. Louise described their accommodations: "The garden runs up the hill behind to the Philosophers wing. We have not been up there yet. I bargained for two rooms, a schafzimmer (bedroom) and a big wohnzimmer (living room) with two writing desks, a table, a bookcase and two sofas, a nice room, the best yet, and (I) got it for the same price I had been paying before."

Explaining her work, Louise admitted that she didn't like the subject of her dissertation. Nevertheless, her goal of completing her studies in one year prompted her to accept the recommended topic.

Adele has been here a week now. We are all settled now as if there had never been a break. I've scarcely been out of the house since moving here. Working mostly in Old French (which I hate) and verifying references in the one hundred and fifty books examined for my dissertation. I had no idea it would take so long. I can't say I think very highly of my subject or of the dissertation itself but as long as they like it over here that's the main thing.

Taking a break from her studies, Louise attended several dances in December, 1899. A letter written at Christmas time, probably to Olivia, described her social life.

A big Christmas tree is in the house tonight and great bowls of punch . . . I shall have a nice Christmas too, one way or another . . . I've just been talking with a Virginian here studying medicine. He has been cheated one way and another, stuck for a hundred marks . . . my he hates it here. He says Heidelberg is as bad as Berlin. I'm fortunate that (her landlords) are fair and honest! I have to pay enough goodness knows but I seem to be better off than most of the others—and I'm taken good care of.

> *I've been talking with a Russian. The Russian waltz is an experience, stunning—takes one's breath out—everything else—quite away. He hates Heidelberg too . . . (it) can't compare to Russia and the Russians.*

> *Social doings are getting to be rather too much for me. I've been to two dances in the last week and am invited to three more in the next two weeks . . . I didn't come here to know people or for social doings or dances etc. Now it's hard to keep out of them. But I shall . . . and will be all right. You needn't worry about me. I hate Germany more and more. All Heidelberg isn't worth a square mile of Nebraska.*

It's easy to imagine Louise whirling across the dance floor in the arms of the Russian gentleman. He must have been fascinated by her beauty and appreciative of her dancing ability—a talent she inherited from her father. Perhaps she indulged in a bit a flirting and accepted the Russian's offer of a cap to wear about town.

In a letter dated December 24, Louise noted that she was spending her first Christmas away from home.

> *This is the day before Christmas. It seems queer to be so far away. Tomorrow will be the first Christmas I've ever spent away from home . . . A sleet has come and spoiled the ice so there'll be no skating for a few days. The town is simply crazy over skating. Everybody is on the ice in the afternoon, or in the morning, off in corners practicing . . . I'm well-fixed for skating clothes because of a blue tailor-made skirt Tude (Olivia) left here. People take me for a Russian. Because I wear a little (Russian fur cap) a splendid cap—(it isn't hers) and what German I speak is said to be with a Russian accent.*

She continued to worry about her fluency in German. "I don't rank very well with those who expect to take degrees when I want to, though I seem to be (satisfactory) in O.E. (Old English.)

In March of 1900, Louise left her studies long enough to watch Heidelberg citizens celebrate the arrival of spring.

> *Today was 'summertag.' Never saw anything like it! It's the children's day celebrated like no where but in Heidelberg. It's in honor of winter's going and summer's coming—the children from miles around march in the procession. They carry long poles shining with confetti and ribbons—all colors—'Maypoles' I suppose. At the top hang pretzels and generally an apple or hardboiled egg or orange is stuck on the top. Some are draped as Christmas trees . . . the old and decrepit winter and the beautiful new one 'summer'. . . From many other trees hung pairs of shoes.*

> *Today there was snow—the (wet) Heidelberg snow which is water before it hits the ground. But the procession took place anyway. The children tramping through the mud afterwards eating pretzels off their maypoles. I believe the city pays for the procession—the maypoles and the Christmas trees. It was almost as much fun as Fast Nache. Carnival times.*

Louise must have considered leaving Heidelberg during a spring break, but professors convinced her to stay. They told her it would be "foolish to go away without a degree when I am so 'near.' Professor Brause said, 'stay' and 'work all this vacation." She ended the letter with encouraging news. "They have promised, at last, to let me sit for examination in July!" They gave their promise with the condition that she work hard all vacation and continue her private lessons in Old French and German.

A concerned Louise wrote, "There are chances and chances that I'll fall through, but I must stay. It would really be a fine thing if I got it . . . It's the dissertation. Professor Hoops likes it. Well–he can see by this. He's editor of a lot of things." Dr. Hoops wanted to publish her dissertation in a philological series. Louise wrote that she would have to pay for the printing. "But he wants it to appear in this series (I will get a lot of advertising this way), and it will be printed more cheaply."

"Isn't this great?" she stated. "It will be quite an honor. Tonight I'm feeling good. This looks like a degree doesn't it?" Louise would be the first woman graduate of the University of Nebraska to earn a Ph.D. Her dissertation, "The Comparison of Adjectives in English in the XV and XVI Century," written in German, of course, was published as a small pamphlet in the philological series, Englishe Studien.

On July 6, (1900) Louise wrote her parents that her exam would come in about three weeks. She had written Dr. Sherman, of her expected degree and received a favorable reply. "I had a nice letter from Dr. Sherman. He will let me teach about what I want. The English wing has been cut down a lot," she wrote.

Whether or not Louise was conscious of it, her success in taking the exam early and receiving her doctorate in one year proved her excellence. Having praised individual excellence in her college graduation speech and also counting herself among the intellectual elite, she was more than relieved to receive her advanced degree, she was jubilant.

Even though she had worked hard scholastically, Louise had kept her resolve to remain active in athletics. Perhaps her statement to her parents that playing sports would help her achieve her academic goals was accurate. She had fond memories of playing competitive games in Heidelberg. In a 1951 "Looking Back" newspaper column, she told the reporter that while in Heidelberg, she was "most proud" of turning the tide for a girls' cricket team that had "experienced consistent defeat at the hands of a boys school team even though the boys were handicapped by 'blind umpires,' skirts and special rules that forced them to pitch left handed, catch with one hand, (and) bat with a broomstick." The girls' team had never won a match until Louise took her turn with the paddle-shaped cricket bat. To her, the bat was just another tennis racket. Standing firm against on-coming balls, Louise prevented the opposing pitcher from putting her out. Fans yelled, "Go it Columbia!"

About her performance on the cricket field, Louise said, "With all those silly handicaps, of course the boys didn't have a chance. But we'd have beaten them anyhow." That same year, Louise had been named 'honorary pitcher' of an American baseball team that played an annual Fourth of July game with the British.

In addition to playing cricket and studying, Louise returned to the tennis courts. She had heralded her entrance to the city by winning the Heidelberg championship, and she celebrated her departure with a second triumph—winning the 1900 local championship. Because of her competitive spirit and hard work, Louise returned to her beloved Nebraska bearing a Ph.D. cum laude, and two more tennis trophies.

Chapter Ten

Ani and the Lifestyle Choice

IN HEIDELBERG LOUISE encountered a personal challenge apart from her studies. She met a young woman whose personality was as strong as hers. This woman, Ani Königsberger , seemed as determined as Willa Cather had been to befriend Louise. Unlike Cather, who had been rash and emotional in attempts to gain Louise's favor, Ani exercised patience and diplomacy in breaking through Louise Pound's reserve. Their developing friendship was an event that must have taken Louise by surprise, arousing emotions that she usually denied.

Early in her Heidelberg stay, Louise reassured her family that she had "plenty" of friends. "The Americans who are studying and one German woman who is perhaps the best, because most in earnest." She referred to Ani, the daughter of Professor Königsberger . Ani's background contributed to the bond that formed between the two young women. Although she was German, Ani had not been raised in the ways of other German girls. As Louise informed her parents, Ani had been reared as an "English girl." Her parents, like those of Louise, had allowed Ani to take part in sports. She hiked and climbed, swam and skated. She also was an artist.

Although her letters to Louise never mention her educational background, Ani's writing reveals a wide range of interests. Because her father was a professor at Heidelberg, Ani, like Louise, was a friend of Dr. Hoops and perhaps had studied under his direction. But the strongest tie between the two, at least in the beginning, was formed through their mutual love of sports. After they met and spent time together, an intellectual affinity encouraged them to correspond for fifty-eight years with interruptions only during the two world wars.

When Louise asked Ani why her parents had permitted their friendship, Ani credited her unique background. In a January 1901 letter, she wrote: "You say you wonder why my parents let me know you . . . Why I always do what I like, I am not educated on German principles, you must remember, my mother was Russian–hers was French, all have seen much, know things, know me and knew the (Heidelberg) girls and they don't want to make life harder for me than they can help."

In her early letters, Ani often expressed affection for Louise and her gratitude for developing a friendship with "a girl." A January 1910 letter stated that she was "off for the Alps and Italy." She hoped to have "a good time this winter–though not with people (girls especially) with men I always get on. They don't seem so small." Ani wrote that it was difficult for her not to have a girl with whom she could talk, yet she couldn't "change it." Her interests outdistanced those of most German girls, creating a void in her life that friendship with Louise had filled. Even after ten years apart, Ani missed Louise's companionship.

Meeting Louise was a central event in Ani's life, one she never forgot or neglected. A 15 August 1900 letter confirmed the camaraderie that existed between them. Describing the view from a mountain peak that she had climbed, Ani had thought of Louise as she watched "the clouds come and cover some mountain then go again and the whole view is so clear . . . I am writing you because I feel like it, you know. I just feel as if that would give you a feeling of it, does it?" While she observed her surroundings, Ani wondered why she had found the courage to invite Louise to walk with her in the hills surrounding Heidelberg. Mystified by her actions, Ani wrote that Louise was the "first and only one" she had invited for a hike in the hills.

One can imagine the two young women wearing sturdy hiking boots that thrust forward from beneath ankle-length skirts as they strode along the trail. If the weather was cool, they probably wore cardigan sweaters over their shirtwaists. At first only the crunch of their boots on dried leaves and stray twigs broke the silence of the forest. Then birds twittered and flitted above them as they climbed uphill.

Anxious to prove that she hadn't made a mistake in asking this aloof, yet beautiful, American to join her in a hike, Ani broke the silence between them, possibly with a question about Louise's studies or a comment on the surrounding terrain. When their conversation gained momentum, slowing their steps, Ani realized that Louise's controlled surface masked a warm, compassionate personality.

Referring to the girls she had known before Louise as "dolls," Ani said that she was grateful to Louise for accepting the invitation to go walking, "it helped me, it showed me a new thing." Louise's friendship caused a "great difference" in Ani's life, creating a "new sensation." She believed that Louise had "the better life," but that she had a good one "for a German girl."

Louise must have written to Ani about her Lincoln friends, because Ani was curious about the quality of their relationship: In the 15 August 1900 letter she wrote: "I wonder what you are with your friends, for whole days and to talk about everything . . ." Expressing a desire to continue their correspondence, Ani wrote, "it would be hard for me to 'lose' you. You help me when I think of you, do you understand?"

In addition to being better educated and more liberated in her attitudes than other German girls, Ani had a congenial relationship with her father. A 12 May 1910 letter stated: "My father is still the one in the family who talks the most, my mother less, then my brother, then I but sometimes I more than my brother . . . I am very much like my father and (we) always get on well. My mother and brother are somewhat alike again in looks."

She stated that she cared little for people, could "do well without them." Yet Louise was "outside of that anyhow, but inside the wall I suppose, got in long ago and got a piece of the wall yourself." Emphasizing the rarity of her tie to Louise, Ani continued describing her interactions with others: "I still care sometimes to see new people wonder what they are like but as a rule having seen them for 5 minutes is enough to convince me that they are just what I expected and am glad to leave them again and think no more about them. Sometimes being with my parents I get to know new people, walk with them, mostly men and get quite intimate (they only, not me) but when they begin to speak of 'us' I wonder if they really think of me as one of them."

Both Ani and Louise differed from their peers and felt set apart from them. Their athleticism and broad educations set them apart from their contemporaries. Yet this separation didn't affect their self-esteem; they seemed proud of their differences–probably because they had been raised to respect themselves and to value their unique personalities and talents.. Louise prided herself in individual excellence, and Ani admitted that she hadn't been raised as others her age. She had been allowed to go her own way.

Having found a soulmate in Louise, Ani expressed her desire to be with her again. (31 August; no year stated.)

> *I want you as much as ever, would you really come if I wanted you for good. I wonder. If we meet again sometime, if it will be the same? There has been much life for each of us between our last meeting, for me rather much and change in things and more in opinion. You know I try hard to change, do I succeed? You know in what not outward things and not in tasks. Had I not met you I would have changed in the other direction.*

Louise had a profound influence on Ani and was probably the only woman with whom Ani had formed a close friendship. She treasured her memories of Louise after returning from a hike. On an undated scrap of stationary, Ani wrote, "Do you know, when one comes just back and is in one's room, it all comes back. Then it's easy to think how we were there and the talks and all. Later it is not so easy."

Their friendship, which appears to be ardent on Ani's part, almost an infatuation, was not an unusual occurrence between women at the turn-of-the-century. Smith-Rosenberg's studies of correspondence between women of that era "revealed the existence of a female world of great emotional strength and complexity. It was a world of intimacy, love, and erotic passion." Yet that passion was not always fulfilled. Since the letters that Louise wrote to Ani aren't available, the essence of their friendship remains a mystery.

Was Louise surprised by Ani's persistence in breaking down her reserve? Possibly, but Ani had several traits that favored a relationship with Louise. Both women had a unique and privileged background. Their families had encouraged their daughters' intellectual and athletic pursuits and had the financial resources to secure their daughters' educations. Both families belonged to an intellectually and socially prominent segment of society, the Pounds in Lincoln and the Konigsbergers in Heidelberg.

Ani was enterprising in closing the distance that Louise preferred to keep between herself and acquaintances. She must have asked provocative questions. One can picture her waiting patiently for Louise to respond. But her most successful lure was inviting Louise to walk with her in the hills surrounding Heidelberg. Any athletic activity produced a positive reaction in Louise. She was ready and willing to hike with Ani.

Aside from their common interests and attitudes, Louise may have allowed herself to enjoy a friendship with Ani because she realized that on a personal basis, the relationship would end when she left Heidelberg. Under the protection of a foreign country, Louise relaxed into intimacy with another woman, a companionship that was concealed from her brother's questions and that could not generate gossip among Lincoln's elite.

Ani's letter mentioning her friend's reserve also gave insight into why neither Louise or Ani had married. After observing an acquaintance's behavior with a man, Ani wrote on 11 October 1902, "One girl has been queerly treated by a man, nothing serious, but small things count anyhow and she does not seem to resent it and behaves for him as before. As neither you nor I would ever behave for a man at all."

A following March 1902 letter written during Ani's visit to Berlin discussed marriage again. "They all wonder why I don't marry. There are such nice young men: such good position, such rich men and the girls marry (them.) They don't care about personality think of everything else first. It seems not very delicate and as if they did not think very highly of themselves don't you think?"

Probably Ani and Louise had discussed marriage and men during their hours together. Both women possessed strong personalities and considerable self-confidence. Watching other women's coy behavior toward men disgusted Ani, and she assumed Louise would also condemn such actions. Quite likely, Louise and Ani's standards for life-long partners were so high that few men of their time and acquaintance could meet them, although later, Ani married a physician.

As a New Woman, Louise may have deliberately chosen not to marry. New Women most frequently avoided marriage from the 1870s through the 1920s. Smith-Rosenberg stated that during those decades "between 40 and 60 percent of women college graduates did not marry," yet only 10 percent of all American women remained single. Those who dedicated themselves to a career realized that the responsibilities of running a household would end their professional aspirations.

Jean Bethke Elshtain's biography of Jane Addams (*Jane Addams and the Dream of American Democracy*) quotes Addam's description of the dilemma young women faced in choosing marriage or a career:

> *She could not have both (marriage and career) apparently for*
> *two reasons. Men did not at first want to marry women of the*
> *new type, and women could not fulfill two functions of profession*

and home-making until modern inventions had made a new type of housekeeping practicable, and perhaps one should add, until public opinion tolerated the double role. Little had been offered to the unmarried women of the earlier generations but a dependence upon relatives which was either grudged or exploited, with the result that the old maid herself was generally regarded as narrow and unhappy and, above all, hopelessly embittered.

Louise was dedicated to a life of scholarship and teaching and intended to contribute to the world's store of knowledge. Remaining true to her goals motivated Louise to concentrate on building a professional career at a time in life when other women worked hard to attract husbands. In expanding the folklore field and championing the use of American English over British English, she made her mark in the language field. She also served as a model for individual excellence.

Whether or not her family cared that she didn't marry is unknown. Probably, Laura Pound would have welcomed grandchildren, but she also had many interests outside her home. Her work with community organizations continued to absorb her until she died. The students living in the Pound home after Stephen Pound's death were considered part of the family, and Laura would have felt fulfilled without her daughters' marrying and producing grandchildren. Although Roscoe married, he and Grace had no children.

How did men feel about Louise? Her classmate, Alvin Johnson, admired and respected her original and brilliant mind, yet he didn't court her. Whether or not any young man dated Louise steadily isn't recorded. They must have appreciated her graceful movements on the dance floor and her agility on the tennis courts. It's possible that her self-assurance posed a threat to her male competitors, and they bypassed Louise in search of more pliable mates.

The derision of New Women by the press at the turn-of-the-century also may have discouraged men from contemplating marriage with such a self-confident and brilliant young woman as Louise.

Marks stated that the attempts by the press to "tame the rambunctious feminist spirit and return it to its domestic sphere . . . contributed to popularizing the goals and manners of the New Women" who wanted the advantages of their brothers: education, suffrage, careers, shorter hair, and rational dress. The uncomplimentary cartoons and poems probably succeeded in alienating traditional-minded men against the adventurous New Women who romped through the pages of magazines such as *Puck.* A poem published in the 6 March, 1895 issue of the weekly magazine reflected the editorial opinion of New Women:

The New Woman

The lovely and graceful new woman
On man will with patronage look—
But when she mends clothes like a tailor
And cooks like a frisky French cook
Then men will look fondly upon her
In all her sweet lights and her shades
Oh! Then she will be the new woman—
Of those kind there will be no old maids.

Louise realized that marriage and a career weren't compatible at the turn-of-the-century. Compromise isn't a word one associates with Louise Pound, nor is the term, second-rate. To achieve recognition in her professional field would require research and writing in addition to her teaching duties, leaving little time for the domestic responsibilities of a traditional marriage. Like the American artist, Mary Cassatt, Louise's decision to remain single may have been deliberate. As Cassatt devoted her life to art and her immediate family, Louise devoted herself to teaching and to her parents and sister.

CHAPTER ELEVEN

Productivity at the University

A FTER WINNING HER Ph.D. in one year, Louise returned to
her beloved Nebraska. Once again, she enjoyed the familiar
comfort of 1632 L Street even though the family shape had altered.
Since his marriage, Roscoe no longer lived at home. In 1900, he was
a professor of law at the University of Nebraska, and a year later he
also served on the Nebraska Supreme Court. Olivia taught Latin,
English, and history at Lincoln High School, and Louise faced a
classroom of University students again. The two sisters, companions
since childhood, continued to live at home, and as always, they enjoyed
a close relationship.

Stephen and Laura Pound also spent their final years at 1632 L
Street. Stephen Pound practiced law until his sudden death in 1911.
Laura continued to be a vital force in civic affairs, serving once again
as DAR regent in 1900-01. She entertained family friends, University
professors, and public officials in the stately Victorian residence and
enjoyed working in her rose garden during the summers. In 1922, at
age 80, she wrote a memoir of her childhood in rural New York. She
died in 1927 after a brief illness.

As always, the Pounds were interested in local and world affairs and kept themselves informed on current events. When Louise attended summer school at the University of Chicago in 1898, she had written Olivia asking for news of the Spanish American War. That small conflict which Secretary of State, John Hay, referred to as a "splendid little war" changed, briefly, the United States' international status. The war lasted only a few months, from April until August, but terms of the Treaty of Paris allowed the United States to claim Puerto Rico, Guam, and the Philippine Islands, while Cuba became independent. This outcome set the country on the road to imperialism, a path that Lincoln native and 1900 Democratic presidential candidate, William Jennings Bryan, campaigned against.

To appease Democrats supporting the gold standard, Bryan had chosen Adlai E. Stephenson of Illinois as his vice president. His choice alienated the Populists, allowing the Socialist and Prohibition parties to gain strength and deflect support from the Democrats. The Republican party won Nebraska votes, both popular and electoral, thus helping the team of William McKinley and Theodore Roosevelt win the election.

As staunch Republicans, the Pounds, like other Lincoln conservatives, disagreed with Bryan's political views but tolerated his prominence in the city's life. Bryan had built a grand farm home east of Lincoln and was a popular speaker at local church gatherings, picnics, and banquets. His daughter, Ruth, was acquainted with Louise Pound. According to Knoll, Ruth had a "colorful" personality and was an accomplished athlete who mastered jumping hurdles, a feat which earned the admiration of Louise.

William McKinley's second term as president lasted less than a year, ending in 1901 when anarchist, Leon Czologosz, assassinated him. Under the leadership of Theodore Roosevelt, the country ended its flirtation with imperialism, yet remained a world power taking over the building of the Panama Canal in 1903. Construction of the canal began in 1906 and took eight years to complete.

Meanwhile the mood of the country changed. Many citizens felt economically oppressed and resented organized wealth and big business. Roosevelt dealt with the problem by enforcing anti-trust laws. Perhaps the country's mood along with the down-to-earth attitude of Roosevelt encouraged Louise's interest in word derivations as she began her study of American speech patterns. It was an unexplored field, ready for investigation, and Louise needed a specialty if she intended to make a lasting impression in the linguistic field.

The future for female university professors in the early twentieth century was never secure or comfortable. Many women, like Louise, were New Women whom men resented. Those attempting to make a name for themselves within male professions were considered intruders. Often male colleagues thought their female counterparts should be at home taking care of husbands and children, or, if unmarried, looking after their aging parents.

To advance their careers in male-dominated professions such as college teaching, New Women often explored untried areas within established fields. Louise Pound's training in linguistics and philology caused her to notice language variations taking place, and being Louise, she was enterprising enough to take advantage of those deviations.

Always in tune with the world around her, Louise would have noticed that by 1900 the use of telephones began to change the way Americans talked. Telephone conversations were more informal than letter writing and gave rise to new expressions. Schlereth wrote that "give me a ring" or "I'll give you a buzz" entered American speech. The telephone appealed to the public's imagination and inspired greeting card verses, vaudeville skits, and popular songs: "Drop me a Nickle Please," "Hello Central," "Give Me Heaven," "Call Me Up Some Rainy Afternoon," and "All Alone by the Telephone," were a few of the catchy titles.

Along with observing the expressions that evolved from telephone use, Louise must have been aware of differences in the lines spoken by actors and actresses. Accompanied by Olivia, she attended the theater productions that came to town.

At the turn-of-the-century, Lincoln remained the cultural center of the state. Olson and Naugle wrote that discussion clubs, literary societies, and the opera house were the key elements of Lincoln society. The Funke Opera House had a reputation as "the most ornate building west of Chicago" and was the scene of performances by touring metropolitan companies. The Lansing Theater also attracted top stars. Slote reported that in a week's time five or six plays featuring quality stars often were performed.

Louise entered her classroom in 1900 with the title of adjunct professor of English, a step up from her former role as instructor. She taught under the direction of Lucius A. Sherman, who continued as Chairman of the English Department as well as the graduate school. Knoll described Sherman as "a rather pathetic old man clinging to outmoded ways." Although changes in the teaching of English were taking place nationwide at this time, those changes didn't come to the University of Nebraska until Sherman's retirement in 1929 at age 83.

A reaction against the narrow Germanic methods which made "English as hard as Greek," gained momentum during the first decade of the new century. Graff contended that professors had been more interested in their research specialties than in inspiring their students. English education had been a "pouring in" process with students acting as "passive buckets" in an apathetic atmosphere.

Although Louise was well-trained in the Germanic tradition and taught Old English, Middle English, as well as Chaucer, General Survey of English Literature, and other philological subjects and literature courses, she was not a boring teacher. A former student, Arthur Kennedy, recalled taking philological classes under Louise in 1904. "Her courses," Kennedy wrote, "moved along with a clarity and finish that gave to the earnest seeker after philological learning a real satisfaction . . . It was only after many years that I came to realize how young she was in years at that time, and how mature in her erudition." (In 1904, Louise was 32 years old.)

Because of her fascination with words, Louise joined the American Dialect Society in 1901. She had been introduced to the organization during summer sessions at the University of Chicago in 1897-98. A Chaucer course that George Hempl taught piqued her interest. Along with his teaching of Chaucer, Hempl stressed living American dialects which preserved words, phrases and pronunciations of the past. No doubt, Hempl stimulated Louise's interest in American language, an interest she passed on to her students, encouraging them to study word origins and folklore.

Louise provided an in-depth account of her attitude toward language variations in a publication of the American Dialect Society, *Dialect Notes*.

> *Most people, especially those possessing a certain degree of education, are prone to look upon these variations simply as the bad usage of the ignorant, and therefore as something to be avoided and done away with as soon as possible. The idea that they can have any serious value to the scientific student of language is strange to a surprisingly large number of people. The truth is, however, that these variations represent just the class of facts on which the scientific study of language rests. Many of them are survivals from older periods of the language; many new words are formed or adopted to meet a real need arising from new conditions, and so ultimately gain a place in standard English; and many variations in pronunciation illustrate phonetic changes which are constantly going on in language development, and furnish valuable data for arriving at conclusions concerning the laws which govern such changes.*

A few of the articles she wrote during the years following her Heidelberg studies indicated her awareness of current speech patterns. "Dialect Speech in Nebraska" and "Traditional Ballads in Nebraska" reflected her interest Nebraskan's varying speech patterns and in folklore. "The Southwestern Cowboy songs and the English and Scottish Popular Ballads" discussed the influence of British and Scottish ballads on American cowboy songs. "Word Coinage and Modern Trade-Names" arose from her curiosity about word derivations.

Anne Cognard wrote that "Louise Pound was writing about American authors and Nebraska folkways at a time when scholars in the field of English studied seriously only English writers and classical Greek literature." Louise, Cognard contended, "pioneered" less respectable fields. Nevertheless, her research continued to carve new niches in already established subjects. "She was a scholarly purist," Cognard claimed, "but her interests were widespread, and her intellectual curiosity began with the fields and flowers, the native grasslands and vistas, the ethnic stories and folk songs of her own roots, Nebraska."

In *Guide to Nebraska Authors*, Evelyn Haller agreed with Cognard that Louise investigated areas considered unimportant by many English professors. Discussing Pound's attitude toward language, Haller stated: "When she began her trail-blazing work in etymology and modern changes in the English language as spoken in the United States, she was investing in what was not considered respectable by philologists either in England or the United States." Louise had never feared crossing the boundaries of accepted practices in scholarship, teaching, or sports. It is paradoxical that she managed to achieve her goal of individual excellence while studying the language of common people.

1900 WAS A fine time for Louise to return to her University position. Enrollment had reached 2,200 and would continue to increase in the following years. In 1910, the student population was 4,000. The University was a growing institution, and the new chancellor, E. Benjamin Andrews, gave it a form that "persisted through the next century." Under his leadership, the University built a student activities center and succeeded in getting state money for classroom buildings and laboratories. Five new buildings were erected on the agriculture campus and four on the city campus during Andrews' tenure.

Prior to Andrews' arrival and the subsequent infusion of funds, the University had been in transition. After Canfield's departure in 1895, George McLean accepted the position of chancellor, but Knoll wrote that his "cool manner" proved unpopular with Nebraskans. After McLean's resignation in 1899, Charles Bessey again headed the University.

Disliking administrative duties, yet realizing that the institution needed a strong leader, Bessey had offered the post to Andrews in 1889. But Andrews had declined the position, accepting instead the chancellorship of Brown University. After leaving Brown in 1898, Andrews became superintendent of Chicago Public Schools, and in one year he freed the system from political control. In 1900, he came to Nebraska.

Not afraid of controversy, Andrews hired independent thinkers as staff members, Knoll wrote, thus encouraging a variety of opinions and the ensuing arguments that often verged on quarrels. Edward A. Ross, "a fire-eating young liberal" came to Nebraska in 1902 as a lecturer in sociology. Ross had been dismissed from Stanford for protesting the exploitation of Asian immigrants in building railroads and for opposing municipal ownership of public utilities. Knoll stated that Ross believed "his discussions with Roscoe Pound influenced Pound's fundamental attitudes toward the law."

Harvey Wish wrote in *Society and Thought in Modern America* that Roscoe Pound was "the most scholarly expositor of sociological jurisprudence." Wish contended that Pound "popularized the concept directly or indirectly" among the younger lawyers and statesmen who occupied key posts in Franklin Roosevelt's New Deal administration and who sat on the Supreme Court in the 1940s and 1950s. To these men, the pragmatic test of determining truth and justice seemed more important than the traditional certainty of the law that could only be cited, not made.

At this stage in his career, Roscoe criticized closed systems, stating that legal principles were instruments that should grow and adapt "relative to time and place." Wigdor referred to Roscoe Pound as expressing "some of the most advanced elements of contemporary social theory." Yet later in his career, Roscoe sacrificed his instrumentalist beliefs in favor of "traditionalism, professionalism, and organicism." Wigdor claimed that Pound's thought reflected his personality which blended "boldness and caution."

Roscoe's career advanced steadily, much like the march of his boyhood toy soldiers across the dining room table. When serving as Dean of the University's Law School from 1903-1907, he reorganized the curriculum into a three-year course and introduced the case system of instruction. Knoll stated that Pound also "set up practice courts as laboratories and strengthened the library."

In 1906, Roscoe gave a ground-breaking speech at the Bar Association Meeting in St. Paul, Minnesota. His address revolutionized the legal profession, kindling "a flame of progress," Wigdor declared. Roscoe pointed out the weaknesses of the judicial system, stating that it was "archaic." He believed that concentration on legal etiquette frittered away the court's time, and that putting courts in politics destroyed respect for the bench. His outburst alienated the older bar association members but impressed the younger ones, including Dean Wigmore of Northwestern University.

In 1907 Roscoe accepted Wigmore's offer of a post at Northwestern's Law School. After two years there, he held a similar position for one year at the University of Chicago. He then agreed to take the Story Professorship at Harvard in 1910. In 1916, he accepted the deanship of Harvard Law School.

Andrews' hiring of independent thinkers did not damage his standing with staff and regents. He gained their loyalty and support and also became popular with the students. Understanding the students' enthusiasm for competitive sports, Andrews allowed football to thrive under the coaching of Walter Cowles "Bunny" Booth. The team changed its name from the Bugeaters to the Cornhuskers under Booth's reign and won twenty-four games during the next three seasons: 1901-04.

AN AVID COMPETITOR, Louise approved the elevation of the football team and cheered for their victories from the stadium, but football wasn't a sport that women played. Instead, they played basketball at the University. In addition to her teaching duties, Louise had resumed coaching the women's basketball team, arranging tennis tournaments for girls and helping with track meets. She earned no pay for directing the girls' athletic activities, but the students appreciated her efforts.

Both her athletic and scholastic prowess impressed students. A year after she resumed teaching, she was the subject of a poem that appeared in an April 10, 1901, student publication. Beside the poem, is a sketch of Louise holding a tennis racket, titled "Arrowhead's Gallery of Good Looking Profs."

Dr. Louise Pound

Though she's slight, and looketh fragile
She is wiry and she's agile
And the tennis friends have found
When there're tourney's to be won,
Though she's listed as a Pound
She plays nearer to a ton.
She's at home in Gothic lore,
She knows how the vandals swore
And the Iceland roots of saga
Are as tasty to her tongue
As the yellow rutabagas
That she ate when she was young
She's an athlete; she's a scholar
She is brighter than a dollar,
She won honors from the Germans
In their woman–hating schools
She's a mighty clever maiden
Judged by any sort of rules.

By 1917, the founders of the University of Nebraska Women's Athletic Association awarded her a life membership, and the 1916 Cornhusker yearbook dedicated a poem to her. The verse honored her sponsorship of Girls' Athletics, and like the previous poem, portrayed her as a multi-talented woman, one of those rare individuals who excelled in both sports and scholarship.

Our Favorite

There is a professor named Pound
Who knows more than anyone round
Things she can't do
And succeed with it too,
Are not likely ever to be found

A photograph of Louise accompanied the poem. Holding a muff that matched the fur collar on her coat, she appeared energetic and stylish. A small hat with a feather flaring into the air topped her upswept hair.

Although she was busy in the classroom and on the playing fields, she also found time for fun with her friends. In 1908 she and Marguerite McPhee signed a contract stating that Louise would travel on roller skates from her home on 1632 L Street to 1808 South Seventeenth Street, "during the month of August, on one of the following days, August 17th-Sept 1 inclusive between the hours of 8 a.m. and 8 p.m. having made the whole trip on roller skates, skating neither behind nor being seated in or standing in any sort of vehicle, carriage or automobile, whether run by gasoline or electricity, or by hand or foot as with an Irish Mail." (An Irish Mail was a child's toy with three or four wheels that were activated by a hand lever.)

After completing the journey, Louise was instructed to give a witness of her trip the key from her roller skates. Then she would be rewarded with a cake that Marguerite McPhee had made. The cake required the following ingredients: at least three eggs, one-half cup of milk, one-half cup of butter, one and one half cups of sugar, one and one half cups of flour, along with one heaping teaspoonful of baking powder. "It shall be baked in an oven till done. It shall be neither burned nor soggy. The layers shall be at least nine inches in diameter, and three-fourths of an inch in thickness. Between the layers there shall be a filling of chocolate."

The contract, written in legal form, listed Louise's titles and her memberships in several organizations and referred to her as "expert of the first part." Marguerite McPhee was "inexpert of the second part."

A note discovered among Louise Pound's papers contained the following information about the contract: "Louise Pound won the bet referred to by riding a horse—with her roller skates on. M. McPhee baked the cake and it was eaten by persons herein named." A few of those who signed the contract in addition to Louise Pound and Marguerite McPhee were Harriet Muir, Olivia Pound, Clare McPhee, Sarah T. Muir, and Marguerite Klinker.

WITH LOUISE AS a coach, no basketball team ever lost a game, she declared with pride to *Daily Nebraskan* reporter, Gretchen Shrag. During her ten years as coach and player, the Nebraska girls' team played the Haskell Indian Girls, Missouri University, Minnesota University, and teams from the Omaha Y.W.C.A. and Peru Normal School. The games attracted many enthusiastic spectators and were chaperoned by prominent Lincoln ladies, including wives of the chancellor and governor.

"The health of no girl was ever injured," Louise declared, "for it was only the most skillful who made the teams and the players through participation in the contests had one of the most enjoyable and valuable experiences of their lives." Praising the athletic prowess of the former female students, she added, "In those days, there were track meet champions and champion jumpers, ball and javelin throwers, and shot putters among the girls."

Louise made this statement in 1932, eight years after Mable Lee had become Women's Athletic Director and had ended intercollegiate sports competition for the Nebraska girls. Louise remained adamant in her defense of intercollegiate games and of competitive sports, a belief that sprang from her creed of individual excellence. For Louise, winning was the goal of any contest. It's not surprising that she and Mabel Lee nursed lifelong animosity toward one another.

In 1904, Louise and Mrs. Anne Barr Clapp published their own version of basketball rules for women. The game had originated in 1891 and had many rule variations. When Louise first became involved with basketball in 1895, New Women were throwing off Victorian constraints, and Louise and the teams she coached played by men's rules. By 1904, controversy had arisen again over the danger that athletics posed for women's health, and Louise and Mrs. Clapp devised a new set of rules for the University team.

The regulations were published in a booklet titled, "Rules for Basket Ball for Women as played in the University of Nebraska." Kristi Lowenthal summarized the rules in her thesis: *Mabel Lee and Louise Pound: The University of Nebraska's Battle over Women's Intercollegiate Athletics.*

Teams required at least five but not more than nine players. Games were divided into twenty-minute halves with a ten minute break. (With the teams' agreement this rule could be changed.) After the ball landed in a closed-bottom net, a referee would bring it to center court for a jump ball. Batting, snatching, or striking the ball from an opponents's hands was prohibited, and a player couldn't hold the ball for more than three seconds unless trying to score. The girls could dribble the ball, but they had to throw it rather than hand it from one player to another. Holding, tackling, and pushing weren't allowed, but one wonders if Louise relaxed this rule when she coached.

To reporter, Nellie Yost, Louise stated that the last game the Nebraska girls' basketball team played was with Minnesota in 1910. "Yes, we won!" Louise said. The governor of Minnesota was among the audience of 5,000 people. But the dean of Women thought basketball was inadvisable for the girls' health, and the games ended, Louise explained.

Expressing her belief that athletics and scholarship were compatible, Louise said to Yost: "When I coached the girls' basketball team for

Nebraska I had three Phi Beta Kappas on the team. They kept their heads better." When she was elected to the *Lincoln Journal* Sports Hall of Fame in 1955, Louise repeated her belief that "the best players had the best grades."

Ina Gittings was one of the Phi Beta Kappas that Louise had coached and with whom she had played. Ina, like Louise, was a New Woman. When she retired from the University of Arizona faculty in January, 1955, The *Tucson Daily Citizen* summarized her career.

Ina Gittings had graduated from the University of Nebraska in 1906 with a Bachelor of Arts degree. A year before she graduated, Gittings had begun her teaching career as student assistant in Swedish Gymnastics, a class taught by Anne Barr Clapp. She continued teaching at Nebraska until 1916, when she joined the faculty at the University of Montana.

During World War I, Gittings was a physiotherapist with the Army Signal Corps. After the war, she went to Turkey as a relief worker for the United States Near East Relief Organization. Earning her Master of Arts degree from the University of Arizona in 1924, Gittings remained as a staff member until her retirement. Like Louise Pound, she never married. Yet she had an exciting and fulfilling life and was devoted to her career.

Louise and Ina Gittings stayed in touch with each other for the rest of their lives.

Chapter Twelve

University Conflict and Change

IN 1908, LOUISE was promoted to assistant professor, and Andrews resigned from the chancellorship. The post was offered to Roscoe Pound, but he turned it down. Thereafter, Knoll stated, the regents ended the tradition of finding a "distinguished scholar" to serve as chancellor. Instead, they chose "an obscure local man, Samuel Avery," head of the University's chemistry department. Knoll believed that appointing Avery to the post was a "fateful decision," because it marked the University's withdrawal from the national scene. From that time on, it failed to keep pace with Illinois, Minnesota, and Missouri in enrollment, buildings, and equipment.

Avery had won the chancellorship through dogged persistence. Whenever a vacancy for the office occurred, he applied. By 1909 he had worn down the regents' resistance, and they handed him the job. Avery was not an intellectual, and the more genteel Lincoln residents viewed him as a peasant who lacked the qualifications to head a great university. Although Avery had been a classmate of Louise, she viewed his promotion with skepticism, understanding that he was practical rather than innovative. Knoll stated that Avery considered his position custodial rather than visionary, a view that allowed the University to gradually decline in prestige and national standing under his leadership.

Before Avery took over the chancellorship in 1909, the student body had begun changing. Manley quoted Alvin Johnson's comments about the quality of University students he encountered when he returned to Lincoln as a faculty member in 1906:

> *The student body had changed with the swelling prosperity of the state. There was no longer in evidence the kind of student I had known, particularly one who had walked in from Loup City, a hundred and fifty miles, with a broken ankle, to save a few dollars on railway fare. All students had money and bicycles, and here and there one had a "buzz wagon" a primordial automobile that could carry a crowd of laughing boys and girls to the nearby woods where crickets and frogs squeaked and croaked welcome. The dean of women was growing haggard and gray, breaking up parties on campus benches where young men's wooing was getting too handgrieflich, as the Germans say—too "handgrabbish."*

Regardless of the carefree student attitudes and Chancellor Avery's practicality, the University continued to hold its eminent status for about a decade after Avery's appointment as chancellor. In 1909 Abraham Flexner established the University's College of Medicine which was considered the best medical college in the West. Charles Bessey was elected president of the American Association for the Advancement of Science. While on extended leave in London, Charles W. Wallace discovered important facts about Shakespeare, bringing worldwide fame to the University. Entomologist, Lawrence Bruner, earned an international reputation and was named the "greatest living Nebraskan" by a special governor's committee. Sociology professor, George E. Howard, was elected president of the American Sociological Society in 1917.

Louise Pound's friend, Hartley Burr Alexander, was elected president of the Western Philosophical Association. His ideas on culture had influenced Louise's approach to folklore, a field in which she began to make her mark during the first ten years of

Avery's leadership. Because of his influence on her folklore research, Alexander's career is worth noting.

According to Knoll, Alexander was the intellectual center of the campus from 1910 to 1925. He was one of the most remarkable persons the University had ever produced, "proficient in half a dozen disparate fields of inquiry." Because he was a "visionary" and Chancellor Avery a "pragmatist" the two were at odds. Alexander left the University in 1929 to join the faculty at Scripps College in Claremont, California.

As a University undergraduate Alexander had studied with H.K. Wolfe, an empiricist who believed that knowledge was based on observation of experience rather than on theory. After graduating from the University in 1895, Alexander attended the University of Pennsylvania on a fellowship and then went to Columbia, where he earned his Ph.D. in metaphysics. He returned to the University of Nebraska at Chancellor Andrews' invitation in 1908. Alvin Johnson, a former classmate, had recommended him to Andrews. Both Johnson and Alexander had been among the "independent thinkers" that Andrews recruited.

Knoll described Alexander as a "poet in a fashion now outgrown, an essayist, an anthropologist of North and South American Indians." But his most original accomplishment was planning the iconography of the new Nebraska state capitol. In 1922, Bertram Goodhue, architect of the capitol, commissioned Alexander to supervise the decorative patterns and symbolism to be used in the building. "They agreed that a building should be read like a book," Knoll reported.

Under Alexander's direction, mosaicists, painters, and other artists prepared coordinating iconography and inscriptions for the capitol. Because of his brilliant integration of themes, Alexander was recruited to plan the iconography of Rockefeller Center in New York, the Century of Progress Exposition in Chicago, the public library in Los Angeles, and other American professional buildings. His work in this field was recognized with an honorary membership in the American Institute of Architects.

Louise Pound and Alexander became friends during his undergraduate years at the University. Recalling those years in a 1948 *Prairie Schooner* article, "The Undergraduate Years of Hartley Burr Alexander," Louise wrote that Alexander was "the University's most distinguished professor in the humanities division." The son of a minister who also edited a newspaper, Alexander had grown up in Syracuse, Nebraska. An omnivorous reader, he also set type for his father's newspaper. Louise stated that "he never lost his interest in printing," and he credited typesetting with giving him "excellent training in English composition."

Praising his intense loyalty and helpfulness to his friends, Louise stated that she owed "more to him for his unflagging interest and encouragement than to any other scholar, with the possible exception of (her) Heidelberg professor for two semesters, Dr. Johannes Hoops."

It's unusual to think of Louise Pound as a person who needed encouragement, but Alexander's fascination with native cultures must have increased her existing interest in the customs and folklore of Nebraska. She loved her home state and believed that writers should study the world around them. Mari Sandoz remembered Louise advising her to write about the people and places she knew. Throughout her career, Louise researched and wrote about the folk traditions of Nebraskans. Her final book, *Nebraska Folklore*, remains the only volume published on the subject.

By 1912, Louise had finally been granted a full professorship and by 1916 she had collected enough information on folksongs of Nebraska and the Middle West to compile a syllabus. The January 20, 1916, issue of *The Dial*, a semi-monthly journal of literary criticism and information, published a notice of Pound's forthcoming book, *Folksong of Nebraska and the Central West: A Syllabus*. The journal stated that people interested in "folk-song, all Middle-Westerners, and all who enjoy things human" would find "instructive entertainment in a new number of the Nebraska Ethnology and Folk Lore Series." As the first scholar to collect songs from the middle of the country, Louise broke new ground in the folklore field.

The 89 page book categorized the material by country of origin and by subjects. "Songs of Lovers Reunited," "Pioneer and Western Songs," as well as "Songs of Criminals and Outlaws," were among the listed categories. Louise recorded "the first stanza of most familiar lines of the songs sung by the people of Nebraska, passing by word of mouth from singer to hearer and thus perpetrated," she explained. Indigenous songs, "I Want to be a Cowboy," "The Little Log Shanty on the Claim," and "Bury me not on the Lone Prairie," gave the syllabus a wider audience. Her selections in the syllabus were included in her book, American Ballads and Songs, published in 1922 by Scribner's.

In the preface to the syllabus, the editor, Addison E. Sheldon, explained that the material within the book was "often strangely altered on its journey from the Atlantic coast to the Nebraska prairies." The songs had mostly come from European immigrants who eventually arrived in Nebraska "via the states of the old Northwest Territory through Iowa. The lesser came from Virginia and the Carolinas through Kentucky, Southern Illinois and Missouri . . ."

During the years spanning her promotion to full professor and the publication of her syllabus, Louise Pound's former friend, Willa Cather, had gained a nationwide reputation. In 1913 Cather's novel, *O Pioneers*, was published. Olson and Naugle described the novel as a "memorable regional story that was told simply and spontaneously."

She penned a second novel, *Song of the Lark*, in 1915, whose main character was an opera singer with Nebraska roots. By 1917, another regional novel, *My Ántonia*, assured Cather's continued success as a fiction writer. Even though Louise had given up attempts at fiction, she, too, had been making her mark with scholarly research articles.

Although her name wasn't as familiar to the reading public as that of Willa Cather, nor had she delivered the blow to traditional literary theories that Roscoe fired at established law practices, Louise was gaining ground in her quest to prove her individual excellence. In sports achievements, she had outstripped both Cather and Roscoe.

But she was 34 in 1916, the year that her syllabus was published. That same year, Roscoe advanced to the deanship of Harvard Law School. Louise would have recognized that, physically, she was reaching the end of her prime performing years. It was time to concentrate on her scholarly achievements.

Although in future years, Louise would view the passing of the Victorian Age with nostalgia, she marched in step with change as reflected in her broadening intellectual interests. The new breed of students, more carefree and less hardworking, viewed Professor Pound with some puzzlement. Her friend, Hartley Burr Alexander, described their feelings toward Miss Pound (the title she preferred over Dr. Pound). In his article about Louise, "In medias res-1933," Alexander stated that Louise was well-known among students for her athletic feats, but placing her sports accomplishments ahead of her intellectual interests was deceptive: "athletics was after all just an incident in Louise Pound's personality, a lateral expression . . ."

> *No doubt to the student there appeared to be an incongruity in one young woman of great athletic skill and clear intellectual attainment. But this union in Louise Pound's case, conspicuous as it was, by no means sufficed to explain the hold upon the imagination which she exercised. There was something enigmatical about her personality, almost cryptic, and I think that the feeling that here was an instructor whom no one could quite read was at the bottom responsible for a feeling akin to awe which touched the mind of many a youngster where she was concerned.*

Louise probably didn't notice her students' bewilderment regarding her eclectic personality, nor would she have cared. She simply plunged ahead in all aspects of her life. After giving up tennis, she took up golf, and she never hesitated to serve as an officer in numerous professional groups. She also held memberships in several social organizations, and she played bridge, went to movies, and enjoyed dining out with friends.

In all of her wide-ranging interests, she remained alert to changes taking place, especially in the field of language. She also followed political movements of the day and was undoubtedly relieved when a constitutional amendment allowing women to vote passed in 1920.

CHAPTER THIRTEEN

The Organization Woman

Flying through her University tasks with her usual speed allowed Louise to enjoy a social life outside the classroom and to continue taking part in sports. She'd begun playing golf as soon as the game came to Lincoln. Lincoln Country Club, located in the present Antelope Park region, held the first local Women's Golf Tournament in 1916. Of course, Louise played in the tournament and won the championship.

That same year she also won the state women's golf championship which was held at the Omaha Field Club. She fired an 88 in the finals against Mrs. J.T. Stewart of Omaha. Among Louise Pound's papers, a poem by Constance Rummans praised her win.

To the Champion

She played the course in 88
A record, so the papers state.
About the game, I must confess,
I nothing know—or even less:
Of "brassie shots" I've dimly heard,
And "putts" or "punts" which is the word?
But yet I must reiterate

She played the course in eighty-eight.
They speak about a lovely drive,
And say she made a "six on five",—
Though I'll admit I cannot see
Just what a "six on five" may be
They all declare her game is great—
I can't distinguish well between
"In the rough" and "on the green",
But would I had been there to shout
Some of the times when she "holed out"!
I hail the champion of the state—
She played the course in eighty-eight!
P.S. I do not know which is the worse,
My golf terminology or verse,
But though the first is fearful quite,
The second limping—it's a fright!
The champion I'd congratulate,
Who played the course in eighty-eight.

These golf victories which took place on familiar territory differed from Louise's tennis triumphs that occurred in Chicago a decade earlier. There, she had been competing for the Western Women's Tennis championship and had displayed a single-minded intensity. In the local and state golf tournaments, her opponents often were friends or acquaintances with whom she enjoyed playing, even though she remained determined to take home a trophy.

Louise always relished having a good time and probably was a fun-loving student like her brother, Roscoe. Knoll observed that Roscoe was a jolly student who enjoyed playing pranks. Perhaps he shed his mischievous tendency earlier than Louise. Marriage and concentration on advancing his career probably took precedence over having fun. Louise remained single and lived at home, circumstances that allowed her considerable personal freedom. Her memberships in informal clubs such as the Golden Fleece, Copper Kettle, and Wooden Spoon reflected her versatility and her sense of humor.

If students needed a professor's backing to start a non-academic organization, they didn't hesitate to knock on Miss Pound's office door. In 1917, Louise listened to a trio of red-headed young coeds, Eva Miller, Elizabeth Brown, and Melba Quigley, who wanted to organize a red-head club. Simpson, stated that the girls came to "Miss Pound, whose crowning glory made her eligible, for a sponsor and a name." Agreeing to be a member, Louise and other red-headed coeds met about once a year. "The last time we met there were 98 members present–and Mrs. Samuel Avery, wife of the chancellor, who always attended wearing a red wig," Louise said.

She wrote an article about the Golden Fleece for a 1954 *Nebraska Alumnus* column, "Do You Remember?" She stated that "A hard-boiled committee passed judgement" on those applying for memberships, "fixing the exact tint of the applicant's hair and rejecting the many attempting to chisel in though not genuine reds. Hues of putty, taffy, and ginger, and all suggesting the use of chemicals, were firmly barred." Various prizes were awarded throughout the organization's existence: for the greatest quantity of red hair; the fieriest hair; the most fascinating scintillating golden glow; the most fascinating bob; the most fascinating green eyes; the most devilish dark eyes; the best-coiffed hair.

The Golden Fleece, like many other organizations Louise joined, had a literary theme. Members contributed poems, and a short play was composed and presented at one meeting. Appropriate musical numbers always were sung such as "Brighten the Corner Where You are," and "Sorrel Threads Among the Gold." An unidentified member contributed a lullaby:

> *At night when I go to bed*
> *And when I rest my ruby head*
> *I praise whatever Gods there be*
> *They didn't make a blonde of me*

Louise wrote that "H.L. Mencken penned a panorama piece for red-haired women which was printed later in the *Smart Set*–of which he was then editor." Louise and Mencken were acquainted through their mutual interest in promoting American English. Whenever she attended meetings or had speaking engagements in the vicinity of Mencken's Baltimore home, the two would meet for a meal and conversation. No doubt, their iconoclastic attitudes toward language initiated their friendship. A portion of Mencken's prose contribution to the Golden Fleece organization follows:

Red-haired girls with eyes
that are metallic and full of green, spooky depths, like rain
puddles in a fir-forest.
Red-haired girls with pale, orange freckles of irregular shape, like
alphabet noodles.
Red-haired girls who wear their hair in high,
wild heaps, like red-hot spaghetti.
Red-haired girls with brilliantly black eyebrows–too black,
in fact, to be God's unassisted gift.
Red-haired girls who wear verdigris-green frocks,
and are too intelligent to go into rooms with blue wallpaper.
Red-haired girls, slightly oxidized, riding in Fifth Avenue
busses with larval red-haired girls of the next generation,
their lovely progeny and legacy to culture . . .

Louise informed Simpson that she couldn't remember how long the Golden Fleece existed. "It never was in favor of the deans, because it had no officers, no regular meetings, no established program. But since the chancellor's wife came to every meeting, we were safe." Another reason Louise gave for the group's demise was the size. "It had grown too large to handle. There were 34 at the first meeting; at the last one there were a hundred." The group had planned to invite the Fire Department from Tenth and Q to their last meeting, but that proved impossible. "Ellen Smith Hall was not large enough. Some of the girls gave me locks of their hair on graduation, these for the archives."

Two other informal organizations attempted to gain a campus following, but their existence was brief. Louise wrote that a group called the "dumbbells"–associated with the physical education department–asked her to become an honorary member. The dumbbells lasted only a few days. "Speediest of all was the fate of Nu Upsilon Tau Tau (NUTT) . . ." NUTT was a parody of Phi Beta Kappa. The parent Texas Nu Upsilon Tau Tau chapter attempted to establish a Beta chapter at Nebraska, but the effort met resistance from University officials. The Texas NUTTS, popular with their faculty, were given an annual garden party by the University of Texas chancellor.

Louise reported that on the day the new Phi Beta Kappa members were to be announced, "a group of girls of good scholastic standing" appeared in her office wearing "goobers" (Texan for peanuts) on yellow ribbons around their necks. The Texas chapter had sent the peanuts to the Nebraska fledglings. "I was proud of being considered eligible as a Dumbbell," Louise wrote, "the new NUTTS were queens of the campus in the morning, but by afternoon the Deans had banished the institution ignominiously from the campus. One Dean termed it 'an insult to Phi Beta Kappa,' the other Dean took the goober from about the neck of a member and reduced her to tears."

Responding to the Dean's lack of humor and his intolerance, Louise wrote a letter to the editor of the campus newspaper. Complimenting the Dean's unusual promptness in responding to campus issues, she nonetheless accused him of bringing down a "heavy hand on the campus." She stated that when she had visited Austin, Texas, the previous spring, she had met some of the 'NUTTS' in the Dean of Women's office. The dean's staff had given the girls peanut necklaces which they wore on their necks–"those symbols which were ordered from the necks of our Nebraska girls so promptly."

The NUTTS, Louise continued, were popular in Texas with the faculty, students, and Phi Beta Kappas, and "its appearance was thought to lend zest . . . to Phi Beta Kappa Day." The Nebraska

NUTTS had been rebuked for "lacking a constitution, purpose, and recognition by the student senate committee–so stated the Dean."

Louise questioned whether the committee had been consulted, and in the final paragraph she commented, "May I suggest mildly to our efficient Dean of Men that he give fuller rein to his sense of humor when he is presiding over the destinies of girls' organizations. To me, Nu Upsilon Tau Tau and the Golden Fleece, which has now appeared at another institution, are quite on a par–both functioning on one day of the year only . . . Surely many things on campus need the time and attention of our executives more than do the poor 'NUTTS' or 'Dumbbells' or members of the Golden Fleece, who like to vary the routine of campus life with harmless hoaxes."

The letter revealed Louise's sympathy with the students' need for diversion from the routines of attending class and studying as well as expressing her yen to have a good time. It didn't bother Louise to poke fun at a serious organization such as Phi Beta Kappa even though she was a charter member of the group. Her tendency to create mischief went a step further when she needled the Dean for putting a stop to the NUTTS and the Dumbbells.

Assuming a combative stance against University administrators–as though they were opponents on a tennis court–gave vent to Louise's competitive spirit. According to Knoll, one administrator said that Louise Pound "took ten years off his life, and the women whom she sponsored were not advanced because deans were afraid they would become as difficult as Louise Pound."

Probably with the same friends who had witnessed her ride across Lincoln on a horse while carrying roller skates, Louise and Olivia recruited members for the Wooden Spoon and Copper Kettle Societies. The constitution of the Wooden Spoon Society stated the organization's objectives as "friendly, recreational, and social." Made up of women, the group hoped to "promote the mutual acceptance of Lincoln women who are following or have followed some character of professional work, or who take part in business life." The club did not "expect to interest itself in politics or literature or to devote its meetings to propaganda of any type." Belonging to the Wooden Spoon Society was another expression of Louise's crusade for the recognition of women's role in the workplace.

To be qualified for professional positions, women often needed additional education. The American Association of University Women, the organization closest to Louise Pound's heart, promoted and provided financial aid for women wishing to pursue advanced degrees. She served as Nebraska director from 1906-1908 and was a member of the national council in 1913. In the 1930s she served on the fellowship award committee and was national vice-president, an office she held until 1944. Her support of women's education prompted her to stipulate in her will that between $500 and $1,000 go to the state AAUW organization for the "Louise Pound Fellowship." Olivia's will also bolstered donations in her sister's name, directing that $10,000 be given to the Lincoln AAUW branch to establish the Louise Pound International Fellowship.

Phi Beta Kappa was another scholarly group that Louise supported. From 1889 to 1905, she was the organization's corresponding secretary. She moved into the vice-presidency in 1911 and held the office throughout 1912. She accepted the vice-presidency again in 1925-26-27. In 1915-16, and in 1936-37, she served as president of the organization.

One of her former students, Dr. Leta Stetter Hollingworth, wrote Louise in December, 1916, about a prejudicial item in the organization's publication, School and Society.

I intended to send you a clip from School and Society which comments on the recent action of the council of Phi Beta Kappa. The council, it seems, thinks it is high time some means should be adopted for limiting the proportion of women eligible for membership. Too many women are getting in according to the ideas of the council . . . Can't you express yourself publicly somewhere on the subject?

Although no evidence exists that Louise expressed herself on the subject of limiting female Phi Beta Kappa members, this was a controversy that would have attracted her. One can imagine her staging a letter-writing and verbal campaign against limiting women members.

As a college-level English teacher Louise had belonged to the Modern Language Association since 1906 and served as vice-president and as an executive committee member in 1916. She continued to hold offices and serve on MLA committees throughout her teaching career, and she often presented papers at MLA conventions. Finally, in 1955, nine years after she had retired from the classroom, she was appointed the first woman president of MLA, a long overdue honor.

The professional organizations that Louise joined and the offices she held are too numerous to list. In addition to the groups already mentioned, a few others that interested her were the American Folklore Society, National Council of Teachers of English, Nebraska State Teachers Association (1916 Literature Chairman), American Association of University Professors, and Nebraska Academy of Sciences.

CHAPTER FOURTEEN

The Mentor

❧❦❧

THE YEARS SPANNING 1900-1920 were busy for Louise. She wrote articles and traveled throughout the country giving speeches, activities that established her reputation as a language and folklore expert. At the same time, the University and Lincoln were expanding, but the Pound family began its gradual disappearance from Nebraska.

Roscoe left Lincoln in 1907, and his father died in 1911. Louise and Olivia remained unmarried and childless, and Roscoe and his wife had no children. Although Stephen and Laura had been enthusiastic settlers, none of their relatives followed them to Nebraska, and the Pound family era in Lincoln ended with Olivia's death in 1963.

The ebbing away of the Lincoln Pounds began with Stephens's death on May 14, 1911. Sayre wrote that as Stephen Pound aged he had worked at a slower pace, but always in the "same dependable and understanding way." Describing his final hours, Sayre stated that Judge Pound had been preparing a brief, but at five o'clock he decided "to call it a day and did not intend to work on it further in the evening. He died before completing the brief; a heart attack ended his life during the night.

Did Stephen Pound glance out the window of his study on that mild May evening and enjoy a last sight of flowers blooming in Laura's garden? Perhaps the picturesque view encouraged him to admit his fatigue and put aside his work. He may have sat in a favorite chair and watched clouds scud across the sky as he waited for dinner, or he may have simply closed his eyes and rested. Then he shared a last meal with his wife and daughters.

A newspaper clipping gave the following account of Stephen Pound's death:

> *Announcement of the death of Judge Stephen B. Pound came as a shock to the residents of Lincoln yesterday. Judge Pound was one of the oldest residents of the city and a man who had been in public life since his location in Lincoln in 1868. He had reached the age of seventy-eight years but was still active in professional life.*
>
> *He had been in his office the day before. He was taken ill with heart trouble and died at 1:30 Sunday morning. (May 14, 1911) Angina Pectoris was the cause of death. While Judge Pound had not been in good health for more than two weeks his condition was not regarded as serious. He had been going to the office taking care of business affairs and meeting his friends as usual. Many of his close friends had no intimation even that he was ailing.*
>
> *Judge Pound leaves a wife, a son, Dr. Roscoe Pound of Harvard Law College, and two daughters, Misses Louise and Olivia.*

Stephen Pound's funeral was held in the family home on the Tuesday following his death. Rev. S. Mills Hayes officiated at the 4:00 P.M. service. Burial was in Wyuka Cemetery in Lincoln. Stephen Pound had played an influential role in the settlement and development of Lincoln and the state of Nebraska, but his role as a father was of equal importance. With Laura, he had raised three children who became outstanding educators.

Though Louise wasn't prone to reflecting on her past accomplishments or deliberating planning her career advancement, the death of her father may have caused her to consider her own future. She was 39 when her father died, on the threshold of middle age. Although she still played golf, she'd given up tennis, perhaps to devote more time to her career.

Eventually, Louise would tackle the established theory of ballad origins, toppling an esteemed male professor's assertion that groups of common people joined together in composing songs. Before Louise challenged the male establishment concerning ballad origins, she revealed the compassionate side of her personality, a trait that sprang from her family's Quaker roots and was in tune with the actions of her mother and sister.

For Laura Pound, her husband's death left an empty space in the home that needed to be filled. Speaking to a *Lincoln Journal Star* reporter in 1961, Olivia recalled her mother's 1911 remark: "Mother said then we would share our home with girls needing help to go to high school and college." Through her teaching and administrative positions at Lincoln High School, Olivia encountered many girls who needed a place to live, and she offered several of them shelter at 1632 L Street.

The female students who lived in the spacious Victorian home soon became part of the family. "The big house with carved dark woodwork, fireplaces in parlors, dining room and bedrooms, seemed a haven," reported Mamie Meredith. Long after boarders earned their college degrees and left Lincoln, Mrs. Pound, Olivia, and Louise maintained contact with them. Meredith believed that living with the Pound women influenced the girls' "ideas" and "ideals." Those values were passed on to the children and students of the young women who had flourished under the guidance of Laura, Louise, and Olivia.

One of the girls who lived at 1632 L Street, Anne Marie Rhetus, had been like another daughter in the family. The Pound women welcomed her into their home and encouraged her to finish her education. She remained with them until she had earned a University degree, then she taught school in Arizona.

Replying to Meredith's inquiry about living with the Pound women, Rhetus wrote that there had been many students before her who resided in the Pound home while attending school and more followed after she left. Those students always were welcomed with open arms when they returned for a visit. "Our welfare was always a concern of the Pounds as was our progress." She then recalled the personalities of Laura and her daughters:

Mother Pound enriched the years I was privileged to know her. Like her daughters, she never complained, always saw the best in people; befriended many; exercised a wonderful sense of humor, and constantly improved her mind. She, too, had a 'Green Thumb,' and we shared many happy moments in her rose garden.

Louise, I found was always worth a chuckle; Wee secrets were shared as a bit of 'deviltry,' Olivia shared the joys and sorrows. She served as the 'Listening Post' and with her quiet gentle suggestions 'righted the course.'

To me 1632 L St. was a Haven of Understanding, A Bolster of Morale, a Challenge to do my very best, and a spot where I was appreciated. This spirit of sincerity, love and goodness is a precious memory and continues to support me.

My return was always eagerly awaited. In later years, when students no longer seemed to need a home, the sisters shared the household tasks. It was then my turn to listen for Louise's call to breakfast, which she had prepared. How good that wholesome meal tasted in the warmth of the Pound kitchen.

Rhetus ended her letter attributing her success as a teacher to people like the Pounds: "Great educators and big people who never lost the touch of human kindness."

Whatever factors motivated them to better their future prospects, the girls found additional inspiration during their sojourn with the Pounds. While the personalities of Olivia and Louise differed, it broadened the girls' minds to join in the playful jokes and pranks of Louise and to be reassured or comforted by Olivia's understanding nature. Reigning over this female society, Laura Pound earned the title, "Mother Pound."

On Sunday afternoons, according to Meredith, Louise and Olivia welcomed aspiring student writers into their home and listened to the stories, poems, acts from plays, or chapters from novels the young women had composed. Nebraska author, Mari Sandoz, was among those receiving advice and encouragement. "And Olivia, Quaker devoted to public service that she was, always served delicious hot chocolate," Meredith remembered.

An unidentified individual also wrote of those Sunday afternoon meetings. In a letter addressed to "Mr. Nicolls," the writer stated that the Sunday gatherings were those of the Chi Delta Phi, a national literary honorary group which became part of the Lincoln intellectual scene in 1921. Louise called the meetings to order with her "ear-splitting whistle, made by putting both hands before her mouth, as a sort of amplifier."

This writer's description of 1632 L Street mentioned stained glass windows and walls filled with paintings. "The two living rooms would be well-filled, and we would be served, after the program, with little cakes and delicious hot chocolate made by Olivia Pound in little China cups, gifts from friends in many places . . . A good many girl students were encouraged by these gatherings to begin and to continue writing."

Louise's study formed another memorable image for the anonymous writer: "I remember having tea years ago in this book-lined room–just a few of her former students for there isn't much space left for moving around." The students read "bits from all sorts of fascinating books, humorous as well as weighty ones." Many of the books had been presentation copies from famous authors. In this room, Louise had done her writing. "If her spirit is contained anywhere, it's there."

Because it wasn't in their natures to waste time pining for the past or basking in self-pity, Laura, Louise, and Olivia Pound chose to overcome their grief through helping others. They demonstrated their belief in the value of education by providing a loving and supportive family atmosphere for those in need. The three Pound women also encouraged the literary ambitions of aspiring young writers, dispensing hospitality and advice without expecting anything in return.

CHAPTER FIFTEEN

WWI Humanitarian

WITH THE START of World War I, Louise had another opportunity to exercise compassion and leadership. She acted as head of the National League for Women's Service and served as chairman of its overseas relief activities. As a member of the Food for France Committee, Louise led a group that sent $1,000 worth of soap to French peasants at the suggestion of her friend, Dorothy Canfield Fisher.

She also was listed as a member of the Nebraska State Council of Defense, but it's doubtful that she engaged in, or approved of, the policing activities the council exercised. State and County Councils of Defense were subordinates of the National Council of Defense established to ensure that wartime regulations were followed. Zealous county councils encouraged super-patriotism, recording the names of German families and fingerprinting unnaturalized Germans. Store clerks were ordered to sell merchandise only to people who spoke English, and all telephone calls were to be in English. Ministers of German language churches had to deliver sermons in English which their congregations couldn't understand. German was no longer taught in schools, and German books were removed from libraries. Extremists often burned the banned books.

Prior to the United States' involvement in the war, Nebraskans of German descent sympathized with "the cause of the Fatherland," according to Olson and Naugle. About thirty thousand Nebraskans had been born in Germany and over sixty thousand were children of parents born there. Another group of Nebraskans opposing U.S. participation in the conflict were the "old populist progressives." They felt that the nation should remain aloof from Europe's troubles. Progressive William Jennings Bryan resigned his position as Secretary of State on June 7, 1915, in protest of President Wilson's increased sympathy with the Allies. Nebraska senator, George W. Norris, voted against the United States entering the war.

The most celebrated incident for Nebraskans in the "battle of the home front" was the trial of various members of the University faculty before the Board of Regents. Responding to complaints from various sources claiming that certain members of the faculty failed to support the war, the Board of Regents held open public hearings on the matter and invited the appearance of citizens who had knowledge of unpatriotic words or actions of University faculty members. Lasting two weeks, the hearings rated extensive press coverage and resulted in the resignations of two professors whose criticism of the war had been excessive.

On a positive note, Nebraskans were proud that two men leading the Unites States military in Europe had close ties to the state. General John J. Pershing, commander-in-chief of the American expeditionary Forces, had been commandant of the University cadets and taken classes at the law college. His sister, Mae, continued to live in Lincoln. Charles G. Dawes, purchasing agent for the American Expeditionary Forces, had started his law practice in Lincoln and continued to have financial interests in the city, although he had moved to Chicago at the time of his appointment as purchasing agent.

As chairman of the Overseas Relief branch of the State Defense Council, Louise's wartime activities gave her an opportunity to strengthen her friendship with Dorothy Canfield Fisher. The papers of Olivia and Louise contain several Fisher letters, and five of her letters to Louise have been published in Mark J. Madigan's *Keeping Fire's Night and Day: Selected Letters of Dorothy Canfield Fisher.*

Born in Lawrence Kansas (17 February, 1879), Dorothy Canfield was the daughter of James Hulme Canfield, a university professor and Flavia Camp Canfield, an artist. Canfield left his Kansas teaching post to become chancellor of the University of Nebraska where he implemented changes that ushered in the school's "Golden Era." From Nebraska Canfield moved his family to Columbus, Ohio, where he presided over Ohio State University. He left that position in 1899 to become librarian at Columbia University.

While her father held the presidency of Ohio State, Dorothy earned her bachelor's degree with a concentration on languages, especially French. After completing her Ph.D. in French at Columbia, she was qualified to teach on the university level, but she turned down an offer from Western Case Reserve University in Cleveland Ohio. Not wanting to leave her family, she accepted a position as secretary for the Horace Mann School in New York.

Dorothy also began her writing career at this time, and in 1907 she married John Redwood Fisher. Fisher, a fellow graduate of Columbia, had been captain of the football team and a roommate of Alfred Harcourt. Harcourt later became Dorothy's publisher. The Fishers settled in Vermont on land that Dorothy had inherited from her great-grandfather.

Although she was primarily a fiction writer, producing twenty-two published novels and several short stories, she also wrote eighteen works of nonfiction. She introduced Dr. Maria Montessori's child-rearing methods to the United States in A Montessori Mother, and advocated continuing education for adults in *Why Stop Learning.* She translated Giovanni Papini's *Life of Christ* from Italian as well as Adriano Tilgher's *What it has Meant to Men through the Ages.* A record of Vermont history, *Vermont Tradition,* and several children's books are included in her repertoire.

In addition to writing, Canfield "spent most of her life doing good deeds," Madigan commented. These deeds were performed without "self-consciousness just as great athletes perform well almost because they cannot help it." Her altruistic nature urged her to found a Braille press and a children's hospital in France during World War I and to organize food and soap distribution to the war-ravaged country. During World War II, she organized the Children's Crusade for Children. Continuing her interest in education, she was the first president of the Adult Education Association, and the first woman to serve on the Vermont State Board of Education. Madigan reported that "shortly before Fisher died, Eleanor Roosevelt referred to her as one of the ten most influential women in America."

Before the United States entered World War I, Fisher wrote to Louise about her sympathy for the Allied forces and of her surprise at the anti-German sentiment in Nebraska. In March 1916, she wrote, "I'm surprised by what you say of pro-German in this country." Fisher had given speeches in many New England cities and towns and had encountered only "impassioned sympathizers with the Allies."

The same 1916 letter discussed the Fishers' desire to help the French people. "There is a chance that John and I may go to France to do relief work, children or no children–take them along and settle down somewhere in a quiet place to the south of Paris . . ." In that location she and the children could see John when he wasn't working in a hospital. "This never-ending inaction on our part is getting to be too much for us both," Fisher wrote. By February 14, 1917, the Fishers were in Paris.

After the United States entered the war Louise was in charge of the Women's Overseas Relief, and she questioned Fisher about the best disposition of funds and also about sending a unit of reconstruction workers to help the French. Fisher outlined practical steps for aiding the French:

Louise Pound

(November 19, 1918)

I know you want a really frank and outspoken answer to your inquiry; that's what you wrote for. So I'll say at once that unless you can get a quite extraordinary set of people together for a reconstruction unit, a good deal of their effort will be wasted. I have seen a good deal of the work of such organizations and . . . well, I think the same amount of money and work used in other ways might have had more effect.

The usual difficulty, the prime difficulty is that a good many American relief workers do not speak and understand French fluently. If they do not do this, they really cannot be useful. That is a prime requisite.

Now I have alternatives to suggest to you, either one of which would be most useful. The English Friends . . . have, since the American intervention, amalgamated with the American Society of Friends, who are working under their guidance, and consequently making few mistakes and few wasted motions. Their work is tactful, adapted to the French temperament, they have learned not to try to construct English or American villages where French ones stood (oh Louise, the cases where this has been done, and where the French will NOT live in them) they don't try to make over human nature too fast, and they have an excellent and competent business organization. Any money you might furnish them would be spent so that every cent would count . . .

The other alternative is (to me) more interesting, because more unusual. I don't know whether it would appeal to the contributors to your fund, however, as much. It is this; when the Germans moved out of those devastated regions, they took every single thing away from the pharmacies. There isn't a bottle of the simplest drug left anywhere (something is bound to get forgotten) it is a detail which hasn't been looked after. There isn't any adequate supply (any supply

*at all as a matter of fact) of such indispensable things as castor-oil,
bicarbonate of soda, cod-liver oil, quinine, glycerine, Vaseline, etc,
etc, and oh, there isn't ANY SOAP. If people in Nebraska wanted
to help out in a most undramatic manner, but in a way which
would benefit the lives of the people at once, they couldn't do better
it seems to me than to get a supply of these things and let either the
Friends distribute them, or the Trait d'Union Franco-American
or any other responsible authority. I have asked my doctor to give
me a list of what poor people most use in such ways here in France,
(but I'm writing you before I get it, so that you may get my answer
as soon as possible.) I want to get a list from a French doctor who
works among the poorer classes so that you won't make the mistake
of sending American remedies which they'd be afraid to touch.*

*Anything which has grease or oil in it is terribly expensive,
that is why soap is so dear and so hard to get. The Germans took
every scrap of that, . . . and you've no idea how hard it is for decent
people to live without any soap. It is a matter of health also, and
a very essential element in the effort we all want to make to help
those poor folks back to a normal life.*

Fisher then wrote of Mrs. Griggs, head of the Trait-d'Union
Franco-American, an organization doing useful work in France. She
advised Louise to write to Mrs. Griggs's husband in New York, who
could tell her where to buy the drugs wholesale, or he could get them
for her. "Mrs. Griggs's organization could distribute them and as the
French Government is allowing shipments for her organization to
come through under its name, they wouldn't have to be passed through
the very cumbersome machinery of the American Red Cross."

Dorothy's letter continued: "There, that's the best I can do for you.
In a few days, I will send you the list of drugs most needed (and don't
forget soap too!) Personally I think it would be most picturesque
and interesting for Nebraska to send soap to the devastated regions!
It could just be the state speciality, don't you see, and so much
needed!)"

Following Fisher's suggestions, Louise supervised the collection of food, soap, and drugs for the French people. A newspaper clipping reported the progress of the overseas relief committee under her leadership. To collect food money, the committee erected a booth at the state fair and also sold buttons, soliciting a total of $1500. Money for the soap and drug funds came voluntarily, and by September 1, $600 had been sent to Mr. Griggs in New York, "for the purchase of soap in wholesale quantities and its shipment to devastated France ... Part of the soap coming from Nebraska goes to soldiers who have been mustard-gassed and part for civilian relief," the newspaper stated.

Another newspaper clipping reported the gratitude of the French people who received the soap. The individual delivering the last shipment of Nebraska soap to French citizens reported their reaction: "In making my distributions I told these people that I could give them milk and sugar and soap; and when I said 'soap' there was even more gratitude and appreciation than a prima donna generally shows when some kind friend offers her a diamond tiara. Everybody gasped 'soap' as if it was some unheard of article. The inhabitants had seen none of it for almost four years, except what the Germans were using themselves–which of course belonged to the French.

Her efforts to aid the French during World War I demonstrated Louise Pound's concern for humanity and belied her former classmates' description of her as a "cold" person. After reclaiming their ancestors' Quaker faith, Laura, Louise and Olivia may have been against the war. Yet they had a strong sense of social justice, a feeling that Louise expressed when she organized the collection of food, drugs, and soap for the French. During World War II, she would reveal her compassion for others by corresponding with her students after they left her classroom to serve in the military. She also aided her German friends, Ani Königsberger Phister and Johannes Hoops after the war ended.

Meanwhile during the closing months of World War I the Spanish Influenza invaded the United States. The disease lasted from four to eight days. Patients were advised to remain in bed at least a week and not resume normal work for two weeks. The state board of health in Lincoln sent rigid regulations to local authorities in an attempt to control exposure to the virus. Families infected with flu were quarantined, and individuals violating quarantine were fined from $15 to $100.

After the epidemic struck Lincoln on October 18 1918, it lessened—until the mingling of Armistice Day crowds caused a recurrence. Before the year ended 4,000 cases had been reported, and 219 people had died. The flu claimed twice the number of lives that the war had taken. Copple wrote that "No tragedy in Lincoln history took so many lives." Fortunately, Laura, Louise, and Olivia did not contract the virus, nor did Roscoe. The remaining Pounds with ties to Nebraska survived, and an exciting decade awaited Louise.

Pound residence at 1632 L Street, Lincoln, Nebraska -1895

Steven Pound - circa 1900

Laura Pound - circa 1920

Roscoe Pound - 1920

Olivia Pound -circa 1920

Louise Pound and bicycle (circa 1890)

Louise Pound and Willa Cather (circa 1892)

Louise Pound -1920   Louise Pound - 1945

PART FOUR:
LOUISE POUND IN HER PRIME
1920–1940

CHAPTER SIXTEEN

H.L. Mencken & Challenging The Status Quo

DURING THE 1920s Louise Pound was in her fifties, and her career had reached a high point, reflecting Smith-Rosenberg's observation that "women achieved their greatest professional visibility and political activism" in the years before and after the First World War. In this decade, Louise confirmed her reputation as a leading language expert through the publication of her book, *Poetic Origins and the Ballad*, in 1921.

Her co-founding of the journal, *American Speech*, in 1925, with Kemp Malone of Johns Hopkins and Arthur G. Kennedy of Stanford also gained scholars' respect. Louise received a prestigious appointment in 1927 as representative to the International Council on English, and her promotion of American English inspired H.L. Mencken's writings on the subject as well as his praise and friendship.

Correspondence between Louise Pound and H.L. Mencken took place over a period of thirty years. Through their combined efforts, Pound and Mencken brought American English onto center stage in the United States, nudging aside the awe that many academics held for the British way of speaking and writing. Nowadays, American English stands on its own due to their efforts.

Mencken admired Louise Pound's work years before he initiated their correspondence. Her article, "Word Coinages and Modern Trade Names," that appeared in a 1913 *Dialect Notes* had "delighted" him. Mencken had published a few articles on the American language in the *Baltimore Evening Sun* in 1910 and 1911, but his reading of Louise's monographs and those of her pupils in *Dialect Notes* inspired his further study of the American language.

While most scholars concentrated on the speech habits of specific regions, Louise and her pupils investigated the "general speechways" of the entire U.S. After her first *Dialect Notes* article had been published in 1905, Louise or her students' writings appeared in almost every issue of the publication for the next twenty years. Before the founding of *American Speech*, *Dialect Notes* had been the only outlet for the work of those few scholars who studied the American language.

Dialect Notes was the publication of the American Dialect Society, an organization that Louise had joined in 1901. It owed its continued existence to her efforts during the 1940s. Memberships had dwindled due to the economic depression and the resulting loss of academic teaching positions in the thirties. After Louise accepted the presidency in 1940 letters flew to her concerning the organization's name and whether or not to publish a journal. She supervised efforts to extend the society's interests and to adopt a new name–The English Language Society of America. Judging from the letters Louise received, renaming the society generated considerable controversy. Yet today, the organization is still known as The American Dialect Society.

Biographers of Mencken have stated that he often initiated correspondence and meetings with academics because their knowledge helped him in his work on the American language, but he did not develop friendships with them. He merely "used" them to advance his own writings. When he opened a correspondence with Louise, he was probably interested only in tapping her storehouse of knowledge. Their working relationship, however, developed into a friendship. Comparing their personalities, B.A. Botkin wrote, "... one might draw an interesting parallel between her (Louise Pound) and H.L. Mencken–she a scholar who can be entertaining and he an entertaining writer who can be scholarly."

Through her studies, Louise realized that the differences between the American and English languages were great enough to merit individual treatment. She believed the divide between the two languages would increase, but hoped they would not become completely separate. Other experts agreed with her, and most reputable pronunciation texts of recent years accept American English as it is.

The length and content of their ensuing correspondence revealed that the cynical mind of Mencken had met a match in the eclectic personality of Louise Pound. Their correspondence and friendship endured until a stroke in 1948 left Mencken unable to read or write. After his stroke, the fading journalist had his secretary type notes to Louise.

Revealing the informal tone of their relationship, a November 17, 1921, letter from Mencken to Louise referred to a meeting that Louise planned to attend. Mencken wrote that he'd try to be there, "not for the philological shambles, but to introduce you to two brands of superb malt liquor, and my colossal store of other refreshments. If you are a teetotaler, which God forbid, then name a substitute."

Although prohibition was in effect during the 1920s, the law was widely ignored, and Mechken imbibed. Louise, however, would not have broken the law. After prohibition ended, she enjoyed cocktails after dinner, when entertaining guests at 1632 L Street, and when dining at the University Club.

Born in Baltimore in 1880, Mencken spent his life there. His loyalty to his home city matched Louise Pound's attachment to her native Lincoln. The son of a cigar factory owner, Mencken preferred a journalism career over replacing his father as factory head. After he graduated as valedictorian from Baltimore's Polytechnic Institute in 1896, he worked in the cigar factory until his father died in 1898. Then, at age 18, Mencken became the youngest reporter the *Baltimore Morning Herald* had ever hired. After only four years with the paper, he was appointed managing editor. When the paper ended publication,

Mencken worked for the *Baltimore Sun* papers and continued writing for them intermittently until his stroke in 1948.

As co-editor of the *Smart Set* magazine from 1914-1924, Mencken published many unknown writers who achieved later fame: F. Scott Fitzgerald, Eugene O'Neill, Sinclair Lewis, Theodore Dreiser, and James Joyce. After the *Smart Set* ceased publication, Mencken established *The American Mercury*, a magazine featuring politics, the arts, and sciences. It was the first magazine edited by whites to publish African-American writers including James Weldon Johnson and Langston Hughes.

Often referred to as a libertarian, Mencken viewed the Constitution and the Bill of Rights as sacred documents and passionately defended the First Amendment. He reported on the Scopes Monkey Trial which took place in Dayton, Tennessee, July 9-18, 1925. John Scopes, a young high school teacher, had been charged with teaching evolution in violation of Tennessee law. The trial rated nationwide news coverage and a place in American history books.

Nebraskan, William Jennings Bryan, argued for the Genesis theory of creation, while Clarence Darrow defended evolution. Mencken's libertarian views put him on the side of Darrow and Scopes against Bryan. Stating that Bryan's political aspirations "had gone to pot" forcing him to rely on folks from "remote hills" and "lonely farms" for religious support, Mencken wrote that Scopes' case was lost long before the trial started, and that the Bill of Rights had been "made a mockery of by its sworn officers of the law."

Although Louise Pound and Mencken may have had similar opinions about the Scopes' Trial outcome and Bryan's defense of Tennessee law, no mention of the event appeared in Mencken's letters to Louise. Instead, the messages referred to American English or language-related meetings where he often invited her to join him for a drink and a meal.

While Mencken penned deliberately controversial and antagonizing social and political commentary, he also engaged in scholarly research. His most important contributions to scholarship, were *The*

American Language (1919), revised in 1921, 1923, and 1936, and two supplementary volumes published in 1945 and 1948. Compiling these studies fostered Mencken's link to Louise Pound. He admitted that he could not have written the books without her ground-breaking work.

LIKE HER FRIEND, H.L. Mencken, Louise didn't hesitate to question established doctrines. Along with her study of American language derivations, she continued to research folklore and folksongs. These studies resulted in her sensational book, *Poetic Origins and the Ballad*, which Macmillan published in 1921. Challenging the prevailing theory of communal ballad origins with examples indicating that individuals wrote early ballads, Louise shocked and antagonized the academic community.

Firing the first shot in this literary battle, the book's beige dust jacket contains an explanatory paragraph printed in bright blue.

> *In this book Professor Pound attacks the prevailing theory in regard to the origins of poetry, and especially of the ballad. The theory which the late Professor Gummere set forth with such great skill and which is now held by Professor Kittredge and other scholars is based on the belief that the origin of poetry is the communal dance.*
>
> *Professor Pound takes the stand that (1) poetry and song are not necessarily connected with dancing, (2) that the individual artist appears among primitive people even in connection with communal festivals, (3) that the poetry composed by a crowd never really gets anywhere without individual artistry, (4) that the English and Scotch ballads in most cases never were the products of the dance and offer no support to the general theory, for they were distinctly works of art.*

To establish her theory, Louise used forceful language: "The assumption that the group power to sing, to compose songs, and to dance, precedes individual power to do these things is fatuously speculative." Continuing to advance her theory, Louise argued that folksong scholars had lost their perspective. "Literary historians," Louise wrote, "have dwelt too much, it seems to me, on the festal throng and communal improvisations and the folk dance, when dealing with the beginnings of poetry."

Further illustrating her point in a footnote, she quoted from A. von Humbolt's *Travels in Equinoctial Regions of America*. von Humbolt reported Indians' observations that one monkey always chanted as a leader when howling monkeys filled forests with their noise.

In Cognard's words, Louise uses "Strong, almost curt, solid prose" demanding readers' attention. "Her prose reflects her scholarly and personal interest in diction, is detailed and quite, quite specific." But, Cognard also criticizes Pound's writing as repetitive: "*In Poetic Origins and the Ballad*, Pound states five or six times the disregard she has for Prof. Gummere's theory."

The deceased Professor Gummere put forth the communal theory which had been furthered by Harvard Professor George Lyman Kittredge (1860-1940). Kittredge was a renown Shakespeare and Early English literature authority. When promoting her theory of ballad beginnings against the communal stand of the esteemed Prof. Kittredge, perhaps Louise used the same techniques that she had exercised on the playing fields to win games–scoring points over and over by restating her position.

"Apparently," Cognard observed, "she brought to her studies the same ideal of Greek excellence that she brought to sports, an ideal that demanded of the body and of the spirit . . . a taut and self-appreciating reliance on an internal standard." That standard, whether Louise acknowledged it or not, was founded on her belief in individual excellence.

Pound's creed of excellence formed an underlying premise for her ground-breaking book. In *Poetic Origins and the Ballad*, she questioned whether peasants would possess enough knowledge about aristocratic lifestyles and values to compose lyrical pieces about them. Summing up Pound's conclusions concerning ballad origins, Cognard stated: "As songs progress from inception to use, they get worse. Narrative is a sophisticated, artistic form, an advanced stage." To emphasize the more advanced thinking that produced ballads, Louise devoted a chapter to the possibility that ballads were derived from church music rather than from secular sources.

It's not surprising that reviews of *Poetic Origins and the Ballad* were mixed. Hartley Burr Alexander defended the work of his friend and colleague, summarizing reviewers' comments and adding his own favorable opinion. He stated that "there are those who welcome with a sigh of relief a volume which punctures the envelope of gaseous theory with which sentimentalists have surrounded the ballad question." Defending Louise's hypothesis, Alexander wrote that "Mr. Gerould and the others who sing in his choir" ignored the vast evidence supporting Pound's theory of individual ballad authorship.

Alexander also quoted H.L. Mencken's support of Pound's findings. Mencken considered it "idiotic" to believe that "primitive balladists first joined in a communal hoofing, then began to moan and hum a tune and finally fitted words to it.'"

Alexander's mention of Mr. Gerould referred to Professor G.H. Gerould, author of a book on saints. Gerould took Louise to task for refuting the theory of other scholars, especially that of Grummere. Mainly, Professor Gerould found Louise's writing "bold to audacity," but at the same time lacking in "literary tact." In other words, Louise failed to write in the ladylike, self-effacing style that Gerould expected of women. Probably there was truth in his accusation that she lacked literary tact. In her defense of ballads, she hadn't paused to consider the consequences of her assertions–or if she had, she didn't care about offending Kittredge. Often her verbal reaction, and in this case, her written defense, was impulsive.

Even Mencken expressed a bit of sympathy for Gummere along with his praise for Louise's work. In a letter of May 11, 1921, he wrote:

Your ballad book is anything but monotonous and polemical—the form of it seems to me to be excellent. But I can't help thinking of poor Gummere. To spend a whole life-time cultivating a theory, to come to fame on the strength of it, and then to have it wiped out at one stroke. You leave nothing of it save a faint, delicate perfume.

Did Louise mind the mixed reviews and the criticism of respected scholars? Probably not. After reading their comments she may have packed up her books and marched to her classes or boarded a train for a meeting. Never afraid to challenge authority when proving her point, Louise had exercised the New Women's means of making a name for herself by carving a new niche in an established field.

Louise Pound's theory of individual ballad origins holds true today. Jan Harold Brunvand wrote in *The Study of American Folklore*, that "Pound's group eventually prevailed." But an important outcome of the "ballad war" was the recognition of the need "for more collecting and classification of American materials to be carried out before analysis were further pursued."

By questioning the established theory of ballad origins and gaining respect for her assertion of individual origins, Louise followed the advice she offered a fellow student in her undergraduate years. She had added a "cubic centimeter to the mass achievement of scholarship."

CHAPTER SEVENTEEN

The Jazz Age Arrives

While *Poetic Origins and the Ballad* gained notice from those in the academic community interested in English literary history, Louise Pound's former friend, Willa Cather rose to fame among the general population with her novels. During the 1920s, four of Cather's works were published: *One of Ours* (1922); *A Lost Lady* (1923); *The Professor's House* (1925); *My Mortal Enemy* (1926). *One of Ours* won a Pulitzer Prize even though critics did not consider it among her best efforts. The novel described a World War I soldier's escape from farm life for exhilarating experiences in France.

War novels were popular with the public during the twenties, and several new authors gained a foothold in the publishing world. Earnest Hemingway wrote about his wartime experiences in *The Sun Also Rises.* Hemingway's work portrayed the war as a negative experience that turned his characters into neurotics. John Dos Passo's novel, T*hree Soldiers,* told the story of three young men who had gone to war with optimism but ended up hating it.

F. Scott Fitzgerald, one of the young writers whose work Mencken had published in *The Smart Set,* gained a following among the college-age population with his novel, *This Side of Paradise.* Published in 1920, the book's setting was Fitzgerald's alma mater, Princeton University.

The novel caught the flavor of the new generation and of the Jazz Age. University of Nebraska students weren't immune from reflecting the values that Fitzgerald described in *This Side of Paradise*.

After the war ended, a prevailing atmosphere of unrest spread throughout the country and invaded the University of Nebraska. Knoll referred to the post WWI years as a period of "general disillusion," fueled by "Prohibition and its consequences," and to the "gaudy extravagances" of the younger generation influenced by Fitzgerald's novels featuring carefree lifestyles.

Gale E. Christianson wrote in *Fox At The Woods Edge: A Biography of Loren Eisley*, that in 1924 the University regents ordered Dean Engberg to enforce the rule against students' imbibing alcohol. The proliferation of cars on campus posed another problem for University authorities, who blamed automobiles for producing a negative effect on student morale. Consequently, the regents began restricting the use of cars on and around campus.

In addition to creating unrest among the nation's youth, the war had taken a toll on the country's economy. Nebraska had been hit hard. Farmers had provided food for war-torn European countries at high prices. Many borrowed money to buy more land for growing those crops. But the need for American produce dropped along with prices after the war ended, and many Nebraska farmers faced foreclosures. The University felt the effects of the suffering state economy.

Knoll wrote that the University's budget "came under scrutiny by the legislature" in 1923 and "endured drastic cuts."

The "egalitarian nature of higher education also was challenged" when the University began charging tuition. In 1923 students paid one dollar per credit hour for most subjects and three to five dollars for professional colleges. Knoll wrote that the second issue facing the University concerned the conflict between the College of Arts & Sciences, home of generalists, and the emerging professional colleges.

Willa Cather supported those who complained about the changing national atmosphere that encouraged young people to pursue specific vocational goals rather than broadening their store of general knowledge. Knoll quoted Cather's article which appeared in *The*

Nation, September 5, 1923:

> *Too much prosperity, too many moving picture shows, too much gaudy fiction have colored the taste and manners of many of those Nebraskans of the future.*
>
> *There, as elsewhere, one finds the frenzy to be showy; farmer boys who wish to be spenders before they are earners, girls who try to look like the heroines of the cinema screen; a coming generation which tries to cheat its esthetic sense by buying things instead of making anything. There is even danger that the fine institution, The University of Nebraska, may become a gigantic trade school. The men who control its destiny, the regents and the lawmakers, wish their sons and daughters to study machines, mercantile processes, principles of business; everything that has to do with the game of getting on in the world and nothing else.*

The ensuing controversy concerning the University's direction involved Hartley Burr Alexander, Louise Pound's friend. Alexander was an advocate of general knowledge and an outspoken critic of separating the Teachers College from the College of Arts & Sciences. He considered teaching to be an "art" rather than a "science," Knoll explained. In Alexander's view teaching was a "rhetoric for bringing students into participation in culture."

Alexander expressed his views on secondary education in "Letters to Teachers." According to Margaret Dale Masters' biography, *Hartley Burr Alexander: Writer in Stone*, he believed that public schools should be community centers containing a theater, a library, an arts and crafts section as well as an athletic complex, a restaurant, laboratories and a shop. In his opinion, schools existed to improve the life of a community and should be available to citizens for meetings at any time. Such a complex along with a broad general education would achieve his goal of giving students an opportunity to participate in culture.

Louise, along with Alexander and Cather, was a graduate of the 1890s University which had offered students three courses of study.

Masters described the subject offerings: The classical curriculum included "languages, literature, mathematics, science, ancient history, and philosophy." The scientific course omitted the Latin and Greek. The selected course allowed the student "under the direction of the faculty" to choose their own studies." Most likely, Louise had taken the selected course to earn two diplomas: one in letters, the other in music. As a professor of English she served on the Arts & Sciences faculty, and she must have supported Alexander's desire to keep the teachers' college in the Arts & Sciences department.

This wasn't the first time that Alexander had stirred controversy at the University. During his senior year, he organized fellow students to protest Chancellor MacLean's dismissal of H.K. Wolfe, chairman of the philosophy department.

Wolfe had been Alexander's teacher and mentor. As part of the protest, Alexander wrote a senior play satirizing the chancellor and the Board of Regents. Traditionally the play was presented as part of Commencement Day activities. Although Alexander feared that his actions might cause the University to deny him a degree, he attended the commencement ceremony and graduated. However, he refused to give the customary slight bow to the chancellor after receiving his diploma. Nevertheless, he stayed at the University for another year working as a reader in the English department before going to study at the University of Pennsylvania.

Chancellor Avery probably was irritated that Alexander was the "intellectual center of the campus from 1910 until 1925," Knoll wrote. Alexander presented his vision for the University in a letter to the regents requesting that business and academic affairs be dealt with separately. Stating that scholastic matters should determine budgets, he asked that a provost be appointed to preserve academic standards. Because they favored Avery's practical stance on University affairs, the regents ignored Alexander's letter.

As the University continued its pragmatic course favoring the establishment of professional colleges, Alexander made a last attempt at reform. He planned a reorganization of instruction in the college of Arts & Sciences, which he left in the hands of colleagues to implement, while he taught the 1927 spring semester at the University of Wisconsin. His plan languished.

With University administrators favoring vocational studies over broader knowledge, Louise Pound's comfortable niche, encouraged by Professor Sherman, developed cracks like those in an aging building, especially after Sherman retired in 1929.

Although her fall from administrative favor had begun earlier–when Mabel Lee arrived to direct University women's sports in 1924.

The Mabel Lee Conflict

ALONG WITH PROFESSIONAL recognition as a language expert, Louise also experienced disappointment in her University relationships. One of the most frustrating events concerned her longstanding association with women's sports. Although she wasn't active in supervising teams during the twenties, her belief in competitive game-playing continued to set the standard for the women's athletic program–until Chancellor Avery hired Mabel Lee as director in 1924.

The endless feud between Louise Pound and Mabel Lee began with a group of female students. The girls were physical education majors who considered their course of study inadequate. After the resignation of Anne Barr Clapp as head of women's physical education in 1908, her husband, Dr. R.E. Clapp had supervised the training of both men and women. Under Dr. Clapp, the women's program stressed playing games rather than training students to teach physical education, a policy which resulted in the program's loss of recognition from the American Physical Education Association. Knoll wrote that the young women contended that "games were not training," and they voiced their need for competent teaching.

Nationally, opinions about the effect of athletics on women's bodies had swung backward, favoring the conservation of energy. Many physicians warned women of endangering their child-bearing organs and of developing bulging muscles if they engaged in sports. Although Mabel Lee wasn't a proponent of women shying away from games, she recommended that they play only for the fun of it, avoiding intercollegiate competition. This philosophy put her at odds with Louise Pound.

Why should Miss Pound, an English professor, be involved with the athletic program after she had stopped coaching and playing sports at the University? Even though she had given up tennis and only played golf during the twenties, the aura of her former achievements stayed with her. Her past role as basketball coach and her previous tennis championships along with her prowess on the golf course gave an added dimension to her reputation. Especially in Lincoln, people thought of Louise as an outstanding athlete as well as an academic. Also, the fact that she and her family had a long association with the University and its development encouraged Louise to remain interested in all aspects of its progress, including women's sports.

Both Louise Pound and Mabel Lee possessed determination and were interested in the future of University women's sports. But the gap between their backgrounds and personalities was unbridgeable. Descriptions of Louise Pound written by friends, colleagues, and former students, picture her as an ambitious woman intent on reaching the top of her profession. Forthright and often spontaneous, her reactions to situations differed from Lee's more deliberate and calculating means of dealing with obstacles. While Louise would rush headlong toward an obstruction, confident in her ability to leap over it, Lee would study the barrier, then climb carefully, but confidently, over the hurdle.

Growing up in Clearfield, Iowa, Mabel Lee had been an indifferent athlete. In her memoir, *Memories of a Bloomer Girl,* Lee reported that as a youngster, she had enjoyed running and jumping but when it came time to practice for a track meet, she realized that she didn't want to compete. Yet her interest in sports continued throughout her childhood.

Lee also recalled playing games with her three sisters and neighborhood children without keeping score. She wrote, "What difference was the score or who won?" It was just play, and we did it in a way that we liked." In high school, Lee organized a basketball team that included all the high school girls. When the team was asked to play with the Parsons' College team in Fairfield, Iowa, Lee replied, "We girls are having all the fun we need playing here at home by ourselves and we will not come to play with you."

Because of childhood bouts of illness, Lowenthal reported that Lee's sports activities were often interrupted. Lee admitted to *Lincoln Journal Star* reporter, Don Pieper, that her "three sisters outdid her in "golf, tennis, everything. I definitely was not a sportswoman." It's no wonder that she would come to view Louise Pound's competitive spirit with scorn, and perhaps, unacknowledged envy.

After attending Coe College in Iowa, Lee enrolled in the Boston Normal School of Gymnastics which had become part of Wellesley College by the time she graduated in 1910. Lowenthal wrote that Lee wasn't comfortable at Boston Normal because she felt snubbed by the Eastern girls. Once again, her athletic ability fell short of her fellow students' game skills. Nevertheless, Lee claimed that the experience taught her to be a good loser. Persisting in her studies at Boston, she eventually developed a group of friends, just as she found allies in Lincoln, a city in which she also felt uncomfortable at first.

After leaving Wellesley, Lee served as director of physical education at Coe College. She then accepted the same position at Oregon Agricultural College, but was forced to resign after contracting influenza during the 1918 epidemic. Her next appointment was at Beloit College in Illinois where she remained until accepting the Nebraska post as head of Women's Physical Education.

Mabel Lee's habit of considering her actions carefully and of planning ahead helped her impress Chancellor Avery during her interview. Aware that female physical education professionals often conveyed a masculine appearance, Lee took care to dress in a feminine style. She wrote that she wore her "prettiest hat–the lavender braid one lined in sky blue silk and trimmed by a large pink rose which broke the austerity (of her) pearl gray tailored suit and premature gray hair." She succeeded in her mission to charm Chancellor Avery; the two became allies in the battle to revolutionize women's sports.

She had thought ahead about Louise Pound and had decided not to like her before their first meeting. Realizing that Louise had written the rules for women's basketball rekindled Lee's disdain for them. Lee had scorned the rules years ago. Her memoir contained a strong condemnation of Louise and of her basketball rules:

> *At the turn-of-the-century this woman, a graduate of the University of Nebraska, then 10 years out of college and for most of those years a member of the faculty, had successfully organized, coached and managed intercollegiate basketball for women at the university. Since then she had made quite a name for herself through her various local, state and district championships in tennis and golf. In my early teaching years I had encountered her basketball rules for women and been placed on the offensive about them.*
>
> *When she first called at my office, she inquired if I was familiar with her basketball rules. So this was the creator of the old controversial rules of my student and early teaching years. I had never known where she lived or who she might be and none of my profession had the slightest idea.*

Unlike Mabel Lee, who decided not to like Louise before meeting her, Louise had no pre-conceived opinion of the new director of women's athletics. At first, she endorsed the arrival of Lee, believing that Lee would re-establish intercollegiate sports. She even congratulated Chancellor Avery for hiring the new director.

One can only imagine that first meeting between Mabel Lee and Louise Pound. While Louise may have spoken enthusiastically about her basketball rules and her hope of seeing women's intercollegiate sports revived, Lee probably smiled graciously.

Although she admitted that she was familiar with the basketball rules, Lee most likely remained silent on the subject of forming competitive teams.

Any possibility of a civil relationship between Mabel Lee and Louise ended with the publication of a booklet about women's sports which included the program for the coming year.

Lee's assistant, Mary Wheeler, and a group of students wrote the booklet and dedicated it to Lee. According to her, the girls rushed to give her a copy as soon as the booklet was printed, then they hurried to Louise Pound's office to present her with the second copy.

The question arises of why Lee allowed the girls to scurry to Louise's office. Why didn't she discourage them, explaining that Miss Pound probably wouldn't endorse the new program? Perhaps she wanted the girls to witness Louise's reaction.

After the group burst into Pound's office and handed her the brochure, they probably waited for an enthusiastic response from this professor who was known for her athleticism. Unfortunately they were not aware of Pound's unwavering stand on playing games to win, or of her desire to witness a resurgence of intercollegiate competition in women's sports.

Standing in front of Pound's desk, they may have noticed a furrow gathering between her eyes as she examined the pamphlet. Tension must have grown in the silent room as Louise read the dedication to Lee "aloud with much sarcasm." Any expectation of Pound's endorsement for the revised program ended with Louise slamming the brochure on her desk and saying, "Sissy. Just a sissy!'"

She then turned to the page explaining the Women's Athletic Association's endorsement of sports for all women, ending with the affirmation, "We play for the fun of the game." Again, Pound announced her disgust: "Sissies! All sissies! Bah!'"

Only Lee's account of Louise's reaction to the booklet exists. Perhaps Lee allowed the students to deliver the pamphlet to Louise because she wanted to provoke her into a public display of their differences. Of course, the booklet also confirmed Lee's leadership of women's sports. She did not want help or advice from Louise Pound. Lee was determined to establish a reputation equal to or better than that of Louise in the realm of women's Sports.

Louise probably did refer to the program and its participants as "sissies." No doubt she voiced her objections to Chancellor Avery as well, but Avery supported Lee. When Lee complained to Avery that Louise tried to interfere with her work, he sympathized, saying, "So she is trying to pull you around, too, by the nose."

Knoll compared the differing relationships of Louise Pound and Mabel Lee with University administrators: "Louise Pound was an antagonist who wanted to defeat the men. Chancellors, deans, and chairmen all found Miss Pound difficult." While Mabel Lee also refused to give way to "arbitrary administrative authority," her proteges did not suffer," Knoll observed, but the women Louise Pound mentored were ignored.

Because she always spoke her mind, Louise was Chancellor Avery's nemesis. Yet, her national standing among English scholars and her family's prominence in Lincoln society prevented him from taking official action against her. Also, the fact that they had been classmates possibly influenced Avery. Perhaps he simply accepted Louise as an annoying staff member.

Meanwhile, as Mabel Lee declared war with Louise Pound, she also criticized non-physical education majors and Nebraskans in general:

> . . . *Here in my new home, I found Nebraskans a new sort of people with whom to deal. Never before had I encountered so many snobs, so many people with chips on their shoulders, or so many special-privilege seekers; yet on the other hand never before had I encountered a more wonderful group of dedicated earnest young women seeking an education than the group of girls at the University of Nebraska, who, against great odds, were trying to earn a college degree with a major in physical education.*

Toward non-physical education majors, Lee's condescension verged on scorn: "I was struck by the overweight and lack of sophistication in most of these corn-fed girls, and our physical examination records verified this fact." She conceded that she came to like the girls "for the most part." But it was the "eager, earnest, sincere, grateful, fun-loving, and cordial students along with Chancellor Avery who sold Nebraska to me."

Her initial feelings of being an outsider undoubtedly fueled Lee's resentment of Louise. Not only was Louise an outstanding athlete, who had won prizes beyond Mabel Lee's ability, Louise was also a member of Lincoln's elite–a group that ignored the new director of women's sports. She "found Lincoln full of snobs," Knoll wrote, while "Louise Pound belonged to the right clubs and founded new ones."

Although Chancellor Avery supported Lee in her reform of the Womens Physical Education Department, he also managed to avoid crossing Louise Pound who had "powerful friends." When Avery resigned in 1926, Louise Pound wasn't "displeased," Knoll wrote, but Mabel Lee was "apprehensive."

Lowenthal stated that the feud between Mabel Lee and Louise Pound was "not well-documented" and existed mostly through "rumors and gossip." She also confirmed that "the only material on most of the incidents between the women came from the second volume of Mabel Lee's autobiography, *Memories Beyond Bloomers*, which was published in 1978. Louise had been in her grave for 20 years when Lee's book was published and had no opportunity to defend herself or deny Lee's accusations.

Louise valued scholarship more than bearing grudges. As a person who reacted immediately to provocation, she had no reason to continue waging a campaign against Lee. Her friends may have taken steps to annoy Lee, but Louise concentrated on her main objective: adding to the world's index of scholarly knowledge.

Looking back at Pound's graduation day speech, "The Apotheosis of the Common," her opposition to Lee's belief in sports for all women and playing for the fun of the game was consistent with Louise's belief in individual excellence. Her objections to Lee's sports philosophy and her nagging of chancellors and deans came from her belief in placing individualism above commonality and excellence ahead of mediocrity.

CHAPTER NINETEEN

An International Reputation

THROUGHOUT THE TWENTIES, Louise accepted many opportunities that came her way because of her language expertise. Several universities requested her services as visiting professor for summer sessions. In 1923, she taught at the University of California, Berkeley. In 1928, she was a professor at Yale Linguistic Institute, and in 1929 she taught at the University of Chicago. During the summer of 1930, she instructed Columbia students, and in the summer of 1931 she taught at Stanford. Invitations to be visiting professor which she could not meet came from Wellesley (1926), Wisconsin (1930), and West Virginia (1931).

During her lectureship at Berkeley, the *San Francisco Examiner* (July 15, 1923) honored Louise with a poem:

> *She can quote whole pages of Chaucer,*
> *Or play a sonata by Bach*
> *She can handpaint an admirable saucer*
> *Or best you at tennis a block;*
> *She knows all the Cherokee lingo;*
> *At golf she is like Sarazen;*
> *She can write a trim sonnet or trim a right bonnet,*

Or lecture on old Yucatan.
She's won all the bicycle races
And 'most every learned degree
If I had her knowledge, I'd buy me a college
And be its entire faculty.

A more prestigious honor came to her in 1927 when she was selected to represent the United States at the International Council on English held in London on the 16th and 17th of June. The council meetings would take place at the Royal Society of Literature. A newspaper clipping stated that the council planned to "do its best to preserve the traditions and promote the development of the English language." Dr. Henry S. Canby was the "prime mover" of the effort to reform abuses of English. Fifty eminent professors represented the United States, and Louise Pound was the only woman on the council. Bernard Shaw, the English playwright and novelist, was among the fifty British representatives.

Traveling to and from London gave Louise an opportunity to visit friends along the way. After leaving Lincoln on June 3, 1927, (probably by train), she traveled to Springfield, Massachusetts, to attend a June 6 linguistic conference. On June 7, Louise visited Mrs. Halsey C. Yates at Governor's Island, New York.

A Lincoln paper stated that she sailed on the Berengaria for Southampton on June 8 and would be gone for two months. Her friend, with whom she had lived in Heidelberg, Adele Lathrop, met Louise in London. Benefitting from her friendship with Ruth Bryan Owen, daughter of the notorious Nebraska politician, William Jennings Bryan, Louise stayed at the American Club near Berkeley Square. (Owen was a member of the club.)

In a June 18 letter to Olivia, Louise reported that during the conference, she and about 24 others sat around a table in the rooms of the Royal Society. Never at a loss for words, Louise voiced her opinions. "I talked too, having more comments in mind than the others and thinking of many new subjects," she wrote.

Always aware of women's status in her profession and the world in general, Louise wrote, "The Britons were not expecting a woman delegate and seemed a little embarrassed at first." The only other woman present was the secretary of the Royal Society "who does all the work." She invited Louise to tea after the meetings, and Louise wrote that they "got on well."

While attending the conference, Louise, as stated in her letter to Olivia, did not hesitate to express her opinion about matters the council should consider. A June 18 *London Times* article informed readers that "Professor Louise Pound said she would like to see steps taken to bring national spellings into closer accord, and the council could also do good work in matters of pronunciation."

At the conference, Bernard Shaw sat across the table from Louise, and she enjoyed his humor. She told a *Lincoln Journal* reporter that Shaw "kept us in laughter most of the time." Louise also said that the committee agreed with Shaw's remark that "exactly 42,767,500 dialects are spoken on the British Isles, and that every one of the speakers is certain that he has command of correct English."

Other members of the council agreed with Shaw's opinion about the futility of reforming English. The London Times stated that the conference "managed during its two days of sessions to throw a good deal of cold water on its own project." Continuing to emphasize the complexity of forming language standards, the article added that the remedy for "stale, hackneyed, flabby, and circuitous" writing styles "lies beyond the power of committees and councils."

Although the council hadn't agreed on concrete language objectives, Louise had enjoyed her time in England. Writing to Olivia, she outlined her plans for a few days of personal enjoyment after the conference ended. She intended to "read a few days in the British Museum, to go for a day or two to Wimbledon and to shop Liberty's, Peter Robinson's, Selfridges, . . ." She also hoped to see a few shows, because "all the good theaters are within walking distance, for me." But, she often took the "underground or bus."

At Wimbledon, Louise watched Helen Wills play. Wills verified

Louise's belief that intelligent athletes were the best players. "It is of interest to know," Louise told a Lincoln reporter, "that a Phi Beta Kappa can be a world's champion in tennis."

Helen Wills won the U.S. Women's Singles seven times, and captured the Wimbledon Women's title eight times. Even in France, Wills triumphed over other women four times. Referred to as "Queen of the Nets," she was considered the greatest tennis player of her time. A graduate of the University of California, she later studied art in New York City, where she also exhibited her work.

After her London stay, Louise planned to visit friends in Paris and Heidelberg, but a week of London rain made her eager to return to "Nebraska sunlight" and her "unfinished" work. She boarded the ocean liner, Acquatainia, and sailed to New York where she visited friends. Then she traveled to Baltimore for a meeting with the publishers of *American Speech* and had lunch with H.L. Mencken and his friends.

In her beloved Nebraska once again, Louise resumed her usual summertime routine. Writing sessions in her study alternated with golf games at Lincoln Country Club, along with lunches and dinners with friends. Louise and Olivia probably met with other members of the Wooden Spoon and Copper Kettle societies, and the sisters usually played bridge with friends on weekends. They also enjoyed viewing the latest movies.

Around this time Louise bought her first car. In his letter to Butters, Knoll recalled Louise telling him about buying that first auto. She had written an introduction to *The Iliad* even though she was not an expert in Homer. Playing tennis with a publisher, Louise won more the match, she also won the contract to write *The Iliad* introduction. Louise said that she never knew "who used that little book, but it earned her an old flivver nonetheless."

Thereafter, Louise always owned a car, and she always gave them names—sometimes for literary characters. The first car was referred to as the "Whippet." Later cars were hailed "Henry" (perhaps for an English king) and "Rosinate," (probably for Don Quixote's horse.)

When she resumed her teaching duties in September, Louise

missed the presence of her friend, Hartley Burr Alexander, who had accepted a position at Scripps College in California. She also greeted a new chancellor, Edgar A. Burnett. Like Avery, Burnett was a practical man, and he appealed to the regents, who chose him over Dean Herman Jones. Jones had taken his Ph.D. in government from Columbia University, and in Knoll's words, "had puzzled over how academic standards could be reconciled with popular education, how the good could be kept from destroying the best." Within two years of Burnett's appointment, Jones became president of the University of South Dakota and from there went on "to greater things."

As Dean of the College of Agriculture and director of the agricultural experimental station, Burnett expanded off-campus agricultural experimental stations with the aid of federal funds. Through University extension programs, he made the College of Agriculture a major force in the state. Knoll stated that Burnett was a "man of authority; one did not cross him easily." He lacked humor and rarely smiled. Even serious-minded Mabel Lee considered Burnett an undemonstrative man.

What must Louise Pound have thought of the new chancellor?

No doubt, she judged him, along with Avery, as an unworthy administrator, an authority to be tolerated as well as needled— within limits. After all, she did not want to leave Lincoln or the University. She enjoyed her status as a champion athlete and respected scholar, and she often escaped from the campus routine, traveling to speaking engagements, meetings, and attending cultural events.

During Thanksgiving break of 1927, she boarded a train and traveled to Chicago. There, she visited friends, Mr. and Mrs. Charles C. Dawes, and went to the opera, *Madame Butterfly*. At the Dawes' home, she watched a private showing of the film, *The Big Parade*. She also went to a performance of the Chicago Symphony with her friend and former tennis opponent, Carrie Neely.

At the time of Louise's visit in November, 1927, Dawes was serving as U.S. Vice President under Calvin Coolidge. When his term as vice president ended in 1929, Dawes was appointed ambassador to Great

Britain, a post he held until 1932. Then he returned to Chicago and helped arrange financing for the 1933 Chicago World's Fair.

1927 had been an exciting year in Louise Pound's life, one filled with travels, meetings and visits with friends. As always she enjoyed returning home after her excursions. But 1928 would bring a sobering event into the lives of Louise and Olivia and change the living conditions at 1632 L Street

THE STIMULATING EVENTS that Louise enjoyed in 1927 were overshadowed in October 1928 when Roscoe's wife, Grace, died, and again in December with her mother's death. During a trip abroad in 1922, Grace (Gerrard) Pound had contracted influenza from which she never fully recovered. On Roscoe's birthday, October 27, 1928, Grace died suddenly of a cerebral hemorrhage.

Laura Pound had felt exceptionally well the first week of December 1928 and ventured out to a D.A.R. meeting on Friday afternoon, December 7. But the following day she began to feel ill and went to bed. "Her condition gave no alarm until about 2 o'clock Monday afternoon," an obituary stated. Pneumonia had settled into her lungs, and she died at 8:30 that evening.

Obituaries noted her colonial ancestors and Quaker background as well as her contributions to the social and educational life of Lincoln. Journalists mentioned her influence in founding the first Lincoln public library and her efforts to establish the Hayden Art Club, known as the Nebraska Art Association, in addition to her success in founding the Deborah Avery chapter of D.A.R. She and her husband "often gave of their own time and efforts to foster the success of the state university."

Obituaries mentioned that she had taken classes at the University and had become proficient in German, collecting a large library of German literary works. She also had studied English literature at the University. While pursuing her studies, her personal interest in many young students caused them to refer to her as "Mother Pound."

Many letters of sympathy reached Louise, Olivia, and Roscoe after

Laura's death. Derrick Lehmer, long time family friend, and one of those who benefitted from Laura's influence wrote the following tribute:

> *I was much moved to get the news of the passing of your wonderful mother. What a fine life and how much of the real worth- while matters of this world she had to do with! I can not say how much she meant for me, not only when I was a callow young boy from the farm, but also after I had become wise enough to appreciate what a spirit like hers stood for in this foolish haphazard old world. For every touch of her firming hands I am thankful.*

Adele Lathrop, friend of Louise and Olivia, sent her condolences stating that she would never forget Laura Pound, and that she "admired and loved" her. It was a "wonderful blessing" that she "slipped away quickly" and was "spared a long illness."

Yet, Adele understood that Olivia and Louise would be lonely when facing this "new stage of life–just by yourselves."

Their mother's niece, Emma Sweet, also recognized that Louise and Olivia would miss their mother's strong personality. In a January 25, 1929, letter to Olivia, Emma invited Louise and Olivia to spend the summer with her: "You should drive the whippet (Louise's current car) with Louise to Chicago, and I meet you there and come on to Rochester, . . . You would be quite free from any responsibility about weeds or the house . . . To get away for a long vacation from all the heartbreaking reminders might give you new strength and courage in readjusting your life."

Laura Pound's spirit lived on in her children's lives. Louise and Olivia continued to welcome students into their home not just as boarders, but as members of the family. Those who benefitted from their hospitality were not forgotten; Louise and Olivia always encouraged their visits and letters. The three Pound siblings also reflected their mother's zest for learning through their research and writings which continued gaining national and international prestige. There is no doubt that Laura Pound had a profound influence on many lives as well as on the city of Lincoln.

In addition to her mother's enthusiasm for learning and helping others, Louise inherited Laura's habit of speaking her mind. Witnessing her mother's efforts to save the city library when the mayor schemed for its demise and observing her leadership role in cultural organizations encouraged Louise's outspoken nature. She continued to help and defend students and colleagues, unafraid to interfere with administrative decisions that undermined others.

Chapter Twenty

Speaking Her Mind For Students

A N ENDURING CHARACTERISTIC throughout Louise Pound's life was her willingness to help others. Colleagues, students, and friends benefitted from her efforts on their behalf. She did more than pass on the flame of learning that her parents handed her, she took risks to help others achieve individual excellence. Former student, Evelyn Simpson, believed that Louise was willing to put her job on the line when defending colleagues and students. "There never has been room, nor time, for pettiness in Louise Pound's life. Always she has been willing to jeopardize her own position for the greater good of justice."

Lowenthal credited Louise Pound's "sportsman's creed, with its emphasis on fairness and clean play" for her habit of jumping "into situations where a less forceful, less justice-loving person might fear to tread." Throughout her years of teaching, she often interceded with deans and chancellors to save the threatened job of a colleague. Mamie Meredith commented, "There are others besides myself, who probably wouldn't have found it bearable to remain here if Louise Pound hadn't stayed here to champion just causes, whether popular or unpopular. She, more than almost anyone else I know, is free from envy and jealousy."

Louise also defended Ruth Odell, another University English professor. Odell had written a study of Helen Hunt Jackson, author of a popular 1884 novel, Ramona. The English department chairman, Thomas M. Raysor, condemned Odell's study as "impermissible" and "subliterary." According to Knoll, Louise claimed that "Raysor and all those who were 'homesick for Harvard yard' drove prospective schoolteachers into the arms of Teachers College, where education courses, respected by neither students nor by subject-matter specialists, replaced standard academic disciplines."

Did Louise realize that she was sacrificing her own career advancement when she stormed the offices of deans and chancellors in defense of students and colleagues? Probably not, since helping others was an intrinsic part of her personality. Another former pupil, B.A. Botkin, attributed her concern for others to her "Colonial Quaker heritage" and to her family "with their stress on integrity, truth, service, and sociability." The Pounds did more than most settlers to promote the growth and progress of the state, the city of Lincoln, and the University. They also encouraged and supported individuals, who in turn, contributed to the growth and progress of the state, its cities and institutions.

Administrators may have despaired when they saw Louise Pound striding in their direction with a purposeful expression on her face. They listened to her suggestions and intercessions on behalf of colleagues and students because she was a respected scholar and came from a prominent Lincoln family, but they seldom took action on her requests or followed her advice.

Although they could not dispense with her services or ignore the prestige she brought to the University, Louise Pound's superiors employed subtle ways of punishing her for questioning their policies. In fifty years of teaching she was never chosen to head the English department, nor did she receive sabbatical leave, a grant-in-aid, or carfare to professional meetings. University officials refused to grant Louise permission to attend the 550th anniversary of Heidelberg University in 1936 ostensibly because of the unstable German political situation.

Searching for an English Department chairman, University of Nebraska officials queried administrators of other universities for names of possible candidates. In an undated letter, Professor Orin Stepanek forwarded a message to Louise that he had received from W.A. Neilson recommending Louise for the post. Neilson informed University administrators that it was "absurd for the English department of Nebraska to go outside for a chairman as you have Louise Pound." In Neilson's opinion no one else in the country was as good as Louise. "I have had occasion recently to scrutinize the ranks for our part of the profession for similar purposes, and I should be quite at a loss to make such nomination as you propose," Neilson stated.

The search for an English department head resulted in the hiring of Thomas N. Raysor in 1930, "a distinguished editor of Coleridge" who, in Knoll's words, endorsed "research only when it dealt with original examinations of high literary texts." It's not surprising that Raysor condemned Ruth Odell's study of Helen Hunt Jackson.

Nor would he have approved of Louise Pound's advice to a student who struggled to describe her homestead childhood. Another professor expected the student to use textbook English in relating her experience, but Louise advised her to tell her story in her "own words, in the words and expressions that the people used, in the talk that is natural to the material." This incident, related in Mari Sandoz's book, *Love Song to the Plains,* confirmed Louise Pound's support of wide variations in English usage. In addition to valuing Anglo-Saxon English, Louise respected "the speech of the homesteader, the cowboy, the wildcatter, the ex-convict—all of whom appeared in her classes and were all made welcome," Sandoz noted. To Louise Pound, "language was a growing thing," and she had the courage and confidence to uphold her belief.

Sandoz had followed Louise's advice to write about places and people she knew when she composed a novel about her father, *Old Jules.* Before the *Atlantic Monthly Press* published Sandoz's book, the editor, Edward Weeks, wrote Louise in May 1935 asking her to verify Sandoz's accounts of her father's life. Louise responded favorably to Weeks' request, and *Old Jules* remains a classic novel about life on the Nebraska frontier.

Did Louise resent not becoming the English department chairman? No evidence of her feelings on the issue exists among her papers. If she had a strong desire to head the department she undoubtedly would have tailored her opinions to agree with traditional textbook rules about English usage. She would have curbed her reactions to controversial topics, or at least, modified them to avoid offending deans and chancellors. One can assume that she knew and accepted the consequences of speaking her mind.

Also, Louise knew that, scholastically, she was an asset for the University, and wasn't likely to lose her job. Since she turned down offers to teach at other educational institutions, she must have been content to remain in Lincoln. She always looked forward to returning home from her travels and stated that she stayed in Lincoln because of her family, her friends, and her home. In Sandoz's opinion, Louise Pound's statement of her duty to her family and home fooled no one. Louise stayed, according to Sandoz, because she was "a woman of the Plains, not the geographical Plains so much as of that other vast Plains country–language."

Professionally, Louise was caught in the no-win situation that William H. Chafe described in his book, *The American Woman: Her Changing Social, Economic and Political Roles 1920-1970*. He wrote that women who pursued careers in male-dominated fields traveled an "uncharted course" and "violated the most deeply held conceptions of (their) proper role." No longer serving men at home, they competed against them at work, challenging the "powerful forces of tradition." Lacking signposts to guide her career actions, the woman desiring to forge ahead in her career was caught in a bind. "If she acted demurely and accepted a subservient role, she missed opportunities for advancement. On the other hand, if she anticipated prejudice and compensated by being overly aggressive, she alienated those around her and highlighted the extent to which she departed from the female norm."

In either instance she was "a stranger in a foreign territory, confronting repeatedly the conflict between the passivity expected of women and the assertiveness demanded of men." Louise, as evidenced by her outspoken defense of colleagues and her challenge of established theories in the field of ballad origins as well as her promotion of American English, fit Chafe's description of an "aggressive" woman.

DURING THE 1930s, the University was not a pleasant place to work, and it tested Louise Pound's loyalty. The cloud of hard times that settled over Nebraska in the twenties grew darker after the 1929 stock market crash. Attempting to improve their lot, Nebraska voters joined the nationwide trend of electing Democratic legislatures. Many of the newly elected were "latter-day populists, even levelers," and some, Knoll affirmed, "were anti-intellectuals." Because the chancellor, Edgar A. Burnett, "did not challenge the prejudices of the agricultural interests which he saw as his constituency," the 1932 legislature cut the University budget by a million dollars. Nevertheless, the school remained "intact," although it was "impoverished," Knoll reported.

In 1932, Louise Pound was sixty years old, but her retirement was fourteen years away. The limber young woman had aged, yet she could still run up the stairs to her classroom. Her brick-red hair, worn in a braid around her head, showed no gray strands. Although her 18-inch waist had disappeared, she wasn't overweight. The formerly intense dark eyes now glowed with warmth and compassion in photographs. Louise Pound had matured into a distinguished lady.

Sunday mornings, regardless of whether she was settled into her book-lined study with a cat for company or sitting at a hotel room desk, Louise answered her correspondence. An undated letter from Louise to Olivia written from Chicago's Hotel Del Prado, stated, "I'm at the typewriter as usual Sunday mornings looking after the week's letters, and I have a few advance term papers to read." Letters written to Louise during the 1930s often requested her help which she gave with a generous spirit. Unfortunately, Pound Papers at the Nebraska

State Historical Society contain few letters that Louise wrote, but her personality can be glimpsed from the comments of those who wrote to her, and many of her letters to Benjamin A. Botkin are among his papers in the University of Nebraska's Special Collections Archives.

A common interest in folklore sealed the friendship between Louise and Botkin just as the desire to promote American English had fostered the friendship of Louise and Mencken. By 1928, Botkin had coined a term, folk-say, to illustrate his theory that folklore exists in modern experiences which are revealed through language, a concept that Louise shared. Both Louise and Botkin promoted respect for the differing voices of an area's population.

Benjamin A. Botkin, (1901-1975) was born and raised in Boston. He entered Harvard University at age 15 and graduated magna cum laude at 19. After taking an MA in English literature from Columbia University in 1921, he taught English at the University of Oklahoma for two years before returning to New York City to work in settlement houses. There he taught immigrants Americanization and English. After this experience, he studied with Louise at the University of Nebraska, taking his Ph.D. in 1931. By 1938, he was the national folklore editor of the Federal Writers' Project, and he became chief editor of the Writer's Unit of the Library of Congress Project in 1941.

In 1945, he returned to New York and concentrated on his own writing. Botkin listened closely to his sources, taking into account the nation's different regions, races, and classes. He also stressed the interrelationship between folk, popular, and high culture.

In 1930, Louise and Botkin exchanged letters concerning his possible replacement of a University professor who had requested a leave of absence. At the same time, Botkin would study for his doctorate in English with an emphasis on folklore. A letter Louise wrote to him on April 4, 1930, revealed that she was aware of administrators' feelings toward her. She warned Botkin: "Here's a hint for you! Do not say too much about me, or taking my courses, when you write in to the department. Put the 'soft pedal' on me. I don't know much about our new head (Thomas M. Raysor) but he will be like my colleagues, probably, and surely most of his courses are what it would be wisest for you to take."

Louise wrote to Botkin on March, 19, 1932, about the Depression's effect on the University. "Our faculty is to have its salaries cut next year too. We have been lucky to escape up till this time." She then wrote that seven masters' degree candidates were working under her instruction. "The students are of fine caliber this year and there are more of them in our graduate school." The rise in graduate students occurred because of the difficulty young people had in finding jobs during the thirties.

The same letter referred to a paper Louise had written in a hurry as well as her reluctance to accept speaking engagements:

> *The style of that ballad paper is accounted for by the fact that I had but fifteen or twenty minutes in which to present the paper, and tried to get everything said in that time.*
>
> *I'm no admirer of my style. It doesn't flow along easily enough, and when I force myself to write the results are awful. —and I don't think much of my speaking either. You would be rather reckless to ask me to Oklahoma. I have an invitation to West Virginia this spring, but do not know whether I shall accept.*
>
> *It has been pretty nice to stay off of trains and not to have had a single cold all year.*

This letter portrays her realistic attitude toward her work. Her achievements may have impressed others, but she did not fall prey to an inflated ego.

Botkin verified Louise's continuing interest in her students after they left the University. His article, "Pound Sterling: Letters from a 'Lady Professor," states that she was a teachers' teacher and scholars' scholar" who "followed closely . . . her students' careers and publications, and was intensely proud of the 'Louise Pound alumni association,' as some of us alumni and alumnae dubbed it . . . Through her letters she kept in touch with the members of her group or circle."

Botkin believed that Louise "founded a school" rather than a "legend" as other teachers often did by exploiting their own personalities. Because she had known what it was to be "lonely and under attack" during her pioneering work in poetic ballad origins and American English, she surrounded "her disciples (with) the mutual aid and encouragement that give the scholar a feeling of security and the confidence that comes from knowing one is not alone."

A satisfying tribute came to Louise in a letter from her friend, Dorothy Canfield Fisher. Fisher had visited Lincoln in 1938, and she and Louise had attended a lunch at the chancellor's home. While waiting in Chicago for a train, Fisher wrote to Louise, praising her accomplishments: "You're the prize exhibit Lincoln had to show me after forty-five years."

> *You're a first-rater . . . There is a certain validity about that setting for a first rater that I find enormously reassuring—for Lincoln, for you, for the country, when I think what it has meant for the university, for the city, the state, the west, to have you there, one of them authentically, and standing for the very best in taste with no compromises—I shout hallelujah!*
>
> *They ought to put up a monument to you (probably will). I don't at all mean as recognition or reward for what you've done by staying with them; for judging from the lovely expression on your face, you have your reward, right now. I mean so that your rare example will go on, larger than your life, holding up the light to show the way to civilization.*

Ironically, the only monument existing on the University of Nebraska campus to honor Louise Pound is Cather-Pound Hall, a dormitory named for her and for Willa Cather. Cather's name comes first, although after leaving Nebraska Cather made her permanent home elsewhere—mainly in New York City. Lasting fame, however, was never a goal of Louise Pound. Passing on the flame of learning to her students and the general public through teaching, writing, and speaking, in addition to helping friends, colleagues, and students, reflected the generous spirit of Louise Pound and enriched the lives of those who came in contact with her.

Though she was an exceptional individual, Louise displayed a common tendency of becoming more gentle as she aged. From the time of her father's death when she and Olivia joined in their mother's efforts to nurture young women, Louise focused considerable effort in helping both female and male students to succeed in their studies and professions. Always grateful for her help and her knowledge in the folklore field, Benjamin Botkin remained Louise's friend for the rest of her life.

CHAPTER TWENTY-ONE

The Iconoclast

WHEREVER SHE WENT and whatever her mission, Louise was on the watch for words, for variations in pronunciation, and for regional differences in meaning. Nothing escaped her sharp ear and logical mind. The scientific training she had learned under Charles Bessey's instruction allowed her to categorize and analyze words and dialects as though they were botanical specimens.

When Louise boarded a train and left her beloved Nebraska, she often combined business with pleasure. Along with attending conferences and giving speeches, she visited friends and went to plays and concerts or the opera. Of course, lunches and dinners with associates such as H.L. Mencken provided pleasant interludes that were undoubtedly filled with witty anecdotes.

Louise and Olivia often spent their Christmas breaks away from home; usually they visited an Eastern city that hosted the meetings Louise attended. In 1937, Louise went to Washington D.C., probably during Christmas vacation. While there, she intended to see her friend and former student, B.A. Botkin, who was serving as national folklore editor of the Federal Writer's Project. Instead of visiting him at work, she had tea with his wife and children. In a letter of January

10, 1938, Louise apologized to Botkin for not seeing him: "I had to choose between you and Mrs. Botkin and the children . . . I was glad to see them and enjoyed my stay with them and tea at your home," Louise wrote.

By the late 1930s, Louise had given up teaching summer sessions in other colleges and universities, yet she maintained a busy summer travel schedule. During the summer of 1939, she spoke at Oregon schools located in LaGrande, Baker, Covallis, Eugene, and Salem. Then she attended the Washington State AAUW Convention and spoke at AAUW meetings in Seattle and Spokane. Her last stop, according to the *Lincoln Evening State Journal,* was in Idaho where she spoke at the University of Moscow. She also appeared before groups in Gooding and Pocatello, Idaho. Other 1939 speaking engagements included Denver, Colorado, and St. Paul, Minnesota.

When facing an audience, Knoll wrote that Louise followed the advice Roscoe had given her. "Stand up, so people can see you; talk loud, so people can hear you; and sit down quickly, so people will like you." Adding a bit of humor along with facts in her talks insured that her speaking slate was full.

Occasionally, she left the University when classes were in session. In February, 1940, she took part in a conference concerning a Folk Festival that the *Washington Post* planned to sponsor the following spring. The *Post* of 16 February 1940 published an article, "Louise Pound Praises Post's Folk Festivals." Demonstrating her lack of pretension and her keen wit, Louise referred to herself as the "Mrs. Throttlebottom of American Education" because she had been vice president of so many societies.

"Throttlebottom" had its origins in the 1932 musical, "Of Thee I Sing," a production that Louise may have viewed either in Lincoln or New York. A character in the musical, Mr. Throttlebottom, was a vice-president. From that role, the term "Throttlebottom" came to mean "a purposeless incompetent in public office."

As she raced between a conference on the folk festival and an AAUW executive board meeting, a reporter asked Louise to comment on the spring festival. Louise gave an enthusiastic response that reflected her feelings on the importance of folklore:

It will bring to mind the features of America we've all forgotten about . . . The folksongs and dances are not only valuable for themselves, but they make the past of each region of America very real indeed. The festival is the best way I know to acquaint people with the authentic culture of old America, and its survival in many regions . . . She hopes she can be here this year when the cowboys, hill-folk, Indians and colored singers arrive for their three-day performance. But she is afraid she will have to stay in Lincoln with her classes for a while, 'I've been gallivanting around the country too much,' she said.

The following November (1940), Louise had an opportunity to go to New York for special recognition. She was one of four University of Nebraska graduates cited as "women of distinction" at the Women's Centennial Congress held at the Commodore Hotel November 25-27. Carrie Chapman Catt stated that the career successes of Louise Pound, Edith Abbott, Viola Florence Barnes, and Gladys Henry Dick would have been impossible in 1840. Their achievements symbolized the career progress women had made in 100 years. Edith Abbott served in the graduate school of social service administration at the University of Chicago; Viola Barnes was chairman of the History Department at Mt. Holyoke; Gladys Henry Dick was on the faculty of the Northwestern University Medical School.

Whether or not Louise attended the Congress, the citation confirmed her interest in women's progress. The invitation, an information-packed brochure, mentioned that Lucretia Mott and Elizabeth Cady Stanton had sailed to London in 1840 to attend the first anti-slavery convention, an event that inspired their determination to free their own sex from unjust restrictions. At that time, a married woman couldn't control her own property, make a will, or collect her own wages, nor was she allowed guardianship over her own children in the event of her husband's death.

It's not surprising that Louise Pound had been designated a woman of distinction because she had challenged and often surpassed the achievements of men in both scholarship and sports. Although the intensity of the young Louise Pound had ebbed, she continued to meet the standard of individual excellence she set for herself at an early age. Achieving her goals often tested her endurance, but Louise was persistent in her drive for excellence.

The meetings Louise attended along with her speaking engagements provided her with the recognition and respect that University of Nebraska officials withheld–even though administrators and colleagues in other universities valued her knowledge and experience. Her standing in the academic world outside Nebraska prompted Professor O.J. Campbell of the University of Michigan to seek her opinion about requirements for graduate study in English.

Sharing her recommendations, Louise said that "English has many subdivisions–students should aim for an adequate knowledge of the large subdivisions and detailed knowledge of some." She did not think they needed teaching methods courses because many of the students already were teachers and had taken such courses.

For doctoral candidates she recommended historical study of the literary past and the continuation of research-based dissertations. Mastery of English and composition was another necessity. Also required, in her opinion, was a knowledge of modern French and German, as well as the study of Old and Middle English and some general knowledge of Germanic Philology. She summed up her requirements as follows:

> I shall always feel that it is a good thing for a holder of a doctorate in English to have had at one time in his life, a fairly close view of his whole field, to have had, as it were, his fingers on the main strands.
>
> He can drop those later with which he is not to be immediately concerned. Surely familiarity with "English" as a field of learning involves familiarity with other literatures than English and with other forms of art than English, and with the history of ideas.

Adequate study of the history of English literature involves the history of ideas and the history of culture.

Recommending that the history of ideas and culture be fundamental elements in the study of English literature placed Louise among those professors who resisted the trend toward vocational studies that the University followed under Avery's leadership. She would have supported Hartley Burr Alexander's plan to involve students in cultural activities as a means of expanding their fund of general knowledge. No doubt she voiced her opinions, thus increasing the animosity sweltering between her and the administration–a conflict that she refused to conceal from her students.

In 1941 Louise taught an undergraduate course, The History of English Literature. Robert Knoll, a sophomore that year, referred to the class as an "eyeopener." Miss Pound talked about "herself, her colleagues, the department, the university and all manner of gossip."

During her forthright discussions, Knoll said that Louise made no secret of her battles with the administration. Although admitting her respect for the scholarship of her department head (Thomas Raysor), she nevertheless found him a "difficult colleague." She also felt that the university officials never gave women professors "a good shake," not realizing that her defense of them furthered the cause of their neglect. She made certain her students knew that "she was respected more off campus than she was here at home."

As a lecturer, Knoll said that Louise didn't have much "spirit," unless she was talking about American speech. Then she enjoyed her subject and showed her students how to "take delight" in it. When lecturing on literature, Knoll thought that she did not know "a poem from a dish cloth." Trying to become better acquainted with her, he walked across campus with her and "quoted Milton about the dawn and the rising fog." He was disappointed to notice that "the poetic use of language, for evocative effect and nuance, did not seem to appeal to her. Slang and jargon, yes; poetry, probably no."

She did, however, entertain Knoll and his fellow students when talking about Spenser. She described the *Fairie Queene* using the current slang. "Her knowledge of contemporary terms was so astonishing that we all laughed very loud. She was right up to the minute, and combined the current expression ('that dragon was no ball of fire, and the knight was a pretty green type') so accurately that I have never forgotten."

Knoll estimated that Louise was past 70 when she taught him. (She would have been 69 in 1941.) Clearly "she was getting old," although she had no gray in her hair. Describing her appearance, Knoll said that she wore flat shoes, "and walked deliberately" with a rather heavy gait. Although she wasn't concerned about style, she did want to "look nice." Usually, she wore a "plain brown dress" with a small gold ornament at the neck. "Her brown eyes were very bright behind her (rimless) glasses," Knoll wrote.

While sitting through the classes of "Miss Pound" (the title Louise preferred), students may have been bored, but if they showed an interest in her language research and completed her assignments, they reaped professional rewards. Many of them supplied Louise with American language data that she used in her own studies. Several pupils had the satisfaction of seeing the papers they had written under her direction published in local and national magazines.

Following Miss Pound's systematic method of investigating language, those who studied under her were equipped to carry on further research after they left school. "Probably no teacher was ever happier than Louise when one of her students received recognition for his or her work," stated an anonymous letter-writer.

When Knoll returned to the University as an assistant professor of English in 1950, Louise tried to help him get a start in his career and gave him the etymology of the word "dude" to write up for *American Speech*. "She knew that it was necessary to get me into print," Knoll wrote, "and knew that many young people did not know where to start." Continuing to advise him, Louise said that "Much of what goes as scholarship is simply moving one obscure fact from one obscure journal to another."

Chapter Twenty-One

(Knoll concentrated on literature rather than etymology.)

Those who studied under Miss Pound found it easier to obtain academic positions. Norman E. Eliason, who had been hired by a college in Bloomington, Illinois, wrote to Louise thanking her for "help and advice." When he had mentioned that he was from Nebraska, other professors asked him about Louise. "Dr. Bert Vos of the German department was quite amazed and incensed when he learned that you were not head of the department. He was most enthusiastic in his praises. Professor Stith Thompson has let me draw the conclusion that the leading factor when my appointment was made was the fact that I had most of my work under you and I had been recommended by you."

Although she found satisfaction in her students' academic successes, Louise recognized the danger in "all work and no play" and its corresponding boredom. Not afraid to show students her fun-loving spirit, Louise joined with them in having a good time. In a letter to Mamie Meredith, a former pupil of Louise recalled Miss Pound's lighter side: "With all her erudition, she preserved in every decade of her life, a strictly contemporary viewpoint. It was something that went deeper than collecting up-to-date slang. After a 4 o'clock class in Old English she would sometimes fill "Henry," her little Ford car, with students and take them to the latest movie in town, saying that she felt it necessary to keep up with Rudolph Valentino and Clara Bow ... Almost thirty years later, Miss Pound entertained us at 1632 L by playing her newest record album, *South Pacific*. She played her favorite record twice–it was "There is Nothing Like a Dame."

Another student who read of Miss Pound's impending retirement in 1945, wrote, "The article in the paper today caused me to think back over the good times I have spent with you–the movie (*Joyo*) out in Havelock, the senior picnic at Crete to which we went in Rosinante, (another car that Louise had owned) the hamburger and waffle feeds, and last but not least the luncheon you gave for me on my birthday. We really had lots of fun. How good you were to us!"

Knoll recalled that Louise occasionally contacted the leading sororities "to gather up some girls to go to breakfast with her at the Lindell Hotel." (He stressed that Louise called only the "leading sororities; success breeds success.") As she drove the girls to the hotel, "she scared them almost to death, for already she was a dreadful driver." There, she fed them waffles and pancakes and enjoyed their attention. She had cigarettes in her handbag which she shared with the girls. Louise felt that if a man could smoke in public, "why shouldn't a woman?"

Although Knoll portrayed Louise as taking care to associate only with girls from the leading sororities, he also mentioned that her assistant had graded his student papers. "She by the way looked like Mari Sandoz and must have been such a sandhills refuge." In fact, Louise did encourage less socially prominent young women such as Mari Sandoz.

Christianson described Mari Sandoz as the leader of "a circle of artists and would-be writers" who met in an all-night restaurant located in a bus depot. Sandoz told Christianson that the group discussed the work of local writers: "poems by Loren Eiseley, Mabel Langdon, and Weldon Kees, short stories by Pan Sterling, Dorothy Thomas, Lasalle Gilman, and Lowry Wimberly, and essays by Rudolph Umland. They talked technique, and Professor Louise Pound occasionally took one or more of them into Lincoln's better homes, where they read their original works to polite, if not always, comprehending, upper-class matrons."

Mari Sandoz, along with Dorothy Thomas from her circle, were invited to join Chi Delta Phi, a national literary society with a local chapter in Lincoln. It replaced the languishing English Club and was sponsored by Louise Pound, Marguerite McPhee, Mamie Meredith, and Ruth Odell of the English staff. The *Lincoln Journal Star* of 3 October 1937 stated that Chi Delta Phi, organized in 1921, "consistently maintained an interest in literary performance among the women students of the University of Nebraska."

A few of the prestigious Chi Delta Phi members were: Dorothy Thomas whose short stories appeared frequently in *The Atlantic,*

Harpers, American Mercury, Saturday Evening Post, and other periodicals; Louise Pound whose published articles and books featured American language, literature, and folklore; Margaret Cannell whose essays were published in *American Speech* and other periodicals; Mari Sandoz, novelist, whose book, *Old Jules,* won the Atlantic Prize for nonfiction and was a book-of-the-month club selection; Bess Streeter Aldrich whose well-known novels were panoramas of pioneer life, Mignon Good Eberhart, mystery writer, whose story, "While the Patient Sleeps," won the $5,000 Scotland Yard award; Viola Barnes, whose academic works included *The Dominance of New England.*

Louise found satisfaction in having a good time while helping both men and women advance their careers. Although she appreciated her niche in Lincoln's top social circle, she lacked a pretentious nature and ignored formality in her relationships with students and colleagues. Even though she was a sought after language expert, she remained a "down-to-earth" person.

PERHAPS KNOWING THAT administrators scorned her advice encouraged Louise to concentrate on her achievements outside the University instead of producing mind-riveting classroom lectures. Dictionary publishers were one group seeking her recommendations on new editions of their work. H.L. Mencken continued to welcome her research in preparing a new edition of *The American Language,* and she collected war words for *American Speech.*

A 16 February 1941 clipping among her papers revealed that she was "one of 28 distinguished linguistic, phonetic, and dictionary-making scholars" who had worked with Dr. Edward L. Thorndike, educational psychologist of Columbia University, on his dictionary for young people of 12 to 20 years of age." Louise had accepted the task of pronunciation advisor in compiling the dictionary.

The article stressed the versatility of her personality, stating that although Louise was a consultant in "many linguistic projects, officer in many subject societies, (and was) editor, author, and critic," she also held memberships in several extra-curricular societies proving that she hadn't "shut herself in an ivory tower." Members of the social groups to which she belonged "forgot their awe of her scholarship in her quick and subtle wit . . ."

Her continued association with H.L. Mencken prompted him to write Louise in October 1932, asking her to send information for the Dictionary of Americanisms "in progress in Chicago." He wondered if she would recommend someone to write an article or do so herself. The author would earn $75. Louise must have agreed to write the piece, since a following letter from Mencken informed her that her article would "come along in late November."

Proving her versatility, non-academic editors also sought her help with word-related matters. Perhaps the most unusual and humorous request came from George Grimes of the *Omaha World-Herald* in 1940. He asked her to attend the *World-Herald* Golden Gloves Tourney and write about it. She turned him down, but she responded favorably to Cecily Brownstone, editorial assistant of *Parent's Magazine*. Brownstone asked for Pound's help in researching "children's secret languages: Pig Latin, Double Dutch, Opish–and so forth." A follow-up letter from Brownstone thanked Louise for leads in the area of children's secret languages.

When researching word origins, Louise, like her friend, H.L. Mencken, ignored the social status of informants. In a 27 December 1939 letter to Louise, Mencken wrote that a prisoner in the Richmond, Virginia, penitentiary had been "bombarding" him with news about the dictionary of criminal slang he was compiling. "I have applied to the warden for permission to see it, and hope to have it in my hands in a few days."

In a 21 August 1942 letter, Mencken mentioned the prisoner's (Clinton Sanders'), work again, saying, "Poor Sanders is working hard, but such specimens of his lexicon as I have seen do not indicate that he has much gift for dictionary making." Nevertheless, Mencken hoped to get Sanders some help "if he is ever released," and "make a useful book of his collection."

Louise also corresponded with Sanders whose word investigations included "words of the fighting forces" and shipbuilding terms. After sending Louise a list of shipbuilding terms, he gave her permission to use them in an issue of *American Speech*. Perhaps Mencken and Pound's letters to the prison parole board helped convince them to release Sanders from his sentence and place him on parole. After he left prison, Sanders found employment at the Norfolk (Virginia) Shipbuilding and Dry Dock Corporation as editor of the plant newspaper.

In an interview for a 5 August 1951 newspaper column, Louise recalled Sanders, saying "not all word authorities are inmates of educational institutions." When the Nebraska criminal statutes were being revised, Louise was asked the meaning of "watchstuffing," a crime listed as punishable in an ancient code. After consulting every authority she could find, even her brother, Roscoe, she wrote to Sanders who was still a prison inmate at that time. Sanders solved the mystery for her with an accurate definition: "In the early days . . . Hawkers sold watches that looked all right but the man who bought one soon found it wouldn't run because of its 'stuffing' or lack of it."

While Louise continued teaching, traveling, and collecting word origins and trivia, she also was aware of the rising tension between Germany and Europe. Through her correspondence with Ani and Dr. Hoops, she knew about Hitler and the rise of Nazism.

She recognized that another world war was possible, and war, as always, would change local and national conditions. Certainly, she knew that the University would, once again, undergo change.

PART FIVE:
WORLD WAR II & BEYOND
1940-1958

CHAPTER TWENTY-TWO

Changes at Home & Abroad

D URING THE EARLY morning of September 1, 1939, shouting
in the streets may have awakened Louise Pound. Newspaper
boys cycled through Lincoln's residential streets around 3:00 A.M.,
shouting, "Extra! Extra!" according to Neale Copple's *Tower on the
Plains*. Hitler's forces had invaded Poland, insuring the start of World
War II in Europe.

In 1939, September 1 fell on the Friday of Labor Day weekend—the
last days of freedom before University classes resumed. Weekends for
Louise and Olivia usually were filled with social events. They often
played bridge with friends, went to a movie, and had dinner or lunch at
the University Club. During this holiday interlude, their conversations
with friends probably centered on the world tension that Germany's
invasion of Poland created. Louise must have pondered the effect of
Hitler's Nazi party on the lives of Ani Phister and Johannes Hoops.

Their letters, especially those of Ani, had given Louise insight into
the feelings of Germans who opposed Hitler's regime. In October
1933, Ani had written about Hitler's rise to power. She and her
husband, a physician, had been traveling and when they reached
Baghdad, they heard of "the new reign of Hitler and only slowly

understood . . . It is the most astonishing reign of terror in a highly civilized country . . . We who don't live in that country, cannot yet understand how it could happen and (how) it keeps its power, as most of the Intelligentsia are against it."

Ani stated that letters were no longer private and that many of her friends, "either Jews or with some Jewish grandmother, or former Socialists or Democrats have lost their positions and are without possibility to earn their living." She asked Louise for help in finding work for those who had lost their jobs: "any position from a cook general up to a teacher or professor let me know, because the need is great and absolutely undeserved."

By 1937, Louise heard from Dr. Hoops, who planned to lecture at the University of California that summer. He wrote of his need for additional speaking engagements as he made his way across the U.S. to California. "When I was in America in 1933, I was invited to lecture at two universities of the south. I was then prevented from accepting the invitations, but if they should be renewed, I shall probably be glad to accept them now, as, owing to our scarcity of foreign exchange, I shall in all probability be permitted to buy and take with me only a small amount of American currency, so that every opportunity of earning additional dollars would be welcome for our journey."

A 25 October 1938 letter from Ani stated that she and her husband were in Hong Kong where he worked as a physician. They planned to go on furlough to Germany and gather up things they had stored which she would either "give away or take with us."

She hoped they would not have trouble in Germany. Then she described changes that had taken place in Heidelberg: "Already 33 Heidelberg has changed much; the Neckar canalized, without any current, the skating place closed up. I daresay in the hills the Hitler Youth will tramp about in large bands."

Samuel Eliot Morrison's History of the American People, referred to Hitler's hold over the German population as a phenomenon which even the Germans found hard to explain. In Morrison's opinion, Hitler overwhelmed the German tradition of culture and decency with his hatred of Jews, Christianity, democracy, foreigners, and "in general everything that was good, true, or beautiful."

Nevertheless, a division between Germans who embraced Nazism, and those who rejected Hitler's policies had begun taking place during the politically unstable period that followed World War I. In his memoir, *Defying Hitler*, Sebastian Hoffner stated that generally the non-Nazis came from the cultured class who found sustenance and pleasure in books and music. Through independent thinking, they formed personal philosophies that disagreed with Hitler's beliefs. Ani Phister and Johannes Hoops were part of the cultured class that had rejected Nazism from its beginning.

In the war's early years, the U.S. population disagreed about taking part in the conflict, but participation in the war was taken for granted by 1941. Nevertheless, Knoll wrote that University English professor, Thomas N. Raysor, and a history professor, Glenn Gray, both Anglophiles, took action against the isolationist America First groups. Circulating a petition they intended to send to Washington urging U.S. assistance to England, Raysor and Gray encountered resistance from Senator Hugh Butler, who, like many Nebraskans, remained an isolationist. Perhaps Chancellor Chauncey Boucher also was an isolationist because he refused to respond when the military inquired about using University facilities if the U.S. became involved in the war.

Knoll's assessment of Chancellor Boucher's leadership was negative. Boucher had been dean of the college of Arts, Literature, and Science at the University of Chicago (1926-35) and president of the University of West Virginia (1935-38) before coming to Nebraska. The University board of Regents had hired him in 1938 without looking into the reasons for his departure from the University of West Virginia.

At Chicago, Boucher had restructured undergraduate education, and he attempted to reorganize West Virginia according to the same plan. His plan eliminated freshman, sophomore, junior, and senior grades and replaced them with upper and lower division classes. Instead of taking course examinations, students took general comprehensive tests, and interdisciplinary classes were requirements for all students.

When Boucher attempted to force the Chicago University system of study upon West Virginia, he encountered faculty resistance and responded with arrogance. Hiring and firing professors at will, he violated tenure rules and precipitated an investigation by the American Association of University Professors. As a result, he lost the respect and backing of West Virginia's board of governors and began applying for other positions.

Boucher was a dignified appearing man and assumed the role of college president with ease. Knoll wrote that "he presided at public meetings with dignity." But Boucher's formality and coolness blighted his dealings with others, and his unapproachable air caused people to avoid him—reactions that he encouraged. When he arrived at the University he announced that "he had no desire to engage in public discussion or make personal appearances." Knoll reported that he and his secretary, Miss Mallory, "exchanged messages through the letter slot in his office door."

Of course, Louise Pound wasn't intimidated by Boucher's formality, nor could she resist asking him a controversial question when she met him at a dinner party. That question concerned his experiences as head of the University of West Virginia. Knoll reported that Louise "remembered with some bemusement how defensive (Boucher) was in his reply." Although he was an "innovator," Knoll wrote, "he ignored any relationship between a state institution and the people who supported it."

The Japanese attack on Pearl Harbor on 7 December 1941 removed the issue of the University's wartime participation from Boucher's hands, Knoll stated. The War Manpower Commission announced that the University would take part in the Army Specialized Training Program, (ASTP). In March 1943, the first group of cadets arrived and were housed in Love Library. That same year student enrollment dropped to 4,000, one third of its former number, and 151 faculty were on military leave. "By November 1944, Knoll reported that the University had served 13,769 military men and women.

As the country concentrated on winning the war, patriotism healed divisions between the University faculty and among United States citizens. The city of Lincoln, along with the University, adapted to wartime conditions and contributed to the war effort. Lincoln Air Field became part of Lincoln Army Air Field and prepared over 30,000 aviation mechanics to service wartime planes. Bomber crews, fighter pilots, and combat crewmen received initial training at the air field, then were sent on for advanced combat training.

Lincoln industries also adjusted to wartime production. Copple reported that "the Burlington Railroad shops made special car-loading devices for prefabricated airplane assemblies . . ."

The *State Journal* newspaper set type for the *Congressional Record*, and the Cushman Motor Works made about 8 million nose fuses and 15,000 motor scooters for use on bases and shipyards to conserve gas and rubber."

Nebraskans' reactions to this war differed from their response to World War I. The suspicion of German Americans that had been rampant during the Great War had almost disappeared, perhaps because the German immigrants had been here a long time and were well-integrated into communities. The policy of relocating Japanese immigrants didn't affect Nebraskans, since few Japanese lived in the state.

The war brought welcome prosperity to Nebraska and boosted its recovery from the Depression. The defense plants located in the state included the Martin Bomber plant in Omaha, ordnance plants in Grand Island and Mead, and the Naval Ammunition Depot in Hastings. The Army Air Corp built training bases at Alliance, Ainsworth, Bruning, Fairmont, Grand Island, Harvard, Kearney, Lincoln, McCook, Scottsbluff, and Scribner. Inland prairies became concrete runways surrounded by temporary wooden barracks.

These bases and plants brought in workers from all over the country. Indians were recruited from reservations, and Blacks came from the south to fill jobs, while military personnel populated training bases. The towns were stretched to the limit to provide utilities for the newcomers—all needing water and electricity as well as services such as grocery stores and beauty parlors. A housing crisis erupted. Old houses were converted into apartments, and workers lived in chicken coops and carriage houses. The Sioux and Chippewa Indians working at Hastings Naval Ammunition Depot erected their tepees on depot grounds, while Blacks resided in specially built barracks.

Rationing of necessities started in 1942. A few of the rationed products included meat, butter, coffee, canned food, gasoline, and shoes. Other manufactured goods were scarce because plants were re-tooled to produce war supplies.

Since military personnel needed recreational facilities, USO's sprang up and were run by volunteers from community clubs. The volunteers sponsored dances, handed out milk, coffee, and cookies and sometimes played cards with the lonely soldiers. The USO women of North Platte furnished millions of cookies to soldiers passing through the town on troop trains, an act that brought them national fame.

According to Dorothy Weyer-Creigh, prosperity for Nebraskans continued after the war ended. Although many of the imported workers returned to their home states, enough remained to replace those Nebraskans who did not come back from war zones. Finally, state residents had enough money to mechanize and electrify their farms, build new homes, buy new cars, and home appliances. Most important, the drought had ended and crops were good.

During this world-wide conflict, Louise helped individuals instead of organizing aid for international groups as she had during World War I. Continuing to teach at the University even though she was nearing her seventieth birthday, she also carried on her research of American English. Corresponding with H.L. Mencken, she contributed to his American language studies, and she collected "war words" for *American Speech*.

Interested in the wartime role of her former students, Louise exchanged letters with many of them. As her correspondence files show, she helped both men and women. Former pupil, Robert Luebs, wrote thanking her for urging University officials to grant him a degree with honors. In April 1943, Louise had written to the University Committee on Graduation with Distinction recommending that Luebs be graduated "with distinction" or with "high distinction." She maintained that his work on his paper went beyond "mere research." He is at Fort Leavenworth–has written the paper with more haste than he wished. He discussed it at an advanced class very well. Held listeners attention and had read many more books for English 199 than he mentioned in his bibliography." Her help resulted in Luebs gratitude and an exchange of letters with him throughout the war.

Along with Luebs, a former woman student corresponded with Louise during and after the war. Dorothy Jane Hughes, a University of North Dakota teacher, had taken graduate courses under Louise before volunteering to serve in the WAVES–the women's branch of the Navy. Judging from her letters, Hughes and Miss Pound must have had several conversations about women being able to perform the same duties as men, and in some cases, do the jobs better than men.

Women studying for graduate degrees under Miss Pound's supervision received her support and encouragement because she understood the obstacles they faced. In her 1920 article, "The College Woman and Research," Louise stated a fact that was generally unrecognized: "The customary explanation when women graduate students do brilliant work, better work sometimes than their male associates, is that they must be 'selected women' the 'few best,' while their male co-workers are not a selected class, choosing their line of work because of a special bent for it, but are in the work by chance. When a man does well, it is taken for granted that he is typical. When a woman does well, (so strong is the tradition), it is still thought to need explanation; and it is taken for granted that she is not typical but the product of special circumstances."

Probably, because she was one of the first female professors in America, Louise took a special interest in helping other women in her profession such as Dorothy Jane Hughes even though the generation of new women had changed by 1930. In most respects, Louise fit the younger generation of New Women, exhibiting the same self-assurance they possessed.

This second group was just as political as the first, according to Smith-Rosenberg, but "they placed more emphasis on self-fulfillment, a bit less on social services, and a great deal more on flamboyant presentation of self." These women, like Louise, fought for "absolute equality with men," and were among those applying for aid from organizations with which Louise was affiliated: The Guggenheim Foundation; The American Association of University Women; The American Association of University Professors.

Although Hughes was not applying for aid, her letters are a testimony to the encouragement she had received from her teacher and mentor, Miss Pound. Knowing that Louise would be interested in her work, Hughes reported her daily schedule in October, 1943: "We hit the deck at 5:30 and report to our duty stations unfailingly. There is something magnificent in the fact that the Navy is asking as much of its women as of its men in this district. I wish you could share with me the delight of being treated as a man's equal."

Comparing her civilian occupation as a teacher to her navy career, Hughes feared that she would have to make a great adjustment when she returned to teaching. "Security prevents my discussing my work in any detail," she wrote, "but I find that being nurse maid to an aircraft carrier as well as a host of smaller vessels is an enchanting experience."

Referring again to her navy duties in December 1944, Hughes shared her satisfaction over the WAVES performing better than men in an identical task. "I must tell you that the Women's Reserve at our activity have won a minor victory in the endless battle of rights for women. We've convinced our commander that a certain type of work we are doing, hitherto thought to be entirely and exclusively a man's job can be competently performed by women. As a result our Ensign-in-charge asked for more WAVES instead of sailors."

Hughes wrote a postwar letter with news of her teaching position at the University of Oregon; Louise had recommended her for the job:

(June 12, 1946, Eugene Oregon)

I waited to be notified officially before writing to you: I have been asked to return to the University of Oregon next fall as a full-time instructor! My chairman tells me he has good reports of my teaching this spring. You can imagine how happy I am.

This has been an extremely busy but pleasant term. I love it here! As soon as I finish correcting final examinations, I shall try to complete my investigation of the names of ships. Freshman themes have kept me away from the study.

It is good to think that the University of North Dakota will not claim my declining years! Here, I am happy to report, there is less prejudice against women. Furthermore, my military experience has given me courage!

I've been hearing quite a bit about your visit to Eugene, particularly from Dr. Alice Ernst, our specialist in versification. Those I've talked with wish you would come again soon; may I start agitating? I hope you are as happy as I am. Soon I shall write again, enclosing views of our beautiful campus. In the meantime, I send best wishes for a pleasant summer.

Sincerely,
Dorothy J. Hughes
P.S. Your telegram brought me here. I shall always be grateful.

Louise's support and encouragement of female students and colleagues marked her as a woman ahead of her time. The female liberation of the sixties remained decades ahead when Louise first began agitating for equal treatment of women in academia. She was one of those who are seldom acknowledged for their role in building momentum for the progress women have made in the last century.

CHAPTER TWENTY-THREE

Enjoying Life Still More

L OUISE ANNOUNCED HER impending retirement in a 10 June 1945 letter to Botkin.

> *I'm subsiding in the Univ. this spring 'to enjoy life still more.'*
> *My health is fine, as usual, and I don't 'need a rest.'*
>
> *My brother (older) still teaches full time at Harvard, but I think*
> *I'd better stop (before I have to). I began early and goodness knows*
> *should have taught long enough by this time. The newspapers are*
> *full of 'obituaries' of me!*

It's likely that the end of the war influenced her decision to retire. Someone else could teach the veterans who would be flocking to colleges on the G.I. Bill. Perhaps she assumed that the University would accommodate the influx of former military personnel by lowering academic standards. A letter from Ani hinted that Louise had no desire to teach the returning soldiers. In 1947, Ani wrote: "I too am glad you stopped teaching under these circumstances–naturally it lowers the standard of the universities but those boys who come into civilization again have to learn something. I had noticed in China that some of them could not even write orthographically."

In addition to the reference in Ani's letter about Louise's reluctance to teach the returning veterans, comments in Louise Pound's 1942 *Nebraska Alumnus* article and her remarks to reporter Evelyn Simpson questioned the values of the present generation. In her article, Louise praised the Victorian period for "its peace and order, and its serene expectation of a world which was to grow consciously better and better. No one thought of world wars." Campus life fifty years ago was "unaffected by the influence of Hollywood . . ." She praised the faculty and the "tonic atmosphere" of the 1890s University and declared that the "Members of the class of 1892, suppressing a faint nostalgia, may well feel fortunate to have attended the institution then."

During her interview with Simpson, Louise also criticized modern day activities for girls. "Nowadays we have prom queens, dream queens, pep girls, a Goddess of Agriculture, Kosmet Klub Sweethearts, all of them contests staged and managed by men. In the days of Ruth Bryan Rohde (daughter of William Jennings Bryan), she enjoyed prestige and acclaim for her success as high jumping champion—something she accomplished on her own, and there were rewards in many other athletic lines and for poetry and essay writing." Louise added "ours will never be a great literary period.'"

Relinquishing her teaching role didn't lessen the demand for her services as a language expert. An unusual letter dated June 5, 1945, from former student, V. Royce West who, like Louise, had studied with Dr. Hoops at Heidelberg University, offered her a new career as chairman or as one of several directors of an Institute Committee on Flour Milling in Language and Literature.

West was Director of Public Relations for Pillsbury Mills and used his training in philology and literature to study "the lore of milling, the language of milling through the ages, and milling in literature and art." He hoped to develop a non-profit Pillsbury Institute of Flour Milling History and publish educational studies in the field that would benefit students pursuing language-related degrees.

Although Louise was known for researching words used in unique settings and may have been flattered by West's offer, she had no desire to add another responsibility to her life in retirement. From her experience as an officer in several organizations she would have realized the negotiations required in setting up and managing West's proposed committee. If she intended to relax and enjoy life, as she had written to Botkin, Louise would–and did–turn down West's offer.

Simpson's portrait of Louise in retirement reviewed Pound's accomplishments and gave a candid report of Louise as an individual. In closing the piece, Simpson revealed the ways in which Louise kept herself busy:

> *Now that she is retired 'to enjoy myself' one might expect Miss Pound to relax. Perhaps she will, to a certain extent, although present writing commitments will keep her busy through the summer.*
>
> *She has been offered contracts for several books. Why doesn't she accept? 'Why should I? It would mean a lot of work. I can have more fun mowing the lawn. I am a fair carpenter too, and I learned only recently that I can make cement or concrete. The trellis screening the yard was about to fall down, so weakened had the supporting posts become. Something had to be done about it and I decided to try it myself.' (The project was very successful.)*
>
> *Besides these time-consumers, Miss Pound can always fall back on bridge. She never lacks for company, if she wants it, for Sister Olivia, until last year principal for girls at Lincoln High School, shares the old Pound family home at 1632 L Street. And Louise Pound always has her constant companions of a lifetime–books– four roomsful of them.*

Louise welcomed retirement for reasons other than her disappointment in the new generation of students and the decline of academic standards. She had met her self-imposed goal of individual excellence, and she had added to the world's store of knowledge. If she had regrets, they were not about her achievements or her teaching career, but over her choice of subject-matter.

A friend, Isobel McMonies Klopp, had written to Louise, saying:

> *I remember, of course, that you told me in April that were you to teach again you would choose science. But I feel sure you enjoyed the English work, although at intervals you encountered many of us who just didn't have the 'spark' to arouse. And you made it for us a memorable experience.*

While she may have realized that her practicality and her knack for organizing material was better suited for science than for the imaginative thinking involved in literary studies, Louise had applied scientific logic to her research of words and ballad origins. Her method brought her recognition as an authority on word origins and derivations as well as respect for her folklore research.

It is doubtful that she had regrets about her unmarried state. Women of her generation understood that having a career cancelled the possibility of marriage and children. In addition, most men did not consider marrying a career woman. Also, the women realized the difficulty of running a home and managing a career at the same time. Public opinion was against it, and modern appliances that eased homemaking tasks were inventions of the future.

During the war, Louise and Olivia had gained experience in home maintenance because help was hard to find. Workers continued to be scarce following the war, and the sisters tended the aging house themselves. As Louise explained in a letter to Botkin (January, 12, 1947), "Keeping up the three-story Pound home, which is upwards of sixty years old, with little help available, takes a lot of time. I seem rather to enjoy it, the outdoor part especially."

In addition to housekeeping chores, Louise and Olivia continued traveling to conferences and cultural events in other parts of the country. Now, Louise had time to resume exchanging letters with Ani and Professor Hoops, correspondence that the war had interrupted. In the post-war years, Louise provided much-needed assistance to Ani in regaining her mother's jewels and a valuable stamp collection. Ani's postwar letters to Louise form a story in themselves.

THE FIRST NEWS Louise received about Ani's war experiences arrived in November 1945. Although the message was sad, Louise must have been relieved to learn that her friend had survived the conflict. Writing a few days after her husband's death, Ani expressed her despair. The fact that she trusted Louise to understand verified the strength of their relationship even though an ocean had separated them for nearly fifty years.

"My dear old friend," Ani wrote in November 1945, "It is a sad letter I am writing to you to-day–My husband died on the 14th of November of stones in the pancreas." She stated that her husband lived to see the "downfall of the Nazis and Japan. That was his last joy." Ani assured Louise that she and her husband had been happy together and had been "real friends and comrades, so, though you knew me as an independent woman, I feel my loss badly and am terribly lonely."

Because her father was a Jew, Ani feared persecution and left Germany in 1941. Her husband departed in 1942 after a Nazi official warned him that he should divorce Ani or "bad things would happen to him." The couple lived in Hong Kong for a time, then they moved to China and resided at Peitaiho Beach for five years.

In the letter announcing her husband's death that had reached Louse through the American Red Cross, Ani wrote that she planned to sell her property in China and go to Locarno, Switzerland, where she had cousins and friends. She didn't want to return to Germany because she believed the Nazi spirit lived on in the young people who had been "forcefully trained into cruelty and sadism."

According to Haffner's memoir, the politically unstable era in Germany following World War I had produced a generation unable to "live from within themselves." They relied on the mental stimulation of political uprisings to give their lives meaning. Nevertheless, Haffner contended that those individuals who managed to wean themselves from the "cheap intoxication of the sports of war and revolution," developed their own personalities. "It was at that time, that invisibly and unnoticed the Germans divided into those who later became Nazis and those who remained non-Nazis."

As non-Nazis, Ani Phister and Johannes Hoops had formed their own opinions through reading and reflection. Dr. Hoops had always encouraged friendly relations between Germany and other countries. Ani, too, had an open and independent mind about the cultures of other nations. Neither she nor Professor Hoops felt animosity toward the United States as evidenced by their continued friendships with Louise.

When resuming her correspondence with Louise, Ani had asked United States Marine Chaplain, Cpl. Samuel F. Pughse, to write her friend and send the letter through the American Red Cross. Explaining her distrust of the Chinese postal system, Ani informed Louise that "most correspondence was snapped up by the Japanese during the war, and later on Peitaiho was often cut off–the communists had destroyed the line, bombed the bridges etc., so that much correspondence . . . was lost and when we sent letters from China the postmaster stole the stamps and the letters . . . even if the letter was registered.

Chaplain Cpl. Pughse, who was on duty in China with the 6th Marine Division, informed Louise in December 1945 that the Phisters had been at Peitaiho Beach during the Japanese occupation and "of course their experiences had told on them." He had visited with the doctor and Ani to learn the recent history of that part of China. "The doctor was in poor health," Cpl. Pughse wrote, "but made us welcome and we had a most enjoyable talk with him and his wife . . ." When the chaplain and his friend called on the Phisters a second time, they learned that the doctor had died. Cpl. Pughse advised Louise to place her letter to Ani inside an envelope addressed to him and send it by air mail. He ended his letter stating that Ani seemed "most anxious" to hear from Louise.

Louise replied to Ani's letter but her friend did not receive it until April 1947. Nevertheless, she trusted Louise to help her regain valuable stamps and jewels that she had given to a Marine, David Roads, for sale in the United States. When Roads failed to answer Ani's questions about the fate of her valuables, she turned to Louise for help.

Roads had written one reply to Ani's inquiries in a letter that she forwarded to Louise. In his 18 October 1947 message, Roads claimed that he had written Ani three letters which must not have reached her. After receiving her request that he send the stamps to Louise, Roads agreed to do so. Then he excused his slow action regarding the sale of the jewels. "I have not lost my interest in helping you, but have proceeded very slowly so as to get the best of the bargain for you." He explained that the jewel broker had been "in the east for a month (of) vacation." Roads wrote that he was now waiting to learn whether to sell the jewels separately as antique pieces or keep them together for sale as a group.

Ani must have been relieved to hear from Louise again because she had stopped trusting Roads to dispose of her possessions in an honest and fair manner. She was especially grateful to learn that her old friend was willing to take an active role in regaining her valuables. Perhaps Ani understood that Louise would enjoy the challenge of retrieving the stamps and jewels. Unlike University officials' resentment of Louise's interference in administrative matters, Ani asked for and welcomed her intervention.

Writing to Louise in February 1947, Ani referred to the stamps. "You see the American man ... David Roads, to whom I gave them does not seem very trustworthy to me any more. That is why I asked him to send them to you. He wrote me that he was offered ($)25 for the whole lot." Ani wrote that some of the "really old and rare" stamps from Germany were worth more than $25 by themselves.

Typical of her letters to Louise, Ani's writing roamed from one topic to another with no paragraph breaks. She must have been a talkative individual, one who took charge of conversations. Like Louise, she did not hesitate to express her opinions, but she revealed more about her personal life than Louise did in her existing papers and letters. Possibly, Louise was candid with Ani about her inner thoughts, knowing that the letters would not be returned to Lincoln. She may have asked Ani to destroy them, or at least, never to return them.

In the same letter (February 1947), Ani began to describe her departure from China, perhaps in response to questions Louise may have asked in a 27 January card she had written to her friend. Ani mentioned receiving the card, then began the story of leaving China, an ordeal that she finished explaining in later correspondence. "After many difficulties with the Chinese authorities, in getting passage etc. at last things cleared up and permit, passage, passport etc. came quickly and I left Pei tai ho the 8th of November and reached Marseilles the 9th of January."

Now in Switzerland, she had a room in a "single ladies' house and use of bath and kitchen," but she was "looking for a small house or flat in some village higher up." She wrote that she was content in Switzerland, where she had spent many happy years in her youth. "I still love the mountains, but won't be able any more to climb them or at least the real high ones. One ought to be still strong and to enjoy to look at them."

She bathed in ice cold water every morning, but missed her daily dip in the sea, a ritual she had established in China. But that was all she missed of that country. "The rest of China is better to forget." She feared that when the Marines departed, the "last remains" of civilization would "disappear in out of the way places."

When Ani first arrived in Switzerland, she had learned about her brother's death in Germany. "He had been suffering for years of gastric troubles and still hoped to come to Switzerland . . . but fate meant it otherwise." She found it hard to be "sorry for someone who dies nowadays in Germany, it is easier to be sorry for those who are alive." She was referring to those Germans who had not agreed with the Nazi regime. But she had no pity for those who continued to believe in the Nazi system and hoped for its return.

Louise probably inquired about the conditions that Ani's brother experienced under the Nazis because Ani wrote that her brother was "not a Nazi casualty though they did what they could to make him one . . ." He had lost his professorship, and the ministry had cut his pension to the minimum, and his physical instruments and books had been stolen, presumably by the Nazis. "He had some serious gastric trouble and the food he got was not what he ought to have had," Ani wrote.

After referring to her stamp collection and telling Louise to send it back to her, Ani gave Louise news about Professor Hoops. "I once read in China that Prof Hoops had been chosen as rector of H. University, but since I have heard that it is not so. He must be well over 80. The wife was a Nazi, not he," Ani wrote. She referred to Hoop's wife as "always a bit of a fool."

She informed Louise that only two bridges had been destroyed in Heidelberg during the war, but "many remnants of old and better times are gone." She feared it would not be the last time "our once so peaceful world has such upheavals. It is like the wheel of life in families up and down in about three generations." She believed that Russia and America were now on the "upward path."

Addressing her own circumstances, Ani wrote that after searching for six weeks she had found "a tiny house" in the hills above the sea. It was "scantily furnished and very old-fashioned", but it had a garden on the mountainside and was near a river. The climate was rather mild, although snow still clung to the mountainside—"A very rare thing for here in the south of Switzerland."

Finally, Ani again expressed her doubts about Roads' reliability regarding the sale of her jewels. At the same time she revealed that while in China she had been attacked in her home while her husband was away, "and badly battered but got over it." Perhaps the beating caused her to give the jewels to Roads to take to the U.S. because she feared the Chinese would steal them.

Now, Roads had failed to send the price list that she had requested for the jewels, and she had written him asking that he return the gems to her or send them to Louise. He had not answered her last three letters, and she feared that he intended "to make away with the things."

Ani asked Louise, "if you pass Denver by chance, just try to see him (Roads) and pick up the things (jewels) yourself and let me know what is the matter with him ... The jewels are all genuine gold platin, stones and pearls. The list is plain." She ended this letter, simply, "Ani."

By 13 April 1947, Ani had received a letter from Louise containing her curriculum vitae. Ani wrote, "I was very interested indeed and am glad you sent it." Then she compared their two lives:

> *I sum it up that between us we have seen and done most of the things worth while. But our two lives have been as different as possible. Yours was a quiet one, though in Heidelberg I thought yours would have more excitement than mine. Mine has been full of everything like traveling, danger, bodily strain, painting, books, people of all classes and races, hardships the last years, a good husband who liked the same things as I. Now I want quiet and rest though not yet too much of it. My eyes are said to be blue now! My fathers too turned from brown to blue in his old age. I am thin, never got too fat, my fattest time was when you knew me. I still love swimming and cold water, and hate dusting!*

It is doubtful that Louise or her American friends and acquaintances would have agreed with Ani that Louise had lived a "quiet" life. In demand as a speaker, an editor and writer, Louise had rushed from one project and engagement to another with the speed of a gazelle. While her life never was in physical danger, she met and mastered both intellectual and physical challenges.

Continuing her 13 April letter, Ani wrote, "I wonder if we would meet by chance in the street, would we know each other? It certainly would be good to meet, but I quite see you don't want to travel now in Europe and I certainly don't want to travel just now either."

Perhaps Louise did not want to visit Ani in Switzerland because she realized meeting each other might break the bond formed by their correspondence. In person, the relationship might change. Yet Ani's understanding of Louise's reluctance to take a journey abroad demonstrated her tolerance of others' lifestyles, a characteristic that had been strengthened through her travels and wartime experiences.

Ani had traveled extensively before the war, and in her letters to Louise she had occasion to refer to her knowledge of world cultures.

> *I have passed the Suez Canal 6 times and twice by Siberia, which used to be so quick and interesting, as I still had relations in Moskau. I have not heard from them for years. No letters pass. That is the only country I want to see again. But I won't. Germany I don't want to see. It would hurt too much to see all these ruins and to hear of more and more people who have either suicided or died in concentration camp. Lots of our friends have. I am glad I have seen so much of the world. It makes a war seem more senseless still, seeing that all races, if you take the individual, have a common meeting ground, suffer under the same limitations, have the same wishes in life and makes politics seem like a useless game of chess only good for the practice of the players.*

Using a map of the U.S. Ani wrote that she had looked up the places where Louise had speaking engagements. "It is a wide range," she stated, "and you drive yourself. Good for you."

Referring to the state of education in Germany, Ani said that during the war children had worked in factories or on the land, and schools were closed. A shortage of coal during the past winter had closed the schools again. Formerly, education in Germany had been good and the children liked to learn. "The teachers now are mostly old and not properly trained," she wrote.

Finally, Ani wondered if Louise or a friend "could get an answer from this David Roads in Denver." She had written him three times since November and had not received a reply. From an earlier letter he had sent her, she knew that he was a student at the University of Denver, "having been given a three year course free by the state." She worried that Roads had "stolen all the things and tries to get away with it." Revealing her tenacious personality, Ani wrote that she wanted "to get at" the matter.

Whenever she asked Louise to help in retrieving her stamps and jewels, Ani apologized, saying, "Sorry to trouble you." But Louise probably did not mind investigating Ani's missing jewels. In this mission, the two friends exhibited their lifelong determination to succeed in whatever challenge that confronted them. Louise may have assured Ani that she would take steps to retrieve the jewels when she traveled to a folklore conference in Denver that summer (1947).

By 29 April 1947, Ani had received two letters from Louise; one that Louise had sent to the Red Cross in China on January 17 and the most recent one that she had written.

In her replies, Ani describes her lifestyle in her new home, saying that she has started painting again, "which I have not done now for 7 years and it seems to come out all right." She intends to take long walks and continue her sketching as well as tending to her house. " . . . there are so many things starting a house, small as it is, again. I sold everything in China except the things I love, too much bother and cost to take things with one nowadays." Amazed by her electric cooking range, she comments, "Well, it makes life ever so much easier and is a great thing."

On 15 May 1947, Ani penned a letter to Louise announcing that the stamps had arrived, "complete and unhurt." She thanked her friend for the "trouble" she took and for adding stamps to the collection. Again referring to the poor mail service in China, Ani wrote that she had written many friends there, but had received no answers, though she was certain they would have replied if the letters had reached them.

Ani expressed her gratitude for her peaceful life "after those last years of excitement and troubles." She still had no word from Professor Hoops, nor had the "Denver man," David Roads, answered her letters, even though she included a return postcard.

She had written to the Denver post office to find out whether her registered letters had been delivered to Roads.

Roads may have become disgusted with the stream of letters that Ani sent regarding her valuables and simply ignored her requests. But he underestimated her persistence, and he certainly did not know that her friend, Louise Pound, had joined the effort to retrieve the jewels. Louise took action on 14 June 1947. Writing to the Dean of Student Affairs of Denver University, Louise stated Ani's case:

> *David Roads is a GI student at Denver University. He attended during the past year and is probably registered for the summer session since he's supposed to have three years at college as part of his 'bill of rights.' His home is at 3419 Stuart Street.*
>
> *I am sorry to bother you by asking you to interview him. He will respond if you call him in? When he was a soldier in North China he knew a close friend of mine, Mrs. Max Phister, at Peitaho Beach.*
>
> *Mrs. Phister talked often with Americans there, soldiers and others. After Dr. Phister's death and after conditions became so unsafe in her area she had a long and difficult time getting out of China and finally reached Switzerland. She entrusted her jewels to David Roads. He was to bring her jewels to this country for her. There was also a stamp collection. This he sent me a number of months ago at her request, and I forwarded it. But her three letters or more about her jewels have brought no response. Nor has one I wrote. Apparently he will not answer or send them.*
>
> *I hope you will not mind calling him in and learning his explanation, if he has one. (I hope he has not pawned or sold them.) Will he not lose his government money if we have to engage an attorney, or have him arrested, or whatever is the proper procedure in a case like this? I would like to avoid this if possible. Dr. Phister*

practiced in Hong Kong before the war, then moved their home to Peitaiho Beach in North China. Although German, they were always anti-Nazi, very much so.

I shall be in Denver for the Western Folklore Conference in July but I do not wish to delay in taking some sort of action until then. And I need advice.

There is no record of the Dean's reply to Louise. She probably forwarded to Ani any communication she received from him. Either the dean or Roads must have given Louise the jewels, because she then contacted an American woman, Mrs. Cecile Bovell, who lived in New York City and who had known Ani in China. Mrs. Bovell, according to Ani's letter of 20 November 1947, "had a beautiful voice 2 years ago and gave also singing lessons. She is full of life and energy, good looking, very helpful, a charming husband and two (now grownup) boys." Mrs. Bovell received the jewels from Louise and had them appraised. But there was difficulty about paying duty when the valuables entered the United States.

Mrs. Bovell wrote to Louise on 28 October 1947:

I'm sending you and Mrs. Phister, a list of the jewelry you sent to me last week. I received it Oct. 25th. What memories our dear friend must have sent along with her beautiful things! It will be a pleasure to do anything I can to help.

The man who is to appraise the pieces, must have proof of the payment of duty before we can enter into any business transaction re: sales. Have you the information or any papers on this?

This was such an obvious requirement that I can't see how I hadn't thought of it myself! The absence of some of the pieces

Mrs. Phister gave to the marine in China, may be explained by his payment of the duty. I hope so, because I'm anxious to sell the things and send the money to her.

Will you please, send on any information you have on this matter as soon as you can conveniently do so?

Bovell enclosed a list of the jewelry and stated that she had sent a copy of her letter to Ani Phister. In that letter, Bovell reported the amount of money the jewels would bring, because Ani wrote, "Mrs. B. did very well indeed for my jewelry."

The ordeal of regaining her jewels and having them sold finally ended for Ani by 15 December 1947. Ani wrote to Louise that Mrs. Bovell had already sent the money for the jewels–"things moved quickly." She ended the letter with a comment on friendship: "You know the Russian proverb: a friend is worth more than a hundred rubbles. You and Mrs. B. have proved this."

Earlier in that same letter Ani referred to a comment Louise had made about finding it difficult to imagine Ani wearing jewelry:

> *You wrote once you cannot imagine me in the jewelry. True I never cared to wear it much. Just when I had to in Peiking or Hong Kong because everybody did. I liked the things for their beauty but was not attached to them as I am sometimes to some things I bought some-where in the old days of travelling . . . quite a lot of really good things I sold to an American major in Pei tai ho, who understood beauty in his quiet Norwegian way. Maybe you meet him sometime. The world is small enough.*

The letters that Ani wrote to Louise in October, November, and December 1947 also mentioned sending food parcels to Germany. Recovering from wartime hardships that included lack of food, Germans, especially those in the Russian-held zone, welcomed aid from Allied countries. Ani knew of many former professors, including Dr. Hoops, who were in need, and she passed their names on to Louise.

For Louise, helping the needy was a natural impulse that had been strengthened by her mother's example. Sending food packets to Germany offered her and Olivia an opportunity to give aid beyond the local level. At first, they sent money to Ani who assembled the packages and sent them on to Germany. Later, Louise sent at least one package through the U.S. CARE agency to names that Ani supplied.

Louise finally received a letter from Dr. Hoops written on 17 July 1947, saying that he was "greatly relieved and happy" to learn that Louise had asked "Mrs. Pfister, nee Ani Königsberger," about him. Continuing to express his gratitude for her contact, he wrote, "I had so often thought of you during the last few years and wondered what your feelings towards me might be after all that had happened between our two countries. From your inquiry about me I think I may conclude that the friendly relations which have connected us for half a century have not been broken by that ghastly war."

Reporting on his university career since the war started, Hoops wrote that he had resumed his lectures at Heidelberg University during the winter of 1939-40. When the American forces occupied Heidelberg in March 1945, he held the post of rector during the transition period but gave it up when the university reopened. He had retired from his chair but planned to continue giving lectures.

By 17 July 1947, Hoops had received a CARE package from Louise. CARE (Cooperative for American Remittances to Europe) was formed in the U.S. in 1945 for the purpose of sending food and other basic goods to war-ravaged European countries.

Expressing his gratitude Hoops wrote the following:

The CARE package which you announced on your postcard of October 2 has safely arrived. It was a most delightful surprise, and I wish to thank you most heartily for this rich and valuable gift. The parcel contains so many good things—flour, sugar, coffee, chocolate, apricots, and raisins, whole milk and eggs, margarine, and canned meat—all groceries we can't get here.

My wife is extremely happy to have all this nourishing and useful food for the household; she sends you her heartiest greetings and thanks. You have no idea what these things mean for us in the present time of distress, especially in this wintry season and after a summer with a long, catastrophical period of drought that has ruined all our crops, so that we have no vegetables at all and hardly any potatoes.

Hoops then wrote that he and his wife still lived in a house built for them in 1906. Their daughter and elder son, along with their families, also lived with them. Their youngest son, whom Louise had known, had been killed in the war. The war years had been especially hard for Dr. Hoops because he had "always fostered a friendly international feeling and worked all (his) life for a mutual understanding between the peoples of Germany, the United States and the British Empire."

Wanting to let Dr. Hoops know that she remained active in the folklore and linguistic fields Louise sent him copies of papers she had written along with an article written about her. He also had received an invitation from the Lincoln Kiwanis Club to attend a meeting where they planned to present Louise with the medal for Distinguished Service. Explaining his inability to attend the meeting Hoops wrote, "I should have been happy to be present on this occasion, or at least to send an airmail letter that could have been read at the meeting; but we are not yet allowed to send airmail letters abroad; so I could send an ordinary letter, which I hope, was forwarded to you."

Along with sending packages to Hoops and other German intellectuals needing aid, Louise sent Ani books. A few of them provoked Ani's comments, especially the works of John Gunther. An American author, Gunther had become well-known during the 1940s and 50s for his nonfiction books describing the political situation of specific countries. A few of the books shared similar titles: *Inside Europe* (1936), *Inside Asia* (1939), *Inside Latin America* (1941), *Inside U.S.A.* (1947).

In a 2 April 1948 letter, Ani wrote that she liked *Inside U.S.A.* "Some things I skip; but about Negroes, Indians, and life I read. I am not so interested in industry; though I know it is of immense importance." She wrote that she knew "*Inside Europe,*" but did not "care so much for it." Louise probably asked her what kind of books she would like, because Ani said that she did not "care for murder stories if they are not exceptionally good." In later correspondence, (16 July 1949) Ani told Louise not to send her *Readers' Digest.* "It is not my style. I get it occasionally from a friend, but it means nothing to me perhaps too American for a European who lived long in Asia."

With the ordeal of selling jewels and regaining the stamps behind her, Ani's correspondence with Louise fell into a more relaxed style. She continued commenting on the world political situation, describing her daily routine, and she often referred to her own past experiences. Louise must have questioned Ani for further details about getting out of China, because her reply on 25 May 1948 finally gave specific information of the trying experience. A series of lucky circumstances eased her exit.

At first, Ani had been advised to ask the displaced persons bureau for help in leaving the country, "but as I was not a displaced person, that was of no use of course, though they promised to help me get a passage. After waiting a while she "lost patience," and wrote to a Chinese Travelers' Officer in Tientsin. "By chance he was a patient of my husbands and I got an affirmative answer by return of post and the assurance he would do all he could for me. And he did!" Then Ani recounted her journey to Switzerland:

> *I received the permit to enter Switzerland the last days of August and had passage to Hong Kong for November which is very quick these days. They had written for me to Hong Kong for passage to Europe and I got that two days after my ship reached Hong Kong.*
>
> *In HK I had friends where I could stay as there is a great shortage of accommodation. The rest was easy. I had a cabin on the French ship with two very nice nuns (who wanted more help from me than I from them.) . . . In Marseilles I had no trouble with anything as the agency Havas was looking after my luggage and sent it on to Locarno. It took weeks to arrive but nothing was stolen which is the great point. When I left Pei tai ho beach a very nice American Major (Norwegian) lent me a trunk to take everything to the station which is half an hours drove from PTH (in the old days a train ran but Japanese and Chinese stole the rails and then the sleepers.)*

*. . . One very funny Chinese thing happened to my luggage. As
the train in PTH was late and only stopped for two minutes to reach
connection, my luggage could not be put on the train. I did not like
to leave it to the mercy of the coolies of the station as that usually
spells theft or disappearance. But a thickset smiling coolie came up
to me and asked whether I knew him. I could not remember him as
one generally looks not so much at their faces. So he put his sleeve
up and showed me a deep scar. Then I knew. I had to press his arm
while my husband sewed a deep cut. And he said he would look after
my luggage. I made a sign that nobody will steal anything and he
wrote some Chinese characters on it. And so the trunks and boxes
came through unhurt. That is very Chinese. But if things go on like
now in China that too will disappear. The Japanese did their best
to make the Chinese hate and despise the whites.*

The drama of wartime had ended for the two friends, and Ani's
remaining letters portray an idealistic life. She had enough money
to maintain a comfortable, but simple lifestyle in Switzerland, an
existence she preferred. A few years after she settled there, she began
spending summers in higher elevations. But always, no matter where
she was, Ani looked forward to the arrival of letters from Louise and
to composing her replies.

In exchange for the books Louise sent, Ani returned watercolors
that she had painted, probably landscapes, since she often wrote
about taking her art supplies and hiking into the hills to find inviting
views. Sending packages to German professors also occupied her time.
Louise continued sending money to Ani, who arranged for supplies
to be forwarded to former professors and friends in Germany.

Ani had retreated to higher altitudes and cooler temperatures by
16 July 1949. She wrote Louise that she was in one of her favorite
places. Describing her lifestyle, she said that she got up early and took
a long walk or went sketching, a routine she had followed during her
previous visits. Now, because of her age, she returned to her hotel for
lunch and a rest, then she went out again until it became too cool.

Back at the hotel, she ate dinner and visited with the hotel owners, her friends of fifty years.

Referring to her age, Ani wrote that although she still walked well, she didn't enjoy carrying her rucksack of painting supples. "But I do it and get used to it again. But anyhow the years show. Well one can't expect to keep the strength of youth for more than 70 years!"

After discussing Eleanor Roosevelt (Ani didn't like her) and describing her own physical condition, Ani wrote that Dr. Hoops had died. She didn't list the cause, but her comments indicated that he may have had a heart attack or stroke. "Poor Dr. Hoops, he died without pain and without knowing it. He would have felt it to leave his ailing wife alone in this crazy world." His son had been an active Nazi and was finding it hard to get work. Hoops' wife probably was probably financially dependent on her son.

The two friends corresponded for nine more years—until Louise died in 1958. Their exchange of letters is a separate part of Louise's life, a connection to more than the past, but also a recognition of her unrealized self. Ani was Louise's alter ego, someone with whom she could drop her public facade and reveal her inner feelings.

Chapter Twenty-Four

Final Honors

AFTER HER RETIREMENT in 1945, Louise enjoyed well-earned honors. While she was pleased to have her work rewarded, she maintained her usual poise when accepting the honors.

The Kiwanis Club of Lincoln awarded her the 1947 Distinguished Service Medal, and in 1948 the University Alumni and Regents included her in their choice of Distinguished Alumni. The following year, 1949, the University of Nebraska Press published *The Selected Writings of Louise Pound*. At a 1951 spring banquet of Kappa Kappa Gamma, Louise received the Special Alumnae Achievement Award, an honor bestowed on members reaching the highest level in their professions. In 1955–at age 82–she earned two additional accolades: election to the presidency of the Modern Language Association and to the Nebraska Sports Hall of Fame. She was the first woman to wear the mantle of MLA president, and the first woman included in the Nebraska Sports Hall of Fame.

Louise was chosen for receipt of the Kiwanis Distinguished Service medal based on her outstanding literary accomplishments and her achievements in the sports world. Although one by one, she had given up sports, she had continued to break barriers in the language field through her endorsement of American English and literature at a time when few universities included those subjects in their curriculum.

The Kiwanis award ceremony stressed the unique choice of a Distinguished Service recipient who had led the "quiet and unworldly life of a scholar." Praising Louise for cultivating "language as a precise instrument of thought and expression" and for cherishing "words as the exact representations of ideas," the presentation text also stated that she had studied "our mother tongue from its earthy origins to the subtle transformations even now taking place in the mouths of ordinary men and women." For Louise the most satisfying words in the address confirmed that she had fulfilled her professional ambition of adding "to the world's knowledge by the discovery of new truths."

Additional accolades were heaped upon Louise for wearing her "honors lightly," and for refusing the "ponderous or bookish" halo donned by many scholars. Favoring simplicity in her word choice, Louise shunned the lengthy or obscure terms that many professors used to signal their superior educations. In writing and speaking she aimed to inspire her listeners whether they were students, colleagues, or lay people interested in the subjects she addressed.

Providing an example of accessible material, *The Selected Writings of Louise Pound* reflected her scientific approach to the study of language. The book's topics were divided into six sections: "Literary," "Linguistic," "On Vocabulary and Diction," "Folkloristic," "Educational," and "Miscellaneous." In the foreword, Pound's former student, Arthur Kennedy, emphasized the importance of her contribution to the "establishment of scholarship in the realm of contemporary, and more especially, American speech, folklore, literature, and culture in general."

Louise had evolved from a reserved young woman, whose college commencement address protested the lowering of standards, into a confident adult whose creed of individual excellence embraced simplifying spoken and written language. After fifty years of dealing with students, administrators, and colleagues, and, at the same time, lending an ear and eye to language usage, Louise concluded that the "law of life is change and growth."

She told *World-Herald* reporter, Bruce Nicoll, who questioned her about the material in *Selected Writings*, that "language itself undergoes mutations, usually in the direction of condensed and simplified expression." She marveled at Americans' fondness for renaming objects with eccentric labels. "We look at a vacuum cleaner," she said, and "we don't call it that. No it's a contraption, a gadget, a jigger.'"

In her article, "American Euphemisms for Dying, Death, and Burial," Louise noted that Americans avoid using the word, death. "The superstition that to name a thing is to gain power over it seems to receive little credence when death and its trappings are concerned. It appears that one of mankind's gravest problems is to avoid a straightforward mention of dying or burial. Phrases used in referring to death," Louise informed Nicoll, "attempt to evoke gentle emotions and to find in death and burial a melancholy romance or noble dignity." She listed a few terms:

"Joined the great majority," "called home," "launched into eternity," "gave up the ghost," Perhaps the most inappropriate reference to death came from a rattled clergyman who said as he pointed at the corpse: "This is only the shell–the nut is gone.'"

Selected Writings received favorable comments from a broad range of individuals. Reviewing the book in the 2 July 1950 *New York Herald Tribune*, George Genzner referred to her work at Heidelberg University under Professor Johannes Hoops: "Disciplined by him in the great tradition of philological study, she has been a pioneer in applying its methods to fresh subjects and infusing into it a renewed spirit of enterprise." Genzner mentioned that none of the thirty-nine papers were long and some were quite "succinct." Although the book was interesting mostly to friends and former students of Louise, Genzner concluded that "any reader who leafs through *Selected Writings* will surely find something amusing or stimulating as well as informing to reward his search."

Mention of *Selected Writings* appeared in the "Belles-Lettres" column of the *Saturday Review* (16 May 1950). The columnist referred to Louise as "an erudite scholar" and "an observer of wide interests who writes with invigorating humor and unpretentiousness." In the reviewer's opinion the most important group of papers in the volume were those on the English Ballad. "Pound's theory–that ballads are relatively late and are not communal in origin–is now generally accepted, though it has not percolated down into all important school texts." Such words must have satisfied Louise, especially after the critical reviews that had followed publication of *Poetic Origins and the Ballad* in 1921.

Friends, of course, wrote laudatory letters about *Selected Writings*, and some recalled their student days with Louise. Dorothy Canfield Fisher replied to a letter that Louise had included when she sent Canfield the book. "Gracious what vitality you do pack into your letters! This one has your voice, almost your bodily presence so completely I feel as though you had stuck your head in the door of my study and given me a friendly hail! It has done my heart good," Fisher commented.

Fisher also wrote that she wasn't surprised at the book's success and that Roscoe and Olivia deserved credit for insisting that Louise consent to publishing her work.

Recalling student days at the University of Nebraska along with compliments on *Selected Writings*, H.M. Beldon of Columbia, Missouri, wrote a letter to Louise on 16 July 1952. He referred to the book as a "ragbag of interest and accomplishment" revealing "a lifetime record for a scholar to be proud of."

Beldon remembered Louise as a "versatile young woman who danced and played tennis and read themes and knew the literature of the present as well as the past." In addition to Louise, he remembered Willa Cather and Dorothy Canfield, but for him, Louise had been "the central and significant figure."

On 10 January 1950, Marvin Van den Bark of the University of Oklahoma penned words of praise that must have sounded like music to Louise Pound's ears. "Pound's book is a peach ... All her work has life in it–and none of the ground-out to-do that characterizes more scholarly writing." Praising the versatility of her life, he said that Louise had "traveled many roads."

Following these awards, Louise gradually dropped professional obligations. Writing to Botkin on 19 October 1952, after giving a speech in Texas "on the occasion of a college anniversary," Louise vowed to make no more addresses, but she qualified her vow with the words, "I hope." She also reported her resignation from writing a column for *American Speech*, stating, "Twenty-seven years is enough!" In July of 1953, she expressed her enjoyment of "having no deadlines or driving tasks but leisure, something I once had no use for."

Her leisure was interrupted in 1955 with her election to the presidency of the Modern Language Association—the first woman to hold the office, an honor she mentioned in a letter to Botkin. Writing on 6 February 1955, Louise also reported her "unexpected election to the Nebraska Sports Hall of Fame. Here I am alongside a celebrated baseball pitcher, a wrestler, two runners, football players, etc., with a real fanfare—and some inaccuracies of course. First woman again—Life has its humors."

With additional honors came responsibilities. As MLA president, she presided at meetings of the Executive Council and at association gatherings. She also made committee appointments and assigned delegates to attend events. At the organization's annual meeting she was required to give a Presidential address which would be published in PMLA. In addition to composing her speech, she also contributed two more articles to journals. Writing again to Botkin (24 May 1956) she restated her determination to stop writing pieces, declaring "1632 L needs enough care to keep me busy."

A third "first" came to Louise when Benjamin Boyce of Duke University introduced her at the MLA meeting held in Chicago's Palmer House Hotel. For the first time in the history of the organization, a resolution was passed regarding a president. The resolution congratulated Louise for the "achievements of her long and useful career." She had "astonished a nation of scholars unused to the company of ladies who knew quite as much as they did." Once again praises were heaped upon Louise for her ability to be a "social creature," "a wit," and a "champion in athletic sports."

Louise began her presidential address, "Then and Now," with a personal anecdote that prepared listeners for her informal speaking style. "Once before at a gathering of a learned society, seeing an upright gadget before me, I talked with extreme care directly into it for half an hour, moving neither to the right nor to the left, only to find as I went down from the platform that it was a lamp." One can imagine the audience chuckling and sighing with relief when they realized that Louise would not lecture on an abstract concept. Instead, she displayed her usual humor combined with sensibility. Assuring MLA members that she would not exceed her "allotted time," she quoted Gertrude Stein's remark about a long-winded speaker. "She's the kind you like the better the more you hear her less.'"

Giving a brief history of her association with MLA, Louise stated that her department head, Dr. L.A. Sherman, had asked her to prepare a paper to read at the fourth session of the Central Division which met in Lincoln in 1898. At the time, she was an instructor in the English department and wasn't a member of MLA. Nevertheless she prepared and read a paper titled, "The Relation of the Finnsburg Fragment to the Finn Episode in Beowulf." After hearing her work, a professor suggested that she submit it for publication, but Louise ignored his advice because she wasn't familiar with the appropriate journals. "Perhaps I should have tried to print my venture," she said, "for its conclusions were those ultimately prevailing."

In 1906, she joined MLA paying dues of $25 for a lifetime membership. She stated that her membership came six years after her studies in Heidelberg. Explaining the early years of MLA which accounted for the "Then" section of her address, she said that she looked back on those days with nostalgia because one could attend all lectures of the three divisions: English, Romance, German. "Now we migrate from room to room, sometimes from building to building hoping to hear, if we can, the papers in the special research or discussion groups that interest us. This only to find that those we wish to hear come simultaneously. These changes in the structure of the society did not come, of course, from changes in policy but resulted from increasing enrollment, and beyond question they have advanced professional training and scholarship among us."

When Louise began the "Now" section of her speech, she kept listeners' interest with another humorous remark: "Time passes and we must turn to the present. It is a tradition that givers of presidential speeches 'cultivate their own gardens.' I shall try to do this in a limited way, although my audience may think mine a weed patch rather than a garden."

Referring to language changes in the time of Shakespeare, she said, "If linguistic usage was on the loose in Shakespeare's day, really to the ultimate gain of the language, it is still more on the loose among us. In his day the innovations were largely in the direction of word borrowing from the classical and romance languages. The changes of today, departures and shifts of emphasis, are too many to review." The present tendency to "speed up expression," through using fewer words, substituting initials for full names, and compressing long words into shorter versions, "accelerates the tempo of the language," Louise stated.

In contrast to the shrinking of language, Louise spoke of the tendency of technical communication in many fields to elaborate and expand and to use specialized jargon:

> *In official jargon food becomes units of nutritional intake, the poor are the underprivileged, or those in lower income brackets. To mend or revive is to recondition, rehabilitate, reactivate. To an educator of high status, a baby sitter is the custodial supervisor of juvenile activities and recreation. All is not literature that litters but there is considerable litter about our official language as there is about professional jargons in general.*

Her observations about language remain accurate today. Word watchers keep an eye on changing usage and definitions in the journal that she helped establish, *American Speech*. The American Dialect Society also continues to monitor American words. "People will always be word conscious," Louise remarked. "After all it is in language that science, citizenship, education, and welfare are recorded as well as history, fiction, drama and poetry."

H.L. Mencken was among the friends of Louise who sent congratulatory notes on her MLA presidency. Mencken's letter was written by his secretary, Rosalind Lohrfink. He had suffered a stroke in November 1948 that impaired his speech and writing. The note from Lohrfinck, dated January 6, 1955, expressed Mencken's opinion that Louise, above anyone else in America, was "entitled to the presidency."

An interesting letter to Louise from Kathryn McHale of Washington D.C. congratulated her on the MLA presidency and informed her of Mencken's death which had occurred in January 1956. McHale, a member of the Subversive Activities Control Board, recalled Louise's "dissertation" on Mencken during an Atlantic crossing when the two women played bridge together. McHale also enclosed clippings that explained the "two Menckens–the writing Mencken and the real Mencken." The writing Mencken was "cynical, skeptical, iconoclastic, hardboiled, hypercritical, contemptuous." The real Mencken was "just the opposite." Louise knew the "other Mencken," who always helped acquaintances sell a story or an article, or get a job.

His friendship with Louise appeared to be genuine, and Mencken often remarked that he could not have written *The American Language* without her spade work. Edgar Kemplar, one of Mencken's biographers, wrote the following: Between 1919 and 1944 more books and articles would be written on American English than in the hundred and thirty years preceding, and *The American Language* would be linked with the works of Professor Louise Pound as a prime mover of the movement."

Although Louise accepted her final honors with grace and dignity, she continued her no-nonsense attitude toward life. She and Olivia realized that the upkeep of their home would eventually outreach their physical capacities, and they also watched institutional buildings begin replacing their neighbor's homes. In 1957 the sisters decided to sell their house within the next few years. But the burden of parting with the family home would fall on Olivia's shoulders. Louise spent her final years at 1632 L Street.

CHAPTER TWENTY-FIVE

Slowing Down

D URING THE LAST decade of her life, the constant motion
that propelled Louise Pound's accomplishments began to
ebb. Refusing speaking engagements and organizational offices, she
concentrated on savoring the present and found increased pleasure
in social affairs. Perhaps because of her age, she reflected on past
events.

In a letter of 3 January 1956, Louise shared her memories of
the Golden Fleece with Margaret Gettys, a former member of the
organization: "What a wonderful personnel was that of the good
old Golden Fleece. Remember the glittering panorama that H.L.
Mencken wrote for us and later printed in his *Smart Set*?" Louise
recalled with pride that the organization had no constitution, no
regular meetings, and no noble purpose. The existence of the Golden
Fleece perturbed the Deans. "But they could do nothing," she wrote,
"since Mrs. Chancellor Avery donned a flaming wig and attended
our gatherings faithfully. How it all comes back. My own fleece has
regenerated into insipid brown."

On April 10, 1957, Louise and Olivia merited a special program
presented by members of the Wooden Spoon Club. They produced

a series of skits based on Pound ancestors. "These Are Your Spoons" featured Hallelujah and Hosanna, life-sized twin dolls representing the Pound sisters' Quaker forerunners. Willa Cather's sister, Elsie, former colleague of Olivia and friend of both Louise and Olivia, was one of the skit's authors.

The newspaper clipping reporting the event contained photographs of the sisters. At the time, Louise was 85 and Olivia 83. Louise still wore her hair in a braid wound around her head. Olivia's short white curls emphasize her long face. Of the two, Olivia appeared to be older, probably because of her hairstyle. But Louise's statement about her hair being an "insipid brown," indicated that, like her mother, Louise's hair never turned gray, and the lack of fading hair gave her a more youthful appearance.

After Louise had celebrated her 85th birthday in June 1957, she was one of several authors honored at a party. The *Journal Star* article "Author features Authors At Party," published on 8 July 1957, contained two inaccuracies. It stated that Louise had given the luncheon and that it occurred in July. Louise, revealing that her mind remained alert, wrote a note on the clipping stating that the party occurred in June. "I did not give it," she wrote. "It was cooperative."

The celebration had been held in observance of the recent publication of *Roundup*, an anthology containing articles about Nebraska and profiles of noted residents as well as excerpts from works of the states' famous authors. The book contained two articles about Louise. Botkin had contributed a piece, titled, "First Lady of Letters: Retrospective–1957." Hartley Burr Alexander had written the second article, "In Medias res–1933." Writing to Botkin on 2 June 1957, Louise reported that she had "fared well in the *Nebraska Roundup* ... I drew far more than my share. The two greatest produced by Nebraska are (Hartley Burr) Alexander and my brother, neither of whom was awarded space as themselves–himself I should write."

Although Louise considered Roscoe the most successful family member, he marveled at her achievements. Confirming his respect, Roscoe had honored his sister's 85th birthday in 1957 with an article about her accomplishments. His tribute appeared on the front page of the June 30, 1957, *Boston Globe*. Roscoe stated that in Nebraska he was best known as "Louise Pound's brother." He also reported that Louise had "achieved distinction in so many and such diverse fields that one can only enumerate some of them and note that any one of them would suffice to put her brother on the map."

As evidenced in the 1894 Willa Cather episode, the Pounds were a cohesive family. After Cather wrote the scathing article about Roscoe, the family rallied around him. She was no longer welcome in their home, and Louise had ended their friendship. Even though Roscoe lived most of his adult life away from Lincoln–in Chicago and Cambridge–the Pound siblings remained close and supportive of one another. While Louise often mentioned Roscoe's accomplishments in this last decade of her life, she did so in an admiring, rather than a competitive, manner.

A touch of envy may have colored her referral to Roscoe's continued travels and lectures. After the honors she achieved in her 82nd year, she realized that she couldn't maintain her former pace, and noted that Roscoe, though older, managed to sustain a momentum that eluded her. Nevertheless, she was proud of his accomplishments, and that pride overcame any envy she felt toward him.

In a 10 January 1958 letter turning down an invitation from Chancellor Clifford Hardin inviting her to speak at the University Honors Convocation, Louise compared herself to Roscoe:

> *I feel honored indeed at being asked to give the Honors Convocation address in April. I wish I might accept. My brother at 87 seems to tour about giving speeches on the Atlantic coast or quite recently in Oklahoma. At 85 I don't trust myself to write a good address on some timely topic or to deliver it–would be inadequate. I have refused many invitations to speak, of late.*

Not forgotten as an athlete, Louise was invited to be the guest of honor at a golf celebration in Omaha. When golf records were turned over to the Nebraska State Historical Society in 1965, they included a July 1956 handwritten letter of regret from Louise. "Please do not count on my presence if the temperature is difficult, in the 90s for instance," Louise wrote. "A few years ago it would have seemed easy to drive to Omaha and back, as I have done so many times. Now it takes too much vigilance. I'm very well, but it's quite possible to become tired and prefer to subside." Louise was realistic about her increasing tendency to feel tired, a natural consequence of aging, and a signal that her heart was growing weaker. Nevertheless, she probably regretted her loss of vigor.

Another indication of her increasing frailty appeared in a letter to Botkin (2 June 1957). "Did Mamie tell you her nominating committee (Am. Names Society) offered me the national presidency for 1958. I refused. Three such presidencies (are) enough! Am. Folklore Society, Am. Dialect Society, and MLS." Louise asked, modestly, "How did I happen to be given them?"

In her correspondence with Ani Phister, who continued to live in Switzerland, Louise had reminisced about the beginning of their friendship. Ani replied on 15 October 1954. "I was glad to get your letter, a letter which brought old times back . . . Yes we met for a short time and kept our friendship for more than half a century. Remembering everything: circumstances, surroundings, youth, it does seem strange that though our lives ran in such different canals (that is not a good word, channels would be better), we just kept on." Recalling that their countries had been twice at war "meant nothing," Ani wrote, "because personal feelings always don't bother about such outside conditions." She felt that "governments educated their children into overdone patriotism and that way lay the root of war in the young minds."

Louise continued sending her friend books and stamps. Ani liked Virginia Woolf's novels, Orlando and Mrs. Dalloway, and requested more of Woolf's work. She also enjoyed Mari Sandoz's novels, and observed that she could "feel" that Sandoz had "Swiss blood."

On 27 May 1952, Ani agreed with Louise that some modern

writers buried their stories in obscurity. "It is just the same with modern German ones. If you start one it seems very difficult to follow and very deep. Once you have caught the jargon one wonders why the author has not used a simpler language for the well-known old ideas."

At the turn-of-the-century Louise Pound and Ani Königsberger Phister had represented the controversial New Women—but the day of the accomplished New Women had passed. Ani expressed her opinion of modern women in a letter to Louise (23 July 1955.) "What a change all over the earth has made since our youth! I wonder if the freedom women have gained has been to their good." She agreed with Louise that it had been better to pass their lives in a time with "a more serious outlook." Continuing her discourse on feminism, Ani wrote, "Sure they have more chances to work, to do more interesting work, but it seems to me to be more unrest, more discontent among them and certainly on the whole marriages are less happy, less congenial."

As early as 1932, Louise had voiced her opinion to reporter Gretchen Schrag about the new generation of college women. "At present about the only prestige a girl can win is to be made by men students a "sweetheart" or a "prom queen of the west," and this not for achievement or skill or superiority of some kind, but by masculine selection, mostly on the basis of personal appearance or clothes," Louise said. She ended the interview listing her sports accomplishments, but she emphasized that scholastic responsibilities always had top priority in her life.

By 4 April 1958, Ani complained to Louise, "I don't know how long it is since I had word from you." Ani had been in Spain for three months, and letters tended to get lost or delayed for unknown reasons, she explained, yet she hoped to hear from Louise again. "Both of us have reached a rather ripe old age and so our correspondence may be broken off suddenly!" Ending her letter with concern for Louise, Ani wrote, "How are you? Just write me a note—let me know."

What was the state of Louise's health in the spring of 1958? In April she had refused Chancellor Hardin's invitation to speak at the

University Honors Convocation because she didn't trust herself to write and deliver a good address. Ani's April letter voiced concern about not hearing from Louise, and the last letter that Louise had written to Botkin was dated January 21, 1958. He had planned to stop in Lincoln on his way to Berkeley, and Louise invited him to dinner. "I'll gather up Mamie (Meredith) . . . for a good dinner and reunion. Don't let anything happen." Botkin's visit was canceled, "and there was no stopover in Lincoln, no dinner, no reunion," he wrote. "And there were no more letters from Louise Pound."

She was tired. Her heart was wearing out. Like a spinning top losing its momentum during its final gyrations, Louise Pound's life cycled toward its close. Sensing that death was near, Louise picked up a pen and edited her will.

CHAPTER TWENTY-SIX

The Last Days

SEATED IN HER study surrounded by floor to ceiling books on three walls, Louise may have slipped into a reflective mood, a state of mind that her recent honors had encouraged. Writing her MLA presidential speech had given her an opportunity to relive past events, and the recent articles featuring her in *Roundup* along with the Wooden Spoon skit brought to mind the many friendships she enjoyed.

Reflecting on those friends and considering Olivia's age and physical Condition, (she, too, was slowing down) Louise decided to change her will. According to a newspaper article, she specified that "between $800 and $1,000 should be paid to the University of Nebraska Press to help fund publication of her studies in Nebraska folklore. A University staff member should collect and edit the "dozen or so" pieces to print, Louise directed. Another change provided between $500 and $1,000 for the "Louise Pound Fellowship" sponsored by the Lincoln chapter of the American Association of University Women.

If Olivia did not survive Louise, $6,000 would be divided among friends. Louise may have paused, leaned back in her chair and glanced out the window, noticing the neighborhood changes, as she remembered special friendships. Then she decided which individuals to name as possible heirs. Marguerite C. McPhee, with whom she had signed the mock legal contract in 1908 requiring her to skate from 1632 L Street to 1808 S. 17th Street, was to receive a portion of the $6,000. The second recipient, Mamie J. Meredith, was a close friend and a University colleague with whom Louise shared her complaints about the English department. The third beneficiary, Elsie Cather, was Willa's sister and a friend of Louise and Olivia in addition to being Olivia's colleague at Lincoln High School.

Louise also considered the disposition of her books and papers. In a letter to Mamie Meredith (28 February 1959) Olivia wrote that Louise "wouldn't have wanted her special books to go to the (University) library," preferring that they be given to members of the (English) department who could use them. But Olivia discovered another notation on Louise's will directing that her books were to be sold. Pinned to the will was a list of dealers in technical and rare books. Louise had already sold many of her books to Louise Stegner of Omaha.

Why didn't she want to leave her books to the University Library? She had received a request from the assistant library director, Bernard Kreissman, that she give her papers to the library. Although Kreissman's 1956 letter did not mention acquiring her books, he probably would have accepted them.

The tension existing between Louise and University officials, especially those heading the English department, had not eased with her retirement. In a letter to Melvin Van den Bark of the University of Oklahoma, Louise recalled her relationship with University bureaucrats as she praised her former colleague, Mamie Meredith. "Mamie Meredith has acquired for herself a national, almost international reputation. She goes happily and unperturbed on her way. The University ought to do something nice for her by this time, but the department seems rarely to miss a chance to do the opposite."

Books weren't the only item on her mind as Louise contemplated the end of her life. The future of 1632 L Street was another concern. When Roscoe had visited his sisters in 1949, the three Pound siblings had been photographed standing near the library window of their home. The newspaper clipping contained their comments on neighborhood changes that had taken place over 57 years. Rolling prairie and open muddy streets had been replaced with pavements and blocks of city buildings. 1632 L was out-of-place among its neighbors–like a formally dressed woman at a sock hop. Bowing to change, Louise and Olivia planned to sell their home within the next few years.

After Louise died, Olivia sold the residence to Mrs. Mary Peterson of Lincoln, who intended to leave the house unchanged as an antique shop. Unfortunately illness forced Mrs. Peterson to sell the property to the Sam Zolot Family in 1962. Before the final sale, Lincoln resident, Mrs. Ruth Henderson, campaigned to give the Pound home historical landmark status. Her efforts failed, and in 1963 the house was demolished and replaced with six medical offices and a parking lot. Fortunately, Olivia died before the house was torn down.

June 1958 was the last month of Louise Pound's life. A letter from Kathryn A. McEwen written to Mamie Meredith (28 June 1958) referred to the illness and subsequent death of Louise. McEwan had hoped that Louise's "wonderful constitution would see her through this–the first illness I have known her to have."

She reflected that Louise's "big generous heart must just have worn out."

It was appropriate that Louise had been spared a long illness; her death was consistent with her lifestyle. As a child she learned and moved quickly; as a young woman, she sped across tennis courts; and as a mature woman, she had raced from classrooms to meetings. As an elderly woman with a weak heart, she died suddenly.

After her hospitalization in June, Louise returned to 1632 L Street. How did she spend those last days in the home that she had shared since 1892 with her family, and finally, only with Olivia. Perhaps she chose a book from her collection and reread the familiar words, and she may have listened again to recordings of favorite music. With her logical mind, she probably also reviewed the events and accomplishments of a lifetime and felt satisfied that she had achieved her personal goal of individual excellence.

Obituaries state that a heart attack caused her death on June 28, 1958. Later, as Mamie Meredith helped Olivia organize Louise's papers, she heard Olivia's belief that Malaria, contracted when Louise visited Willa Cather in 1893, had a role in causing her sister's final illness. In Olivia's opinion, Louise's attempt to cure herself through frantic bicycling caused the lesions that damaged her heart.

Reaching age 86 was a race that Louise lost. She died on June 28, two days short of her 86th birthday. Private memorial services were held at Rudge Memorial Chapel located in Lincoln's Wyuka Cemetery. Dr. Edgar Z. Palmer of the Lincoln Religious Society of Friends led the July 2, 1958, service.

Wyuka Cemetery, an all faith burying ground, was established in 1869 by an act of the Nebraska legislature. Developed as a scenic rural burial site, it followed the pattern of Mt. Auburn Cemetery near Boston which included curved roads, trees, and flower gardens. In fact, Wyuka served as Lincoln's first park, providing ample space for picnics in its picturesque setting. Now it is included on the National Register of Historic Places and is listed as a Nebraska State Arboretum Historic Landscape.

Rudge Memorial Chapel, erected between 1935 and 1938 was financed by Lincoln businessman, Charles H. Rudge, and continues to function as a site for funerals, weddings, and concerts. It was an appropriate setting for Louise Pound's funeral. Prior to Dr. Palmer's homily, Mamie Meredith noticed the stillness that veiled the room—a stillness broken only by birds singing outside the chapel. Throughout the service she watched petals fall from bronze chrysanthemums, reminding her that the life of her friend and colleague had also fallen away.

Using an apt metaphor for Louise, Dr. Palmer compared life to a book. "The substance is between the two covers, yet it is not complete until the back cover has been added." In conclusion, he stated that the "greatest miracle of all life is the spirit: the spirit that is poetry and art and literature and science, and, above all, love." He reminded the friends who had gathered for her funeral service not to mourn the absence of Louise's physical presence, but to remember her spirit with love.

After Olivia and Mamie Meredith sent word of Louise's passing to her friends and colleagues, Olivia received letters of condolence. Ani Phister praised Louise: "My life was richer because of our friendship. Strange it was anyhow that, from such different surroundings we should meet (and) get so near to each other. Our lives were absolutely different, but something in our characters and outlook bonded."

Dorothy Canfield Fisher remembered watching Louise skate. "Was there ever anyone who had a surer mastery of that troublesome outer edge skating? It was far too difficult an art for the fumbling little girl I was to think of trying." Recalling her last trip to Lincoln, Fisher wrote that Louise had seemed "as she always had been, the wonder of the faculty and students."

Fisher expressed her final praise for Stephen and Laura Pound, writing that Louise had "been a unique figure in those frontier days when your mother and father represented on that bleak prairie everything of value that American pioneers had brought from the Old World. And the way your parents brought up you children, they set burning a flame of learning which has never gone out in the memory of those who knew anything of the old days." (Dorothy Canfield Fisher died five months later, on November 9, 1958, from a stroke.)

In addition to widely published obituaries, several journals printed memorials of Louise. Botkin shared his admiration for his former teacher and friend in *Western Folklore*. He praised her versatility and stated that Louise avoided becoming a dilettante because of her "dynamic view of modern historical study." She believed that literature and language were part of the "whole activity" of humankind. Her interest in folklore came naturally, Botkin wrote, "as part of her frontier heritage." He stated that "In her own life, continuity and stability of tradition–family and regional, and to her home city and state prompted her to remain at the University of Nebraska."

Her love of Nebraska and her interest in folklore were combined in the 1959 posthumous publication of *Nebraska Folklore*.

The University of Nebraska Press edition stated that the studies included in the book "were collected and edited by Dr. Louise Pound shortly before her death, June 28, 1958. Except for the correction of typographical errors, they are presented here as she prepared them for publication."

The Foreword written by W.D. Aeschbacher, Director of the Nebraska State Historical Society, stated that Louise always had been "vitally interested in life and happenings close about her, and the study of the folklore of her area became increasingly important." Containing early-day yarns and legends of lovers' leaps, rain-making attempts, strong men's prowess, cave lore, and other colorful stories, the collection has remained the only book written about Nebraska folklore.

Opening the volume with the article, "Nebraska Cave Lore," Louise cited examples of their prominence in mythology. Although Nebraska had no nationally known caves such as Kentucky's Mammoth Caves, the state had more interesting ones than "might be expected" along with lore concerning them. She felt that cave lore should be recorded before it became "utterly lost."

John Brown's cave located at Nebraska City was among those she chronicled. Through her research, Louise discovered facts which shed doubt on the claim that John Brown sheltered run-away slaves in the cave and in his cabin. She contended that he was interested in more spectacular ways of freeing slaves as proved in his 1859 raid on the Harpers' Ferry arsenal in West Virginia. Brown and his followers planned to distribute weapons from the arsenal to slaves, enabling them to revolt against their masters. Captured by Robert E. Lee's troops, Brown was tried and hanged. He was memorialized in the song, "John Brown's Body." The words came from Ralph Waldo Emerson's poem and were set to the tune of *The Battle Hymn of the Republic*.

In "Nebraska Snake Lore" Louise reported only the snake lore collected from Nebraska residents which included, cures, weather signs, luck, dreams, and preventives. One of the deadliest and most feared snakes in the state, the rattlesnake, was said to also possess curative powers. Holding rattles against an aching head would end the pain. Allowing a baby to chew the rattles would help the child's teeth emerge. Killing the first snake seen in spring would bring good luck, and bad luck came after a snake crossed a person's path. A few of the sayings about snakes that Louise recorded follow:

As cold as a snake
As crooked as a snake
As deadly as a cobra
Like a snake in the grass
Lower than a snake's belly

"Nebraska Rain Lore and Rain Making" was a humorous and informative article listing ways pioneers used to induce rain at the turn-of-the-century. In addition to the explosion theory which used explosives to coax rain from the sky, people were encouraged to believe that "rain followed the plough." Pound reported George Catlin's account about the Mandan Indians calling down rain by sending braves to the top of the medicine lodge where they invoked spirits or threatened clouds in loud voices. When one brave failed, another replaced him. The Mandans always succeeded in producing moisture because the ceremony didn't stop until it rained.

Nebraska Folklore also featured strong men in the style of Paul Bunyan, the nationally famous logger of phenomenal strength. In her article, "Nebraska Strongmen," Louise accounted for three powerful males: Febold Feboldson, Antoine Barada, and Moses Stocking. The most famous, Febold Feboldson, originated in a newspaper column of the former Gothenburg, Nebraska, *Independent*. The writer and inventor of Feboldson was a local lumber dealer who used him as an advertising gimmick. Since there were few trees on the great plains,

Feboldson was not a lumber hero. Instead, he wrestled tornadoes, droughts, extreme heat and cold, as well as Indians, politicians, and disease.

Information about Antoine Barada came to Louise from Mari Sandoz who worked for a time at the Nebraska State Historical Society and served as assistant editor of *Nebraska History* magazine. Sandoz recalled that Barada was a "hurry-up man," so impatient that he couldn't wait for anything. He was known as "the strongest man who roamed the shores of the Missouri River." A popular story told of Barada growing so impatient watching a pile driver that he picked it up in his bare hands and threw it over the river. As it bounced along the ground and broke up, the pile driver formed an area known as the "breaks of the Missouri."

The third folk hero, Moses Stocking, owned sheep and was known for intellectual cunning rather than physical strength. He made use of large turnips growing on his land as shelter for his sheep. After blasting a hole in a huge turnip, Moses' sheep ate their way into the turnip where they were sheltered from cold and blizzards and brought prosperity to their owner.

Other sections of *Nebraska Folklore* recount legends of Lovers' Leaps, and the Nebraska legend of Weeping Water. Another article, "The John G. Maher Hoaxes" relates Mayers' hoaxes of a petrified man, soda springs, and an Alkali Lake Monster. For those interested in folk history, Pound's article, "Some Old Nebraska Folk Customs" gives details of Fourth of July celebrations as well as Halloween, Thanksgiving, Christmas, and other holiday observances. Weddings, funerals, and church occasions are among other customs she describes.

Her final article "Folklore and Dialect," discussed the origins of folklore and "local and regional peculiarities of language traditionally handed on and therefore lore." She detailed the beginning of dialect studies as rising from the science of philology. She also included a chronology of the American Dialect Society's development and the founding of the journal, *American Speech*. The article viewed the fields of folklore and dialect with the intellectual and scientific slant that characterized Louise Pound's studies. Through her research, the dialect and folklore of ordinary people gained scholars' respect.

Continuing to fulfill her role as family caretaker, Olivia began sorting through her sister's papers and arranging the sale of 1632 L Street. After Louise's memorial service, Ann Marie Rhetus, one of the "girls" who had lived with the Pounds while attending high school and college, stayed with Olivia, helping her sort papers and settle into an apartment. After Rhetus returned to her teaching job in Arizona, Mamie Meredith assisted Olivia in organizing Louise's belongings. Meredith's letter to Mari Sandoz, (10 September 1958) mentioned the disposition of Louise's papers.

> *Olivia will not give any of the Cather letters to Mildred Bennett for the Cather memorial, and I doubt that she will give any to Bernard Kreissman for Love library . . . I don't know whether she'll destroy that schoolgirl crush letter and of course nothing is being destroyed that belongs in Louise Pound's estate–although she willed everything to Olivia. Roscoe cheerfully relinquished all claims. Olivia said that she's collecting some of L.P.'s hats, dresses, etc. for the Historical Society–they are not considered part of the estate. She will let me read the many letters she is receiving telling of the help given by L.P. to so many students of here–and others and of course she'll preserve these–probably for the Historical Society.*

Many of Louise Pound's papers are in the Nebraska State Historical Society Archives; others are housed in the University of Nebraska Love Library Special Collections. The "effusive" Cather letter and poem, and the correspondence of Louise and Olivia which contained comments on Cather and Mencken are housed at Duke University Library in Durham, North Carolina. Wisely, Olivia placed the Cather material at Duke rather than destroying it.

Olivia died on April 6, 1961, after completing the arduous task of sorting and depositing her sister's papers. Roscoe outlived his sisters, passing away in 1964 at age 93. With the demolition of the Pound home in 1963, evidence of the family was erased from Lincoln, until a new junior high school named in their honor opened that fall. Also in 1963, a University women's dormitory was named Louise Pound Hall. A connecting tower which housed men bore Willa Cather's name.

As Louise Pound raced through life she passed to her students the flame of learning that her parents had given her. Growing up in the rich intellectual atmosphere provided by Stephen and Laura Pound encouraged her to channel her energy into the teaching profession. Inspiring students to view learning as a means of enriching their lives, Louise reflected her belief that the "more you know of anything in all its phases the more interesting it becomes." She often said that the greatest satisfaction she had in life was the success of her students.

Her influence on friends and students was expressed by Mrs.

Robert Lasch. "For all of us, her students and her friends, she is truly immortal. Every day for as long as we live we will see her influence expressed in innumerable ways and the ideas that she implanted in us reflected in turn by our children and students."

EPILOGUE

L OUISE AND OLIVIA are companions in death just as they were
in life; the sisters share a grave in the family plot at Wyuka
Cemetery. The Pound gravesite is impressive in its simplicity. A gray
stone embedded in the ground displays the family name. The absence
of an imposing headstone to mark the family graves seems surprising,
yet it is consistent with their characters and symbolizes their practical
and unpretentious natures. Smooth gray stones mark the separate
graves of Laura and Stephen and the shared resting place of Louise
and Olivia. At noon on a summer day, tree branches wave above
the graves and create a harmony of sun and shadow that encourage
reflection on Louise Pound's life."

What mattered to Louise? She loved her family, her friends, and her
home state of Nebraska. The strength of those ties determined her decisions,
which, in turn, influenced her lifestyle. Her respect for her family's social
standing in Lincoln and her parents' role in building the city's cultural
and intellectual base caused her to continue upholding their values.
Although speculation has risen about Louise's brief relationship with
Willa Cather, it is inaccurate to determine her sexual preference
from the intensity of their three-year friendship. Using present-

day standards to judge the nature of women's relationships in past generations is one-sided and unfair.

Women of the Victorian era often expressed affection for each other in effusive language. Only Cather's passionate words about her feelings for Louise remain. If Louise used such language in return, no record of it exists. She was practical, not sentimental, and it would have been uncharacteristic of her to jeopardize her own and her family's reputation in the community by returning Cather's passion.

Women can admire Louise for breaking barriers in sports and academia. She was the first woman elected to the Nebraska Sports Hall of Fame and the first woman elected to the presidency of the Modern Language Association. She was also the first female graduate of the University of Nebraska to earn a doctorate. She won the Western Women's Tennis Championship in 1897 and held top golfing honors in Nebraska for twenty years. Her sports achievements are too numerous to list, yet she always put scholarship ahead of sports.

She challenged men in any field and enjoyed winning against them, but she didn't hate them. Her friendships with Botkin and Mencken were only two examples of her willingness to help men as well as women further their careers. The most long-standing feud in her lifetime was with a woman. She disagreed with Mabel Lee's belief in playing games for fun rather than for winning them. If these two strong-minded women could have worked together, the result would have benefited University women's sports.

Her athletic feats and academic brilliance may have awed others, yet she was simply following her own standard of individual excellence. Thorough but practical, she concentrated her research in areas that benefitted the most people. Her work with Mencken gave American English equal standing with British English, and she encouraged preserving the folksongs and stories of the past. Aware that she'd led an interesting life, Louise told Botkin that Mencken had suggested that she should write a memoir. After she retired, she admitted that she was "too indolent to bother with it." Perhaps she regretted not keeping a diary and writing the story of her life as well as more books. Instead, she kept newspaper and magazine articles that featured her accomplishments along with correspondence from friends and colleagues as a record of her life.

While it may seem paradoxical that such a competitive individual as Louise Pound could also have an altruistic nature, the written testimonies of those she helped reflect her generous spirit. Her generosity was just one aspect of her versatile and eclectic nature. That nature included a belief in individual excellence, a creed she followed to the end of her life.

ACKNOWLEDGEMENTS

M Y RESEARCH INTO Louise Pound's life has provided me with many unexpected but rewarding experiences and acquaintances. One acquaintance, Dr. Robert Cochran of the University of Arkansas, has also written a biography of Louise Pound. When I contacted him about writing a foreword for my book, he graciously agreed to read the biography and write the foreword. One of the more satisfying moments of the publishing process occurred when I read his words. He understood and expressed the intent of my book perfectly. Cochran's biography, published by the University of Nebraska Press, will appear in 2008.

Dr. Robert Knoll, a retired English professor from the University of Nebraska, has been an inspiring source. Knoll shared anecdotes from his personal acquaintance and friendship with Louise Pound and suggested additional sources. He also read the manuscript prior to publication and advised my editor in correcting factual errors, an effort that I appreciated. Knoll's book, prairie university: A History of the University of Nebraska, has been a valuable source, one that I often referred to for information about the university, its history, and its chancellors.

During the writing of Louise Pound's life, Kate Gleeson, a University of Iowa summer writing workshop leader, agreed to read drafts of my work and guide me through the process of writing it. I thank Kate for suggesting the book's organization and for urging me to look deeper into Louise Pound's character. My editor at

American Legacy Media, Gary Toyn, has encouraged me to express my views on Pound's relationship with Willa Cather in unequivocal terms. In guiding me through the publication process, his support and enthusiasm for the biography and his attention to detail have been outstanding and encouraging. I'm grateful to Bill Wood, of American Legacy Media, for reading the proposal and asking to see the manuscript. My agents, Joan West and Lois Bennett, tended the contract details, answered my questions, and were always ready with helpful suggestions and uplifting comments.

In Neligh, friends Ruth and George Strassler, encouraged me to contact Robert Knoll and have given many hours of technical help in getting the book to market. Many problems have been shared and solved over cups of coffee or tea. As the Neligh librarian (now retired), Ruth processed my interlibrary loan requests promptly. Kate Ostenrude, the current librarian, has listened with interest to the publishing effort. I'm grateful to the local computer repairman, Walt Storey, for retrieving my work from a failing hard drive and for always answering my calls for help.

Correspondence with Colette Carner, a longtime friend in Rockford, Illinois, helped me adjust to lifestyle changes after my return to Nebraska, and she read my first efforts at recording Pound's life. My dentist, Dr. William Petta, gave me valuable advice about creating writing space for myself, and at the same time, he kept my smile intact. Visits to my optometrist, Mark Palmer, were always uplifting because he listened with interest to my latest writing experiences. Members of the Albion Area Writers' Group have provided me with more than encouragement. While sharing our writing joys and sorrows during monthly meetings, we always ended in laughter. Their humor provided a welcome distraction from disappointments. Jerry Guenther, regional editor of *The Norfolk Daily News*, granted and understood my need for leaves of absence from working as a correspondent.

Without archival collections, this biography would not have been written. The Nebraska State Historical Society has at least 35 boxes of Pound family papers. The University of Nebraska Special

Collections Archives holds Louise Pound papers, B.A. Botkin papers, and those of Bernice Slote and Mari Sandoz. All of them contributed valuable information about Louise Pound. The archivists patiently listened and delivered box after box of papers and past issues of magazines, journals, and yearbooks. Terri Raeburn, former archivist at the historical society, made certain that I received requested copies on the day I asked for them because she knew I was from out-of-town. Through my membership on the Nebraska United Methodist Historical Commission, which Terri now directs, she continues to keep in touch with my progress on the biography.

In Lincoln, personnel at Wyuka Cemetery guided me to the graves of the Pound Family and gave me a tour of Rudge Chapel, the site of Louise Pound's funeral. Friends, Nora Houtsma and Marilyn Jorges of Rogers' House in Lincoln provided more than bed and breakfast, they also listened to my latest discoveries from the archives and cheered me onward, assuring me that, one day, the biography would be published.

When in Lincoln, I also shared meals and received encouragement from my daughter, Kristin, and her husband, Rob McEntarffer. Rob urged me to contact Robert Knoll, and he spread news of my biography writing effort among Lincoln's education community. During the seven years that I worked on the book, I took breaks to celebrate the birth of two grandchildren. Esme and Guy always provided joyful distractions and continue to do so.

My daughter, Alison, also a Lincoln resident, often spends weekends with us while she tends her native seed acres. At the same time, she serves as my media specialist, solving word-processing and other computer-related problems.

Always ready with loving support and encouragement, my husband, Ken, has shared my love of words throughout our marriage. Wherever we've lived, our homes have been filled with books, magazines, and newspapers.

Last of all, I'm grateful for the company of my Sheltie, Annie, who faithfully follows me to my office everyday and keeps me company.

BIBLIOGRAPHY

Books:

Bacon, Margaret, Hope. *Mothers of Feminism: The Story of Quaker Women in America.* San Francisco. Harper & Row. 1986.

Bennett, Mildred. *The World of Willa Cather.* Lincoln. The University of Nebraska Press. 1961.

Bode, Carl. *The New Mencken Letters.* New York. Dial Press. 1977.

Brunvand, Jan Harold. *The Study of American Folklore: an introduction.* Third Edition. New York, London. W.W. Norton & Company. 1986.

Cather, Willa. *My Ántonia.* Boston. Houghton Mifflin. 1918.

Chafe, William H. *The American Woman: Her Changing Social, Economic, and Political Roles,* 1920-1970. London, Oxford, New York. Oxford University Press. 1972.

Christianson, Gale, E. *Fox At The Woods Edge: A Biography of Loren Eisley.* New York. Henry Holt & Co. 1990

Cognard, Anne, M. *Louise Pound, Renaissance Woman. Perspectives: Women in Nebraska History. Nebraska Department of Education and the Nebraska State Council for the Social Studies.* Special Issue

Copple, Neale. *Tower On The Plains: Lincoln's Centennial History 1859-1959.* Lincoln. Centennial Commission Publishers. 1959.

Cox, Gerry; MacDaniels, Carol; Helzer, Chris. *Guide to Nebraska Authors.* Dageford Publishing Co. 1998.

Creigh, Dorothy, Weyer. *Nebraska: Where Dreams Grow.* Lincoln. Miller & Paine. 1980.

Elshtain, Jean Bethke. *Jane Addams and the Dream of American Democracy.* New York. Basic Books. 2002.

Graff, Gerald. *Professing Literature: An Institutional History.* Chicago, London. University of Chicago Press. 1987.

Graff, Jane, Coordinator. *Nebraska: Our Towns: East Southeast.* Dallas. Taylor Publishing. 1992.

Haffner, Sebastian. *Defying Hitler: A Memoir. Translated by Oliver Pretzel.* New York. Farrar Straus and Giroux. 2000.

Hart, James D., with revisions and additions by Leininger, Phillip, W. *The Oxford Companion to American Literature.* Sixth Edition. New York, Oxford. 1995.

Hickey, Donald, R. *Nebraska Moments: Glimpses of Nebraska's Past.* Lincoln and London. University of Nebraska Press. 1992.

Johnson, Alvin. *Pioneer's Progress: An Autobiography.* New York. Viking. 1952.

Johnson, J.R. *Representative Nebraskans.* Lincoln. Johnsen Publishing Company. 1954.

Kemplar, Edgar. *The Irreverent Mr. Mencken: An Informal History of the Man and His Era.* Boston. Little Brown & Company. 1950.

Knoll, Robert E. *Prairie university: A History of the University of Nebraska.* Lincoln. University of Nebraska Press. 1995.

Laughlin. Clara, E. *So You're Going to Germany and Austria.* Boston, New York. Houghton Mifflin Co. 1930.

Lee, Mabel. *Memories Beyond Bloomers.* Washington D.C. American Alliance for Health, Physical Education, and Recreation. 1978.

Lowenthal, Kristi. *Mabel Lee and Louise Pound: The University of Nebraska's Battle Over Women's Intercollegiate Athletics, A Thesis.* July 1999.

Madigan, Mark, J. *Keeping Fires Night & Day: Selected Letters of Dorothy Canfield Fisher.* Columbia & London. University of Missouri Press. 1993

Manley, Robert N. *Centennial History of the University of Nebraska.* Lincoln. University of Nebraska Press. 1969.

Marks, Patricia. *Bicycles, Bangs, and Bloomers: The New Woman in the Popular Press.* Lexington. The University Press of Kentucky. 1990.

Masters, Margaret, Dale. *Hartley Burr Alexander: Writer in Stone.* Lincoln. Jacob North Printing Company. 1992.

Mencken. H.L., *The New American Language with annotations and new material by Rauen I. McDavid, Jr.*, *with the assistance of David W. Maurer.* Alfred A. Knopf, Borzoi Book. 1977.

Morrison, Samuel Eliot. *The Oxford History of the American People.* New York. Oxford University Press. 1965.

O'Brien, Sharon. *Willa Cather: The Emerging Voice.* New York, Oxford. Oxford University Press. 1987.

Olson, James C. and Naugle, Ronald C. *History of Nebraska.* Third Edition. Lincoln, London. University of Nebraska Press. 1997.

Pound, Louise. Sheldon, Addison, E., Editor. *Folksong of Nebraska and the Central West: A Syllabus.* Nebraska Ethnology and Folklore Series. 1916.

Pound, Louise. *Poetic Origins and the Ballad.* New York. Macmillan Company. 1921.

Pound, Louise. *The Selected Writings of Louise Pound.* Lincoln. University of Nebraska Press. 1949.

Pound, Louise. *Nebraska Folklore.* Lincoln. University of Nebraska Press. 1959.

Robinson, Phyllis. *Willa: The Life of Willa Cather.* Garden City. Doubleday & Co. 1983.

Sandoz, Mari. *Love Song to the Plains.* Lincoln. University of Nebraska Press. 1961,

Sayre, Paul. *The Life of Roscoe Pound.* Iowa City College of Law Committee. State University of Iowa. 1948.

Schlereth, Thomas, J. *Victorian America: Transformations in Everyday Life.* New York. Harper Collins. 1991.

Scott, Eugene. *Tennis: Game of Motion.* New York. Crown Publications. 1973.

Sheldon, Addison Erwin, A.M., PhD. *Nebraska: The Land and the People.* Chicago, New York. Lewis Publishing Company. 1931.

Slote, Bernice. *The Kingdom of Art: Willa Cather's First Principles and Critical Statements.* Lincoln. University of Nebraska Press. 1997.

Smith-Rosenberg, Carroll. *Disorderly Conduct: Visions of Gender in Victorian America.* Oxford, New York. Oxford University Press. 1985.

Stout, Janis, P. *Willa Cather: The Writer and Her World*. Charlottesville, London. University Press of Virginia. 2000.

Sullivan, Mark. *Our Times: The United States 1900-1925: The Turn of the Century*. New York, London. Charles Scribner's Sons. 1926.

This Fabulous Century. New York. Time-Life Books. 1974.

Traxel, David. *1898: The Birth of the American Century*. New York. Vintage Books. 1998.

Twain, Mark. *A Tramp Abroad*. London. Chatto & Windus. 1891. Republished by Grosse Pointe Woods Michigan. Scholarly Press. 1968.

Weatherford, Doris. *American Women's History*. New York. Prentice-Hall General Reference. 1994.

Wigdor, David. *Roscoe Pound: Philosopher of Law*. Westport CT and London. Greenwood Press. 1974.

Wish, Harvey. *Society and Thought in Modern America*. New York, Toronto, London. Longmans Green & Co. 1959.

Woodress, James. *Willa Cather: Her Life and Art*. Lincoln. University of Nebraska Press. 1982.

Yanik, Ted, and Cornelison, Pam. *The Great American History Fact-Finder*. Boston, New York. Houghton Mifflin Co. 1993.

Newspaper Articles:

Simpson, Evelyn. "Louise Pound, Sports Champion . . . and Teacher." *Omaha World Herald Magazine*, June 20, 1945. Sec. C. pp. 4-5.

The Daily Nebraska State Journal. June 12, 1892. June 14, 1892.

The Lincoln Journal, August 11, 1898. p. 4. August 12, 1898. p.6. August 13, 1898. p.8. August 14, 1898. p.5. August 20, 1898. p.5. August 22, 1898. p.3.

Schrag, Gretchen. "Miss Pound, English Professor, Reveals Tales of Times When She Had Tennis, Bicycle, Golf Titles." *The Daily Nebraskan*. February 1932. Vol. 31. No. 92.

Anthology Articles

Alexander, Hartley, Burr. "In medias res – 1933." Faulkner, Virginia, compiler and editor. *Roundup: A Nebraska Reader*. Lincoln. University of Nebraska Press. 1957.

Botkin, B.A. "First Lady of Letters: Retrospective-1957." Faulkner, Virginia. Editor. *Nebraska Roundup*. Lincoln. University of Nebraska Press. 1957.

Journal Articles

Botkin, B.A. "Pound Sterling: Letters From a 'Lady Professor." Prairie Schooner. Spring 1959. Vol. 33. No. 1.

The Hesperion. June 16, 1892. Vol. XXI. No. 16. (15 December 1888.) (December 22, 1892. Vol. XXII. No. 5.) (June 15, 1892. Vol. XXI. P.12.) University of Nebraska Special Collections/Archives. Lincoln. Love Library.

The Lasso. February 1, 1892. Vol. 1. No. 5. University of Nebraska Special Collections/Archives. Lincoln. Love Library.

Malone, Kemp; Smith, Eldon C.; Meredith, Mamie J. (Chairman); Louise Pound Memorial Committee. Names. March 1959. Vol. VII. No.1.

Murray, Michael, L. "Benjamin Botkin." *Voices: The Journal of New York Folklore.* Fall-Winter 2001. Vol. 27.

Pound, Louise. "Word Coinage and Modern Trade Names." *Dialect Notes.* Vol. IV. pp. 29-41.

Pound, Louise. "The Class of 1892 ... Fifty Years Later." *Nebraska Alumnus.* May 1942. pp. 4-5.

Pound, Louise. "The Undergraduate Years of Hartley Burr Alexander." Prairie Schooner. December 1948. Vol. XXII. pp. 372-80.

Pound, Louise. "Do You Remember?" *Nebraska Alumnus*. Nov. 1954.

Puck Magazine. "The New Woman." (Poem.) March 6, 1895. Vol. XXXVII. No. 939. p. 41.

Roth, Linda Gage. "Are Sports Harmful to Women?" The Forum. May 1929.

Yost, Nellie Snyder. "Nebraska's Scholarly Athlete: Louise Pound, 1872-1958." Nebraska History. 1983. Winter. Vol. 64. pp. 477-90.

Encyclopedias

Encyclopedia Americana. Vol. 28. pp. 805-06.
Encyclopedia Americana. Vol. 12. p. 621.
Encyclopedia Americana. Vol. 26. p. 494.

Archival Collections

Botkin, B.A. Papers. University of Nebraska Special Collections/Archives. Love Library.

Mencken, H.L. Papers. New York Public Library. Manuscript and Archives Division. Astor, Lenox and Tilden Foundations

Pound, Laura, Papers. Nebraska State Historical Society Archives.

Pound, Louise, Papers. Nebraska State Historical Society Archives.

Pound Louise, Papers. University of Nebraska Archives Special Collections/ Archives. Love Library.

Pound, Olivia, Papers. Nebraska State Historical Society Archives.

Pound Family File. Bennett Martin Public Library. Lincoln.

Sandoz, Mari, Papers. University of Nebraska Special Collections/Archives. Love Library.

Slote Collection. University of Nebraska Special Collections/Archives. Love Library.

Electronic Sources
www.nyfolklore.org/pubs/voic27-3-4/botkin.html
Http://www.unl.edu/libr/libs/spec/botkin.html
http://menckenhouse.org/abouthlm.htm
http://en.wikipedia.org/wki/H.L.Mencken
http://www.law.umkc.edu/faculty/projects/trials/scopes/menk.htm

Personal Letter
Knoll, Robert E. Letter to Mr. Ronald R. Butters. Editor of *American Speech*. Department of English, Duke University, Durham, North Carolina. 7 June 1983.

Notes and Sources

Forward and Part One:

CHAPTER ONE:

Prologue: A report of the Texas folklore festival incident is described by Simpson, Evelyn, "Louise Pound, Sports Champion ... and Teacher," ([Omaha] *World Herald Magazine*, June 1945, Sec. C.)

Page 1: For Laura Pound's description of her childhood dislike of needlework see Pound, Laura, *My Childhood*, Nebraska State Historical Society Archives (Hereafter cited as NSHS Archives,) Laura Pound Papers, Box 2

Page 1: For Laura Pound's description of finding insects on a log during her childhood see Pound, Laura, *My Childhood*, NSHS Archives, Laura Pound Papers, Box 2

Page 2: For Laura Pound's account of her wedding journey see NSHS Archives, Laura Pound Papers, Box 1.

Page 2: "Judge Pound's high character and social position as well as Mrs. Pound's unusual abilities" are reported in Sayre, Paul, *The Life of Roscoe Pound*, (Iowa City College of Law Committee), State University of Iowa, 1948,) p. 38

Page 3: The Pounds were among those families who "tried to keep life very much as it had been in Ohio, New York, Virginia, or Illinois." Slote, Bernice, *The Kingdom of Art: Willa Cather's First Principles and Critical Statements, 1893-1896*, (Lincoln,) University of Nebraska Press, 1997, p. 6

Page 3: Stephen Pound's judicial career summarized in a memorial brochure published after his death is in NSHS Archives. Laura Pound Papers, Box 1

Page 4: Laura Pound's civic activities are listed in a typewritten summary of her life located in NSHS Archives, Laura Pound Papers, Box 2.

Page 4: For a summary of Louise Pound's sports and scholastic achievements see Hickey, Donald R. *Nebraska Moments: Glimpses of Nebraska's Past*, (Lincoln and London,) University of Nebraska Press, 1992, pp. 228-34

Page 4: References to Louise Pound as Miss Pound and Olivia Pound as Miss Olivia came from an interview with Dr. Robert Knoll

Page 4: For Laura Pound's decision to teach the children at home see Sayre, p. 35

Pages 4-5: For comparisons of the Pound children's personalities to those of their parents see Sayre, pp. 15, 38, 54

Page 5: For Roscoe Pound's advocacy of law revisions see Wigdor, David, *Roscoe Pound: Philosopher of Law*, (Westport CT and London) Greenwood Press, 1974, pp. 84, 188

Page 5: For Louise Pound's theory of ballad origins see Pound, Louise, *Poetic Origins and the Ballad*, (New York,) Macmillan Company, 1921, pp. 34-40

Page 5: For Olivia's contributions to secondary education in Lincoln see, NSHS Archives, Olivia Pound Papers, Box 6, and The Pound Family File, Bennett Martin Library, (Lincoln)

Chapter Two

Page 6: For a description of Victorian Americans as "working and striving," see Schlereth, Thomas J., *Victorian America: Transformations in Everyday Life 1876-1915*, (New York), Harper Collins, 1991, p. 343

Page 6: For the "Great West" citation see Traxel, David, *1898: The Birth of the American Century*, (New York), Vintage Books, 1998, p. 66

Page 6-7: For a summary of Stephen Pound's ancestry see Sayre, Paul, *The Life of Roscoe Pound*, (Iowa City College of Law Committee, State University of Iowa,) 1948, p.16-18

Page 7: For Laura Pound's description of Hugh Pound and a definition of the differences between Orthodox Friends and Hicksite Quakers see Pound, Laura, *My Childhood*, NSHS Archives, Laura Pound

Louise Pound

Papers, Box 2, pp. 40-41

Page 7: For Sarah King Pound as clerk of Farmingdale (NY) Quakers, see Pound, *(My Childhood)* p. 80.

Page 7: For Hugh Pound's statement "'I would that thee did not go into the barn tonight," see Sayre, p. 18

Pages 7-8: For Stephen Pound's background and Nathan Pound's personality see Sayre, pp. 14-19

Pages 8-9: For Stephen Pound's career development and settlement in Lincoln see "Life of Judge Pound," "Some Reminiscences," (From an Interview Published in *The Journal* in 1909.) NSHS Archives, Laura Pound Papers, Box 1, Scrapbook

Pages 8-9: For a history of Lincoln see Graff, Jane, Coordinator, *Nebraska: Our Towns: East Southeast,* (Dallas Texas,) Taylor Publishing, 1992, pp. 101-102

Page 9: For the statement about Stephen Pound tending his law studies more conscientiously than he tended his store, see Sayre p. 22

Page 9: For a description of Stephen Pound's literary and sports interests prior to marrying Laura Biddlecombe see Wigdor, p.10

Page 9: For a summary of Stephen and Laura Pound's relationship see Sayre, p. 115

Page 9: For information about Stephen Pound's judicial career see NSHS Archives, Laura Pound Papers, Box 1, newspaper clippings in scrapbook and memorial bulletin

Page 10: For Laura Pound's ancestry and birthplace see Sayre, pp. 17-22, also see Laura Pound's memoir, *My Childhood*, p. 2, NSHS Archives, Laura Pound Papers, Box 2

Page 10: "It was going west in the forties if you went one hundred miles in that direction," see Pound, *My Childhood*, p. 25, NSHS Archives, Laura Pound Papers, Box 2

Pages 10-11: For a description of Laura Pound's favorite childhood school see Pound, *My Childhood*, p. 42, NSHS Archives, Laura Pound Papers, Box 2

Page 11: For an account of sled-riding and sliding on ice see Pound, *My Childhood,* p. 43, NSHS Archives, Laura Pound Papers, Box 2

Page 11: For an account of Laura's interest in plants see Pound, *My Childhood,* p.42-43, NSHS Archives, Laura Pound Papers, Box 2

Page 11: The passage describing Laura's discoveries in the woods is in Pound, *My Childhood,* p. 84, NSHS Archives, Laura Pound Papers, Box 2.

Page 12: For Laura Pound's description of herself at age twelve see Pound, *My Childhood,* p. 84-85, NSHS Archives, Laura Pound Papers, Box 2

Page 12: About Laura learning to read at age three see Pound, *My Childhood*, p. 7, NSHS Archives, Laura Pound Papers, Box 2.

Page 12: Laura learns to read using a geography book. Pound, *My Childhood,* pp. 16-17, NSHS Archives, Laura Pound Papers, Box 2

Page 13: For an account of Laura's mother approving the books she borrowed and read see Pound, *My Childhood*, p. 81, NSHS Archives, Laura Pound Papers, Box 2

Page 13: An account of Quaker schools in Colonial America is given in Bacon, Margaret Hope, *Mothers of Feminism: The Story of Quaker Women in America,* (San Francisco,) Harper & Row, 1986, pp. 59, 89-90

Page 13: Laura's admiration for Edwin Pound appears in Pound, *My Childhood,* pp. 80-81, NSHS Archives, Laura Pound Papers, Box 2

Page 14: About the Universalist faith practiced by Laura's parents see Pound, *My Childhood,* p.89, NSHS Archives, Laura Pound Papers, Box 2

Page 14: For an account of the Biddlecomb family's activities during the summer of 1853 see Pound, *My Childhood,* p. 86, NSHS Archives, Laura Pound Papers, Box 2

Page 14: Laura attends Macedon Academy, Pound *My Childhood,* p. 105, NSHS Archives, Laura Pound Papers, Box 2

Page 14-15: For an account of Laura's study at Lombard College see Wigdor, pp. 10-11

Pages 15-17: For an account of Laura and Stephen Pound's wedding journey see Pound, Laura, "A Wedding Trip in February 1869," NSHS Archives, Laura Pound Papers, Box 1

Page 15: A description of Laura Pound comes from Olivia Pound's letter to Paul Sayre (3-18-46.) NSHS Archives, Olivia Pound Papers, Box 1

Page 16: For Laura Pound's further description of her wedding journey and her comparison of Lincoln to Tama, Iowa, see Pound, Laura, "A Wedding Trip in February 1869," NSHS Archives, Laura Pound Papers, Box 1

Page 17: Laura Pound recalls the grasshopper invasions of Nebraska in "Some Municipal History," NSHS Archives, Laura Pound Papers, Box 1. (1920 newspaper clipping.)

Page 17: For a description of Lincoln when Laura and Stephen Pound arrived in February 1869 see Adamson, Elizabeth Little, "Some Early Recollections," 1928 newspaper clipping, NSHS Archives, Laura Pound Papers, Box 1, Scrapbook

Pages 17-18: Olivia Pound describes her mother's dread of prairie fires in an essay, "Laura B. Pound," NSHS Archives, Olivia Pound Papers, Box 1.

Page 18: For a description of Laura Pound taking apart the stovepipe in her first Lincoln home, see "Home Life of the Pound Family," NSHS Archives, Olivia Pound Papers, Box 1

Page 19: For Laura Pound accepting a petition from an Indian in her husband's absence see, "Laura B. Pound," NSHS Archives, Olivia Pound Papers, Box 1,

Page 19: "There was something inspiring in having a share in the building of a new state." NSHS Archives, Olivia Pound Papers, "Laura B. Pound," Box 1,

Pages 19-20: For an account of Laura Pound's actions to save the Lincoln Public Library see Scrapbook newspaper clipping, "Some Municipal History," (4-19-20,) NSHS Archives, Laura Pound Papers, Box 1

Page 20: For a list of Laura Pound's involvement in civic organizations and in organizing the Nebraska Society of the Daughters of the American Revolution, see Scrapbook clipping of her obituary, "Mrs. Laura B. Pound Succumbs to Illness," 12-11-28. The scrapbook also contains an article describing Laura Pound's leadership of the Nebraska chapter of the DAR and the erection of a fountain in Antelope Park, "Nebraska Society Daughters of the American Revolution." NSHS Archives, Laura Pound Papers, Box 1,

Page 20: Comment from a University classmate praising Laura Pound's influence is in Olivia Pound's essay about her mother, "Laura B. Pound," NSHS Archives, Olivia Pound Papers, Box 1

CHAPTER THREE

Page 21: Two rules the Pound children had to follow are explained by Olivia Pound in her correspondence with Sayre, "A Day in the Life of the Pound Family," NSHS Archives, Olivia Pound Papers, Box 1

Page 21: For Laura Pound's teaching advice given to a newspaper reporter see NSHS Archives, Laura Pound Papers, Box 1, Scrapbook clipping "Who's Who in Lincoln," 2-5-22

Page 22: For an account of Laura Pound installing a blackboard on the living room wall see "Family Portrait," University of Nebraska Archives/Special Collections, (Lincoln) Louise Pound Papers, Box 1,

Page 22: "I have never forgotten your kindness to me when I was a boy . . ." (Quote contained in an essay about Laura Pound written by her daughter Olivia,) "Laura B. Pound," NSHS Archives, Olivia Pound Papers, Box 1

Pages 22-23: For the account of the Pound children's home life and Stephen Pound's sense of humor see "A Day in the Life of the Pound Children," NSHS Archives, Olivia Pound Papers, Box 1,

Page 23: For the account of Roscoe enrolling in University German classes see Sayre, p. 35

Page 23: For Olivia's account of the daily lessons she and Louise received from their mother see, "A Day in the Life of the Pound Family," NSHS Archives, Olivia Pound Papers, Box 1

Page 23-24: For Louise Pound's recollection of her mother's teaching, "We learned and believe me we studied," see Simpson, Evelyn, "Louise Pound, Sports Champion . . . and Teacher," *Omaha World-Herald Magazine*, Sec. C, June, 1945

Page 24: For Laura Pound's account of her children learning "regularity and system," see, scrapbook clipping, "Who's Who in Lincoln," NSHS Archives, Laura Pound Papers, Box 1

Page 24: Laura Pound's continued interest in botany is mentioned in a typewritten obituary, NSHS Archives, Laura Pound Papers, Box 2

Page 24: For the Pound children's backyard activities see "Home Life of the Pound Family," NSHS Archives, Olivia Pound Papers, Box 1

Page 25: Louise describes receiving ice skates from New York relatives and teaching herself to use them. NSHS Archives, Louise Pound Papers, Box 18, scrapbook

Page 25: More facts about Louise learning to ice skate are in Simpson, "Louise Pound, Sports Champion . . . and Teacher," and Yost, Nellie Snyder, "Nebraska's Scholarly Athlete: Louise Pound, 1872-1958, *Nebraska History*, 1983, Winter, Vol 64: pp. 477-490

Pages 25-26: For descriptions of indoor activities including *Pilgrim's Progress* board game and military games see "A Day in the Life of the Pound Family," NSHS Archives, Olivia Pound Papers, Box 1

Page 26: For the thank you letter Louise Pound sent to her cousin after receiving ice skates see, University of Nebraska Archives/Special Collections, (Lincoln) Louise Pound Papers, Bio-bib box

Pages 26-27: An account of his parents buying Roscoe expensive equipment for use in his insect collection is given in "Who's Who in Lincoln," NSHS Archives, Laura Pound Papers, Box 1, scrapbook clipping, 2-5-22

Page 27: Another account of Roscoe's insect collection and his parents' purchase of equipment is in Johnson, J.R., *Representative Nebraskans*, (Lincoln) Johnsen Publishing Company, 1954, p. 161

Page 27: Laura Pound describes teaching Roscoe to read in Sayre, p. 35

Page 27: An account of Louise Pound learning to read from a maid is given in Olivia's letter to reading specialist, Grace Munson (6-16-37), NSHS Archives, Olivia Pound Papers, Box 1

Pages 27-28: Louise and Roscoe compete with each other when reading Macauley's *History of England*, Sayre, p. 39-40

Page 28: An account of the Pound children's reading is in Olivia's essay, "A Day in the Life of the Pound Family." NSHS Archives, Olivia Pound Papers, Box 1

Page 28: For a list of the children's favorite books (chosen by their parents), see Sayre, p. 40

Page 29: Sunday afternoon Greek reading sessions of the Pound family are described in Manley, *Centennial History of the University of Nebraska*, (Lincoln,) University of Nebraska Press, 1969, p. 238

Page 29: Olivia describes the three homes of the Pound family in "Home Life of the Pound Children," NSHS Archives, Olivia Pound Papers, Box 1

PART TWO

CHAPTER FOUR:

Page 32: About University of Nebraska Preparatory School: Knoll, Robert E. *prairie university: A History of the University of Nebraska*, (Lincoln) University of Nebraska Press, 1995, p. 8

Pages 32-33: The characteristics of the New Woman: Smith-Rosenberg, Carroll, *Disorderly Conduct: Visions of Gender in Victorian America*, (Oxford, New York) Oxford University Press, 1985, p. 176

Page 33: Cather's quote about University students: Cather, Willa, *My Ántonia*, (Boston) Houghton Mifflin, 1918, Book 3, Chapter 1, p. 258

Pages 33-34: About the Morrill Act and University charter: Knoll, pp. 1-3

Page 34: Description of the University in its infancy: Knoll, p.5

Pages 34-35: University Hall description and construction problems: Knoll, pp. 4-5

Page 35: Student Alvin Johnson views University Hall as majestic and huge: Johnson, Alvin, *Pioneer's Progress: An Autobiography*, (New York) Viking, 1952, p. 76

Page 35: University Hall room arrangements and uses: Manley, Robert, *Centennial History of the University of Nebraska*, (Lincoln) University of Nebraska Press, 1969, p.19

Page 35: Graft in construction of University Hall: Knoll, p. 4-5

Page 35: First two state capitols also victims of unscrupulous contractors: Graff, Jane-coordinator: *Ne-*

braska: Our Towns East Southeast, (Dallas) Taylor Publishing, 1992, pp. 103-104

Page 36:Chancellor Allen R. Benton: Knoll, p.9-11

Page 36: Chancellor Fairfield and professors Church, Emerson, and Woodberry's campaign to raise teaching standards: Knoll, pp. 16-17.

Pages 36-37: Mannatt as Chancellor and his problems with faculty: Bessey replaces him. Knoll, pp. 19-22

Page 38: James Hulme Canfield and University's Golden Era: Knoll, pp. 27-40. Manley, pp.113-125

Page 38: Bessey's teaching style as described by Roscoe Pound: Manley, p. 80.

Page 39: Bessey's belief in Darwin's natural selection theory as applied to plants: Wigdor, David, *Roscoe Pound: Philosopher of Law,* (Westport Connecticut and London) Greenwood Press, 1974, pp. 22, 54

Pages 39-40: Professor Lucius Sherman and his teaching theory and his encouragement of Louise Pound's career at the University: Knoll, p. 32

Page 40: About August Hjalmer Edgren as professor and his part in founding the University graduate school: Knoll, pp. 33-34

Page 40-41: Lincoln and University growth: Knoll, p. 27Olson, James C. and Naugle, Ronald C, *History of Nebraska.* Third Edition, (Lincoln & London) University of Nebraska Press, 1997, p. 207

Page 41: Lincoln as a cultural center: Slote, Bernice, *The Kingdom of Art: Willa Cather's First Principles and Critical Statements, 1893-1896,* (Lincoln) University of Nebraska Press, 1997, p. 207

Page 41: Louise Pound's statement about the optimistic atmosphere of the University during her student days: Pound, Louise, "The Class of 1892 . . . fifty years later," *Nebraska Alumnus,* May 1942, pp. 4-5.

CHAPTER FIVE

Page 42: Louise Pound and Willa Cather co-edit a literary journal, *The Lasso.* O'Brien, Sharon, *Willa Cather: The Emerging Voice,* (New York, Oxford) Oxford University Press, 1987, p. 119

Page 43: Quotation about Louise as "cold-hearted:" *The Hesperian,* June 16, 1892, Vol. XXI. #16.

Page 43: Fostering of competition in 19th Century America and Thomas Edison's quotation about competition: Traxel, David, *1898: The Birth of the American Century,* (New York) Vintage Books, 1998, p. 41.

Page 43: Description of Louise and Roscoe as "jolly and loving pranks:" Knoll, Robert E. *prairie university: A History of the University of Nebraska,* (Lincoln) University of Nebraska Press, 1995, p. 30

Page 43-44: About Roscoe Pound's study and practice of law and botany: Knoll, pp.30-31

Page 44: Roscoe Pound's interest in military drill: Manley, Robert, *Centennial History of the University of Nebraska,* (Lincoln) University of Nebraska Press, 1969, p. 267

Pages 44-45: Louise Pound participates in a women's military drill team. Manley, pp. 267-68.

Page 45: Louise Pound's account of leading the women's military drill team: NSHS Archives, Louise Pound Papers, Box 21 contains a copy of 1895 *Sombrero* article about the women's drill team

Page 45: List of Literary Societies organized at the University of Nebraska: Knoll, pp. 10-23

Page 46: Advantages of literary societies over classroom lectures: Graff, Gerald, *Professing Literature: An Institutional History,* Chicago & London, University of Chicago Press, 1987. p. 44

Page 46: *Hesperian* Account of Literary Societies teaching socializing arts and public speaking: *Hesperian,* 15 December, 1888.

Page 46: An account of the slate system used by men to choose which young women they would escort to a literary society meeting: Manley, pp. 273-74

Page 47: Knoll's recollection of a conversation with a colleague concerning Louise Pound's lack of attraction to men: Copy of a 7 June 1983 letter Robert Knoll sent to Mr. Ronald R. Butters, Editor of *American Speech* regarding the personality of Louise Pound. Knoll sent the copy to me with permission to use it

Page 47: About the GOI (Go Out Independents)–the group of women who attended sporting events and meetings with escorts: Manley, p 241

Louise Pound

Page 48: Louise Pound's description of literary society meetings: University of Nebraska Special Collections/Archives. Pound, Louise, "The Founding of the University" in *Semi-Centennial Anniversary: The University of Nebraska 1869-1919*, (Lincoln) University of Nebraska Press, 1919, pp. 36-39

Page 48: Synopsis of "The Perjured Palladian"–the play that Louise Pound wrote for the Union Literary Society to perform: University of Nebraska Special Collections/Archives: Louise Pound Papers, Bio-bib box

Page 48: Review of "The Perjured Palladian:" *Herperian,* December 22, 1892, Vol. XXII, #5, p.2

Page 48: Parlors and porches serving as gathering places for friends during 1890s: Traxel, p. 23.

Page 48: Olivia Pound's description of student meetings in the Pound home: NSHS Archives, Olivia Pound Papers, Box 1

Page 49: Edison's mass-produced phonograph produced by 1898: Traxel, p. 23

Page 49: The Pound siblings organize a Carroll Club as a parody of popular Browning Clubs. NSHS Archives, Olivia Pound Papers, Box 1, Letter to Professor Sayre, March 18,1946

Page 50: Quotation from Dick Lehmer's letter praising Laura Pound: NSHS Archives, Louise Pound Papers, Box 1, 1916-1929 file

Page 50: List of outstanding students attending the University with the Pound siblings: Knoll, p. 30.

Pages 50-51: Louise Pound's advice to student wondering whether to devote his life to scholarship: Johnson, Alvin, *Pioneer's Progress,* (New York) Viking Press, 1952. p. 96

CHAPTER SIX

Page 52: Porterfield quotation about the class of 1892 as "the brightest that ever mashed peanut shells into a Brussels capret: *The Daily Nebraska State Journal,* June 12, 1892.

Page 52: Louise sewed her graduation gown: Hutchinson, Duane. "Louise Pound's 100th Birthday This Week," *Lincoln Journal and Star FOCUS,* June 25, 1972, pp. 14F-15-F

Page 53: Louise Pound's Graduation Day Speech, "Apotheosis of the Common:" NSHS Archives, Louise Pound Papers, Box 17 Folder 22

Page 53: About the Pound family's opinion of populists as "demagogues:" Sayre, Paul, *The Life of Roscoe Pound,* (Iowa City) College of Law Committee, State University of Iowa, 1948, P. 50.

Pages 54-55: Reference to Pound's speech as a "most scholarly oration:" *The Daily Nebraska State Journal,* June 12 1892

Page 55: Summary of Pound's speech: *The Hesperian,* June 15, 1892, Vol. XXI, p.12.

Page 55-56: Report of Louise Pound's piano performance as part of commencement ceremonies: *The Daily Nebraska State Journal,* June 14, 1892.

Page 57: About early Kodak cameras: Schlereth, Thomas J, *Victorian America: Transformations in Everyday Life,* (New York) Harper Collins, 1991, pp. 197-200

Page 57: Louise Pound's sketchbooks: NSHS Archives, Louise Pound Papers, Box 30

Pages 58-59: Louise Pound's Short story: "By Homeopathic Treatment," University of Nebraska Special Collections/Archives, Love Library, Louise Pound Papers, Bio-bib box

Page 59: Laura Pound describes her mother's inability to vote in a school election in her memoir, *My Childhood,* Laura Pound Papers, NSHS Archives, Box 2.

Pages 59-60: Louise Pound's story "Miss Adelaide and Miss Amy:" NSHS Archives, Louise Pound Papers, Box 17, Folder: Miscellaneous Essays

Pages 60-61: Louise Pound's story "The Passenger from Metropolis:" NSHS Archives, Box 12, Folder: Miscellaneous Essays

Pages 61-62: British introduction of the safety bicycle heralds the new sport: *This Fabulous Century: 1870-1900,* (New York) Time-Life Books, 1974, p. 112

Pages 62-63: Louise Pound wins cycling medals and wears the comfortable clothing adopted by New Women: Marks, Patricia, *Bicycles, Bangs, and Bloomers: The New Woman in the Popular Press,* (Lexington) The University Press of Kentucky, 1990, p. 184, 202-203

Notes and Sources

CHAPTER SEVEN:

Page 64: About Willa Cather's father moving to Nebraska, See Woodress, James, *Willa Cather: Her Life and Art,* (Lincoln) University of Nebraska Press, 1982, P. 26

Page 64: About Willa Cather's adjustment to living in Nebraska see Woodress, p. 32.

Pages 65-66: For Cather's intellectual development and her friendship with Will Drucker, see Woodress, p. 42-43

Page 67: For Virginia Boak Cather being the "spark that drove her household," see Woodress, p. 22

Page 67: For Willa's rebellion against fashion as a revolt against her mother see Bennett, Mildred, *The World of Willa Cather,* (Lincoln) University of Nebraska Press, 1951, p. 3

Page 68: For Cather exhibiting characteristics of the New Women, see Stout, Janis, P., *Willa Cather: The Writer and Her World,* (Charlottesville and London) University Press of Virginia, 2000, pp. 16, 31

Page 68: For Louise Pound's attitude to smoking see Knoll, Robert E.'s, letter to Ronald R. Butters, Editor of *American Speech.* Knoll gave the author permission to quote from the letter

Page 68: For information about Cather and Louise Pound as co-editors of *The Lasso,* see O'Brien, *Willa Cather: The Emerging Voice,* (New York, Oxford) Oxford University Press, 1987, p. 119

Page 69: For Cather and Pound fitting the New Woman category see Smith-Rosenberg, Carroll, *Disorderly Conduct: Visions of Gender in Victorian America,* (New York, Oxford) Oxford University Press. 1985, pp. 176-77

Page 69: For the statement that Louise Pound was the "storm center of Willa Cather's world," see O'Brien, p. 129

Pages 69-70: For contents of Cather's letter to Louise complimenting her appearance at a party and complaining that friendship between women was viewed as "unnatural," see O'Brien, pp. 130

Page 70: For the letter from Willa Cather to Mariel Gere describing Louise Pound's visit with Cather in Red Cloud see University of Nebraska Special Collections/ Archives, Slote Collection, Box 4, Folder 1

Page 70: For the 9 September letter Mamie Meredith wrote to Sandoz concerning Louise Pound's illness after visiting Red Cloud see University of Nebraska Special Collections/ Archives, Mari Sandoz Papers

Pages 71: For contents of Cather's letter requesting that Pound visit her in Red Cloud again, see O'Brien, p. 131

Page 71: For a discussion of expressions of love and affection between mature women see Smith-Rosenberg, p. 53

Page 71: For a description of Roscoe Pound's distance in personal relationships, see Sayre, Paul, *Roscoe Pound,* (Iowa City) College of Law Committee, State University of Iowa, 1948, p. 241

Page 72: For Cather's complaint to Mariel Gere that Louise wouldn't call Cather, "Love," see Cather letter to Gere, June 1, 1892, in O'Brien, p. 145n

Page 73: For the role that Roscoe Pound may have played in ending the relationship between Cather and Louise Pound, see Robinson, Phyllis, *Willa: The Life of Willa Cather,* (Garden City, N.Y.) Doubleday & Co, 1983, pp. 60-61

Page 73: For Roscoe Pound's membership in "Sem Bots" and their ridicule of students of letters at the UniversitySee Knoll, Robert, *prairie university: A History of the University of Nebraska,* (Lincoln) University of Nebraska Press, 1995, p. 30

Page 73: For Roscoe Pound's opinion of Willa Cather's friendship with his sister, Louise, see Robinson, pp. 60-61

Pages 73-74: For a description of Cather's vitriolic attack on Roscoe Pound in the *Hesperian* see Robinson, p. 60

Page 75: For a statement about the future relationship between Willa Cather and Louise Pound, see Robinson p. 60. Cather addresses Louise "warmly," and Pound speaks of Cather in a "mocking tone."

CHAPTER EIGHT:

Page 76: For Louise Pound's passion for "winning" see Robert Knoll's June 1983 letter to Mr. Ronald R. Butters, Editor of *American Speech.* Knoll sent the author a copy of the letter with permission to use it

Louise Pound

Page 76: For Louise Pound beginning to play tennis at age 14, and for her placing greater weight on learning and teaching than on sports see Yost, Nellie Snyder, "Nebraska's Scholarly Athlete: Louise Pound, 1872-1958," *Nebraska History,* 1983 Winter, Vol. 64, pp. 477-90.

Page 76: For a history of tennis in the U.S. see *Encyclopedia Americana,* Vol. 26, P. 494

Page 77: for a description of Lincoln's first tennis club see Millane, Jean, "Dr. Louise Pound Recalls Lincoln's First Tennis Club," *Lincoln Sunday Journal & Star,* March 9, 1944

Page 77: For Louise Pound as city of Lincoln tennis champion and the only female member of the tennis club as well as her games with S.L. Geisthardt and "Jumbo" Stiehm see Simpson, Evelyn, "Louise Pound, Sports Champion . . . and Teacher," *Omaha World-Herald,* Sunday Magazine, Section C. pp. 4-5

Page 77: For the account of Canfield and Pershing laying out the tennis courts see *The Lasso,* Vol. 1, No.5, February 1, 1892, University of Nebraska (Lincoln) Special Collections Archives

Page 77: For an account of Pershing's years at the University of Nebraska see Knoll, Robert, *prairie university: A History of the University of Nebraska,* (Lincoln) University of Nebraska Press. 1995, pp. 34-35,

Page 78: For information about Louise Pound's 1891 and 1892 tennis championships and her participation in intercollegiate championships see Simpson

Page 78-79: For Louise Pound's letter to her parents describing her 1897 tennis championship, see NSHS Archives, Louise Pound Papers, Box 1

Page 79: For the mind set of a competitive tennis player see Scott, Eugene, *Tennis: Game of Motion,* (New York) Crown Publications, 1973, p. 132

Pages 79-80: For a list of the newspaper accounts reporting Louise Pound's Chicago tennis championships during the summer of 1898, see University of Nebraska Special Collections/Archives, Louise Pound Papers, Biography-bibliography box. For complete articles reporting the tennis matches see the following issues of *The Lincoln Journal:* August 11, 1898, p.4. August 12, 1898, p.6. August 13, 1898, p.8. August 14, 1898, p.5. August 20, 1898, p. 5. August 22, 1898, p. 3.

Page 81: for an undated newspaper clipping concerning Louise Pound's Chicago tennis wins published beneath the photograph of Lydia Pinkham see NSHS Archives, Louise Pound Papers, Box 34. (Louise had refused to pose for news reporters.)

Page 81: For information about Lydia Pinkham see Weatherford, Doris, *American Women's History,* (New York) Prentice-Hall General Reference, 1994, pp. 270-71

Page 81: For Louise Pound and Carrie Neely's 1915 tennis doubles championships see Simpson

Pages 81-82: For the letter from Robert Cecil MacMahon, a former classmate of Louise at the University of Chicago see NSHS Archives, Louise Pound Papers, Box 1, File 2

Page 82: For the background of Anne Barr Clapp, head of Women's Athletics until 1902, see Knoll, p.31

Page 82: For an account of basketball reaching the University and the not uncommon incidents of players' having black eyes, see Manley, Robert, *Centennial History of the University of Nebraska,* (Lincoln) University of Nebraska Press, 1969, p. 304

Pages 82-83: For a clipping describing Louise Pound playing basketball at the University of Chicago see NSHS Archives, Louise Pound Papers, Box 18, Scrapbook

Page 83: For Louise Pound's letter to her sister about her bicycle saddle see NSHS Archives, Louise Pound Papers, Box 1

Page 83: For Louise Pound's account of her athletic accomplishments as told to Schrag see Schrag, Gretchen, "Miss Pound, English Professor, Reveals Tales of Times When She Had Tennis, Bicycle, Golf Titles," *The Daily Nebraskan,* Vol. 31, No. 92, 23 February 1932.

Page 84: For Knoll's statement that Louise wanted to "win" and "lead the parade," see a copy of Knoll's letter to Butters Part Three: Career And Lifestyle Changes: 1899-1920

CHAPTER NINE:

Page 86: For an account of Willa Cather antagonizing Professor Sherman see Robinson, Phyllis, C. *Willa: The Life of Willa Cather.* Garden City, N.Y. Doubleday & Co. 1983. p.74

Page 87: for a German degree as the ultimate in higher education causing Pound to attend Heidelberg University for it, see Johnson, Alvin. *Pioneer's Progress.* New York. Viking Press. 1952. p. 156

Pages 87: For a history of German Universities and their setting the standard for scholarship in the Western World see *Encyclopedia Americana*. Vol. 12. p. 621. (Edition?)

Pages 87-88: for Pound's decision to try for her doctorate degree from a German University and for her decision to attend Heidelberg because of Dr. Hoops' encouragment see Pound, Louise. "Then and Now." Publications of the Modern-Language-Association-of-America. Vol. LXXI. March 1956. No. 1. NSHS Archives, Louise Pound Papers, Box 29

Page 88: For the date of Roscoe's marriage to Grace Gerrard and his mother's positive opinion of Grace see Sayre, Paul. *The Life of Roscoe Pound.* (Iowa City College of Law Committee. State University of Iowa.) 1948. pp. 112-114

Page 88: For a description of Louise Pound as stated on her 1899 passport see NSHS Archives. Louise Pound Papers. Box 1. Biographical information file.

Page 88-89: For the description of Louise as "something to look at" on her arrival in Heidelberg, see Simpson, Evelyn. "Louise Pound, Sports Champion . . . and Teacher." *Omaha World-Herald*. Sunday Magazine. Section C. p. 114

Pages 89-90: For Mark Twain's description of Heidelberg and the routines of university students and professors see Twain, Mark. (Samuel L. Clemens.) *A Tramp Abroad.* London. Chatto & Windus. 1891. Republished by Grosse Pointe Woods Michigan. Scholarly Press. 1968. pp. 24-26, 577-588

Page 90: For the view of Heidelberg as enshrining "youth in its last period of care-freeness ..." see Laughlin, Clara E. *So You're Going to Germany and Austria.* Boston and New York. Houghton Mifflin Co. 1930. pp. 99-100

Page 91: About winning the Heidelberg 1899 Women's Tennis Championship, see Becker, Dick. "Louise Pound Named to Journal's Sports Hall of Fame." *Lincoln Journal Star.* February 1, 1955

Pages 91-96: Louise Pound's letters to her family during her year in Heidelberg are found in NSHS Archives, Olivia Pound Papers, Box 1, Folder 1, Olivia Pound Letters 1897-1955

Pages 93-94: For information about Adele Lathrop who shared Louise Pound's Heidelberg quarters see NSHS Archives, Louise Pound Papers, Box 34, Clippings folder.

Pages 97-98: For Louise Pound's account of the Heidelberg Cricket game see clipping, "Looking Back–'Not All Word Authorities in Educational Institutions.'"August 5, 1951. NSHS Archives, Louise Pound Papers, Box 33.

CHAPTER TEN:

Page 99: For Louise's reassuring her family that she has "plenty of friends" see NSHS Archives, Olivia Pound Papers, Box 1,Folder 1.

Pages 99-102: For Ani Königsberger's description of her family background and her feelings for Louise see NSHS Archives, Louise Pound Correspondence, Box 1

Page 103: For an explanation of "ardent" friendships between turn-of-the-century women see Smith-Rosenberg, Carroll. *Disorderly Conduct: Visions of Gender in Victorian America, (*New York, Oxford) Oxford University Press, 1985, p.28.

Pages 103-104: For Ani's 1902 letter about men's treatment of women and Ani and Louise's attitudes toward marriage see NSHS Archives, Louise Pound Papers, correspondence Files Box 1 and 1A

Page 104: For reasons New Women avoided marriage from the 1870s through the 1920s see Smith-Rosenberg. p.253

Page 104-105: For Jane Addams explanation of women avoiding marriage see Elshtain, Jean Bethke. *Jane Addams and the Dream of American Democracy,* (New York) Basic Books, 2002, p.114.

Page 106: For the derision of New Women by the press see Marks, Patricia, *Bicycles, Bangs, and Bloomers: The New Woman in the Popular Press,* (Lexington Kentucky) The University of Kentucky Press, 1990, pp. 1-2

Page 106: For the poem, "The New Woman," see *Puck* Magazine, March 6, 1895, Vol. XXXVII, No. 939, p.41

CHAPTER ELEVEN:

Louise Pound

Page 108: For Louise Pound's letter to Olivia asking for news of the Spanish American War see NSHS Archives, Olivia Pound Papers, Box 1, Folder 1

Page 108: For information about the Spanish Civil War see Yanik, Ted, and Cornelison, Pam, *The Great American History Fact-Finder*(Boston, New York) Houghton Mifflin Company, 1993, p. 360

Page 108: For an explanation of Bryan losing the 1900 election see Sheldon, Addison Erwin, A.M., Ph.D. *Nebraska: The Land and the People,* (Chicago, New York) Lewis Publishing Company, 1931, pp. 777-81

Page 108: For a description of Bryan's position in Lincoln see Olson, James C. And Naugle, Ronald C., *History of Nebraska,* Third Edition, (Lincoln & London) University of Nebraska Press, 1997, p. 253

Page 108: For reference to Bryan's daughter, Ruth, as "colorful" see Knoll, Robert, *prairie university: A History of the University of Nebraska,* (Lincoln, London) University of Nebraska Press, 1995, Picture 29

Page 108: For McKinley's assassination and America's role as a world power see Yanik and Cornelison, *Great American History Fact-Finder,* (Boston, New York) Houghton Mifflin Company, p. 360-61

Page 108: For information about the U.S. role in building the Panama Canal see Yanik and Cornelison, p.301

Page 108-109: For America's brief period of imperialism see Sullivan, Mark, *Our Times: The United States 1900-1925: The Turn of the Century,* (New York, London) Charles Scribner's Sons, 1926, pp 47-55

Page 109: For the dilemma facing women in male dominated professions such as university teaching positions see Chafe, William H, *The American Woman: Her Changing Social, Economic, and Political Roles, 1920-1970,* (London, Oxford, New York) Oxford University Press, 1972, pp. 99-100. Also see Smith-Rosenberg, Carroll, *Disorderly Conduct,* (New York, Oxford) Oxford University Press, 1985, p. 176

Page 109: For telephone slang and popular songs see Schlereth, *Victorian America: Transformations in Everyday Life* 1876-1915, (New York) Harper Collins Publishers, 1991, p. 191

Page 109-110: For a description of turn-of-the-century Lincoln see Olson and Naugle, p. 253

Page 110: For number of plays appearing in a week's time in Lincoln see Slote, Bernice, *The Kingdom of Art,* (Lincoln) University of Nebraska Press, 1966, p.7

Page 110: For Knoll's description of Sherman as "a rather pathetic man . . ." see Knoll, p. 70. For his retirement date see p.77

Page 110: For the source of making "English as hard as Greek," stated by Francis A. March, see Graff, Gerald, (Chicago & London) University of Chicago Press, 1987, p 98-99

Page 110: For reference to students as "passive buckets" stated by Fred Lewis Pattee, see Graff, p. 110

Page 110: For Arthur Kennedy's observation on the "smooth clarity" of Louise's teaching see Pound, Louise, *The Selected Writings of Louise Pound,* Foreword by Arthur Kennedy p. x

Page 110-111: For the background of Louise Pound's membership in the American Dialect Society see the summary of her life written by Norman E. Eliason, Kemp Malone, Alan Walker Read, George P. Wilson, Mamie J. Meredith, Chairman, "Louise Pound: 1872-1958." Bennett Martin Library, (Lincoln) Pound Family File

Page 111: For Louise Pound's attitude toward language research see NSHS Archives, Louise Pound Papers, Box 20, "The American Dialect Society."

Page 111: For a listing of articles Louise Pound wrote see Pound, Louise, *Selected Writings of Louise Pound,* (Lincoln) University of Nebraska Press, 1949, "Bibliography, Professional Activities and Vita" by Mamie Meredith and Ruth O'Dell. pp. 349-361

Page 112: For the statement that Louise Pound wrote about "Nebraska authors and Nebraska folkways when scholars in . . ." see Cognard, Anne M, "Louise Pound: Renaissance Woman," *Perspectives: Women in Nebraska History,* Nebraska Department of Education and the Nebraska State Council for the Social Studies, Special Issue, p. 156

Page 112: For Evelyn Haller's statement that Louise investigated areas considered unimportant by many English professors see Cox, Gerry; Macdaniels, Carol; Helzer, Chris, *Guide to Nebraska Authors,* Dageford Publishing Co. 1998. p. 187.

Page 112: For figures on University enrollment in 1900 and 1910 see Knoll, Robert E., *prairie university: A History of the University of Nebraska,* (Lincoln & London) University of Nebraska Press, 1995, p. 41

Pages 112-113: For Knoll's description of Chancellor George MacLean as "cool" and for Bessey again acting as Chancellor, see Knoll, p. 41

Page 113: For an account of Andrews' past appointments before accepting the Nebraska Chancellorship see Knoll, p.42

Page 113: For an account of Andrews' hiring independent thinkers as staff members see Knoll, pp. 46-47

Page 113: For Edward A. Ross' influence on Roscoe Pound, see Knoll, p. 47

Page 113: For Wish's description of Roscoe Pound as "the most scholarly expositor of sociological jurisprudence," see Wish, Harvey, *Society and Thought in Modern America*, (New York, Toronto, London) Longmans Green & Co, 1959, p. 326

Pages 113-114: For Roscoe Pound's criticism of closed legal systems see Wigdor, David, *Roscoe Pound: Philosopher of Law*, (Westport Connecticut, London England) Greenwood Press, 1974, p 205

Page 114: For changes Roscoe Pound implemented at the University of Nebraska Law College see Knoll, p. 50-51

Page 114: For Roscoe Pound's ground-breaking speech at the St. Paul Minnesota Bar Association meeting, see Wigdor, pp. 188-190. Also see Johnson, J.R., *Representative Nebraskans*, (Lincoln) Johnsen Publishing Company, 1954, p. 162.

Page 114: For a record of Roscoe Pound's career advancement see Sayre, Paul, *The Life of Roscoe Pound*, (Iowa City) College of Law Committee, State University of Iowa, 1948, "Table of Dates," pp. 2-3. Also see Johnson, p. 162

Page 114: For an account of Andrews' encouraging football at the University and changing the team name from bugeaters to cornhuskers, see Knoll, p.43

Page 115: For the poem "Dr. Louise Pound" and the picture of her holding a tennis racket see University of Nebraska Special Collections in Love Library, Louise Pound Papers, Bio-bib box

Page 116: For the poem "Our Favorite," and the photograph of Louise in a stylish hat see NSHS Archives, Louise Pound Papers, Box 18, 1916 *Cornhusker Yearbook*

Pages 116-117: For the account of Louise and Marguerite McPhee signing a mock legal contract for Louise to travel across Lincoln on roller skates see NSHS Archives, Louise Pound Papers, Box 30

Page 117: For Louise's statements about the basketball teams successes and other women's athletic achievements see Schrag, Gretchen, "Miss Pound, English Professor, Reveals Tales of Times When She Had Tennis, Bicycle, Golf Titles," *The Daily Nebraskan*, Vol. 31, No. 92, 23 February 1932

Page 118: For Louise Pound and Anne Barr Clapp's basketball rules for women see NSHS Archives, Louise Pound Papers, Box 26.

Page 118: For a summary of the basketball rules that Pound and Clapp wrote see Lowenthal, Kristi, *Mabel Lee and Louise Pound: The University of Nebraska's Battle Over Women's Intercollegiate Athletics*, A Thesis, July 1999, pp. 53-54

Page 118: For Louise Pound's report of the last basketball game played with Minnesota in 1910 see Yost, Nellie Snyder. "Nebraska's Scholarly Athlete: Louise Pound 1872-1958," *Nebraska History*, No. 64, 1983, pp. 477-87

Page 119: For information on Ina Gittings see "Miss Gittings Retires from UA Staff," *Tucson Daily News*. 8 June 1955

CHAPTER TWELVE:

Page 120: For Andrews resignation of chancellorship and Roscoe Pound turning down the position see Knoll, Robert E. *prairie university: A History of the University of Nebraska*, (Lincoln & London) University of Nebraska Press, 1995, p. 51.

Page 120: For University losing its standing as a leading university, see Knoll, p. 57.

Page 120: For the regents choice of Avery as chancellor, Avery's background, and his persistence in applying for the job, see Knoll, p. 157

Page 120: For Louise Pound's opinion of Chancellor Avery see Knoll, p. 79

Page 121: For Alvin Johnson's comments about the quality of University student he encountered in 1906 see Manley, Robert N., *Centennial History of the University of Nebraska*, (Lincoln) University of Nebraska Press, 1969, p. 237

Page 121: For Flexner's establishing the College of Medicine and achievements of other University faculty see Knoll, p. 58

Page 121-122: For Hartley Burr's influence on Louise Pound's approach to folklore, see Knoll, p. 47

Page 122: For Alexander as the intellectual center on campus from 1910 to 1925 see Knoll, p. 71

Page 122: For Alexander's opinions on education and culture see Knoll, pp. 73-74. For Alexander's background see Knoll, p. 71

Page 123: For Louise Pound and Alexander's friendship see, Pound, Louise, "The Undergraduate Years of Hartley Burr Alexander," *Prairie Schooner,* December 1948, Vol. XXII, pp. 372-80

Page 123: For Mari Sandoz recalling Louise Pound's advice to write about the people and places she knew, see Sandoz, Mari, *Love Song to the Plains,* (Lincoln) University of Nebraska Press, 1961, p. 238

Page 123: For *The Dial*'s review of Pound's *Folksong of Nebraska and the Central West: A Syllabus,* see NSHS Archives, Louise Pound Papers, Box 33, Clippings file

Page 124: For categories listed in Pound's folklore syllabus and the editor's, (Addison E. Sheldon) preface statements see NSHS Archives Louise Pound Papers. Pound, Louise. *Folksong of Nebraska and the Central West: A Syllabus.* Nebraska Ethnology and Folkore Series

Page 124: for a listing of Cather's novels published from 1913-1917, see Olson, James C. and Naugle, Ronald C. *History of Nebraska.* Third Edition. Lincoln & London. University of Nebraska Press. 1997. p. 261

Page 125: For Alexander's explanation of student's view of Louise Pound see Alexander, Hartley Burr," *Roundup: A Nebraska Reader,* Faulkner, Virginia, editor, (Lincoln) University of Nebraska Press, 1957, p. 236

CHAPTER THIRTEEN:

Page 127: For the location of Lincoln's first country club and golf course see "Women Finalists in City Golf Tourney Rivals in Lincoln Sports for 25 Years," Bennett Martin Library, (Lincoln) Pound Family File, Newspaper Clipping, October 3, 1936

Page 127: For the record of Louise Pound's golf championships see "Dr. Louise Pound Named to Journal's Sports Hall of Fame," *Lincoln Journal,* February 1, 1955.

Page 127: For the poem "To the Champion" see NSHS Archives, Louise Pound Papers, Box 33, Clippings file

Page 128: For the description of Roscoe Pound as a "fun-loving" student see Knoll, Robert E., *prairie university: A History of the University of Nebraska,* (Lincoln) University of Nebraska Press, 1995, p.30

Page 129: For Louise Pound's role in starting the Golden Fleece Society see Simpson, Evelyn, "Louise Pound, Sports Champion . . . and Teacher," *Omaha World-Herald* magazine, June 1945, Section C

Page 129: For Louise Pound's descriptions of meetings and activities of the Golden Fleece, see Pound, Louise, "Do You Remember?" *Nebraska Alumnus,* Nov. 1954, pp. 12, 23.

Page 130: For Mencken's prose contribution to the Golden Fleece see NSHS Archives, Louise Pound Papers, Box 19, Scrapbook.

Page 130-131: For the demise of the Golden Fleece, see Simpson

Page 131: About the "Dumbbells" and "Nutts" student organizations see Pound, Louise, "Do You Remember?" *Nebraska Alumnus,* Nov. 1954, pp. 12, 23

Pages 131-132: For Louise's report of the Nutts demise and her letter protesting it see NSHS Archives, Louise Pound Papers, Box 19.

Page 132: For the comment that Louise "took ten years off" a chancellor's life, see Knoll, p. 78-79

Page 132: For information about the Wooden Spoon Society see NSHS Archives, Olivia Pound Papers, Box 5, 1961 Correspondence file.

Page 133: For the offices Louise Pound held in AAUW see Pound, Louise, *The Selected Writings of Louise Pound,* (Lincoln) University of Nebraska Press, 1949, p. 363

Page 133: For contents of Louise Pound's will see NSHS Archives, Louise Pound Papers. Also see University of Nebraska Special Collections, Love Library, Louise Pound Papers, Box 1, Undated clipping, "Authoress Revised Her Will."

Page 133: For Olivia Pound's contribution to the Louise Pound Fellowship Award, see NSHS Archives, Olivia Pound Papers

Page 133: For offices Louise Pound held in Phi Beta Kappa see, Pound, p. 363

Page 133: For Leta Stetter Hollingworth's letter to Louise Pound concerning a prejudicial item in *School and Society* see NSHS Archives, Louise Pound Papers, Box 1.

Page 134: For offices Louise Pound held in the Modern Language Association and a list of other professional organizations in which she held a membership see Pound, p. 362-63

CHAPTER FOURTEEN:

Page 135: For Sayre's account of Stephen Pound's death see Sayre, Paul, *The Life of Roscoe Pound*, (Iowa City) College of Law Committee, State University of Iowa, 1948, p. 34

Page 136: For Stephen Pound's obituary see NSHS Archives, Laura Pound Papers, Box 1, Scrapbook

Page 137: For Olivia Pound's recollection of her mother's decision to fill the "empty space" in their home with girls needing to finish their educations see Bennett Martin Library, (Lincoln) Pound Family Papers, Clipping, Jenkins, Bess, "Frail Olivia Pound Still Teacher at Heart," *Lincoln Journal Star*, February 5, 1961, p.6B

Page 137: For Mamie Meredith's account of the Laura, Louise and Olivia Pound's influence on their boarders see University of Nebraska Special Collections Archives, Love Library, (Lincoln) Louise Pound Papers, Box 1.

Page 138: For Anne Marie Rhetus' letter describing life in the Pound home, see University of Nebraska Special Collections Archives, Love Library, (Lincoln) Louise Pound Papers, Box 1

Page 139: For Sunday afternoon meetings of Chi Delta Phi in the Pound home see NSHS Archives, Louise Pound Papers, Box 33, Clippings

Page 139: For the letter from an anonymous writer describing the Sunday afternoon gatherings in the Pound home and the description of Louise Pound's study see NSHS Archives, Louise Pound Papers, Box 33

CHAPTER FIFTEEN:

Page 140: For a list of World War I organizations in which Louise Pound held memberships see Pound, Louise, *The Selected Writings of Louise Pound*, (Lincoln), University of Nebraska Press, 1949, p. 364

Page 140: For information concerning the activities of the Nebraska State Council of Defense see Creigh, Dorothy Weyer, *Nebraska, Where Dreams Grow*, (Lincoln) Miller & Paine, 1980, pp. 79-81

Page 140: For Nebraskans who were of German descent and "old populist progressives" opposition to the war, and Bryan's resignation as Secretary of State and George W. Norris's opposition to the war, see Olson, James C. and Naugle, Ronald C., *History of Nebraska*, Third Edition, (Lincoln & London) University of Nebraska Press, 1997, p 278

Page 141: For an account of the trial of University faculty members before the board of regents for failing to support the war see Olson & Naugle, p. 281

Page 141: For information concerning Pershing and Dawes' wartime service see Olson & Naugle, pp. 284-85

Page 141: For the five published letters Louise Pound wrote to Dorothy Canfield Fisher about the war see Madigan, Mark J., *Keeping Fires Burning Night and Day: Selected Letters of Dorothy Canfield Fisher*, (Columbia & London) University of Missouri Press, 1993, pp. 49,54, 56-57, 61-62

Pages 142-143: For biographical information about Dorothy Canfield Fisher see Madigan, p.1-2 (introduction)

Pages 144-145: For Fisher's letters to Pound concerning her wartime activities and her advice to Pound about sending supplies to the French people see NSHS Archives, Louise Pound Papers, Box 1, File 2

Pages 145-146: For newspaper accounts of soap collecting and distribution headed by Louise Pound see NSHS Archives, Louise Pound Papers, Box 30, Unnamed clippings file.

Page 147: For information about the 1918 influenza epidemic in Lincoln see Copple, Neale, *Tower On The Plains, Lincoln's Centennial History 1859-1959*, (Lincoln) Centennial Commission Publishers, 1959, p. 114

Louise Pound

Part Four

Chapter Sixteen:

Page 149: For Smith-Rosenberg's findings of women achieving their greatest "professional visibility and political activism" before and after the first World War see Smith-Rosenberg, *Disorderly Conduct: Visions of Gender in Victorian America*, (New York, Oxford) Oxford University Press, 1985, p. 34

Page 149: For information about Louise co-founding *American Speech* see Mencken H.L., *The New American Language* with annotations and new material by Rauen I. McDavid, Jr., with the assistance of David W. Maurer, (U.S.) Alfred A. Knopf, Borzoi Book, 1977, pp. 61-62

Page 149: For Pound's emphasizing the differences between American and British English see, Mencken, *The New American Language,* p. 410

Page 150: For quotations from Mencken's letter which stated that articles of Louise Pound and her students encouraged his interest in language study see Bode, Carl, *The New Mencken Letters,* (New York) Dial Press, 1977, p. 134

Page 150: For Louise Pound's article, "Word Coinages and Modern Trade Names" which influenced Mencken, see *Dialect Notes*, Vol. IV, 1913, pp. 29-41

Page 150: For Pound and her students investigating the "general speechways" of the entire U.S. and for *s* being the only outlet for the work of American Language scholars, see Bode, pp. 134, 64-65

Page 150: For Pound's efforts to prevent the dissolution of the American Dialect Society see NSHS Archives, Louise Pound Papers, 1940s file

Page 151: For Botkins' description of Pound and Mencken's personalities see University of Nebraska Special Collections Archives, Botkin Papers, Box 13A, Folder 1, contains a review of Louise Pound's *Selected Writings.*

Page 151: For Pound's realization that differences between American and English speech were great enough to merit individual treatment see, Bode, p 410

Page 151: For Mencken's Nov. 17, 1921, letter to Louise Pound see New York Public Library, Manuscript and Archives Division, H.L. Mencken Papers.

Page 151: For Louise enjoying cocktails before dinner see copy of Robert E. Knoll's letter to Ronald R. Butters, Editor, *American Speech,* Department of English, Duke University, Durham, North Carolina, 27706. 7 June 1983

Pages 151-152: For facts about Mencken's life and his reporting of the Scopes "Monkey" Trial see the following: http://www.law.umkc.edu/faculty/projects/trials/scopes/menk.htm. http://en.wikipedia.org/wki/H.L.Mencken, / http://menckenhouse.org/aboutlm.htm Hart, James D., with revisions and additions by Leininger, Phillip, W., *The Oxford Companion to American Literature,* Sixth Edition, (New York, Oxford) 1995, p. 427

Pages 153-154: For Pound's forceful language advancing her theory of individual ballad composition see Pound, p.34. For von Humbolt's footnote see page 35

Page 154: For Louise Pound's prose as "detailed and quite, quite specific," see Cognard, Anne M. "Louise Pound: Renaissance Woman," *Perspectives: Women in Nebraska History,* Nebraska Department of Education and the Nebraska State Council for the Social Studies Special Issue, p. 153

Page 154: For Pound stating "five or six times her disregard for Grummere's communal ballad theory see Cognard, p. 154

Page 154: For Kittredge's background see Hart, James D, with revisions and additions by Leininger, Phillip, W., *The Oxford Companion to American Literature,* Sixth Edition, (New York, Oxford) Oxford University Press, 1995, p. 350.

Page 154: For Cognard's observation that Pound "brought to her studies the same ideal of Greek excellence that she brought to sports," see Cognard, p. 160

Page 155: For Cognard's statement "As songs progress from inception to use, they get worse," see Cognard, p. 161

Page 155: For Alexander's defense of Pound's ballad theory which includes Mencken's comments and his criticism of Professor G.H. Gerould's opinion of Pound's book, see Alexander, Hartley Burr, "On Pounding Dr. Pound," NSHS Archives, Box 33, Clippings

Pages 155-156: For Mencken's 11 May 1921 letter stating that Pound "wiped out" Grummere's theory with "one stroke," see New York Public Library, Manuscript and Archives Division, H.L. Mencken Papers

Page 156: For Pound's theory of individual ballad origins prevailing today see Brunvand, Jan Harold, *The Study of American Folklore: an introduction,* Third Edition, New York, London, W.W. Norton & Company, 1986, p. 274

Page 156: For Pound's advice given to a fellow student see Johnson, Alvin, *Pioneer's Progress,* (New York) Viking Press, 1952, p. 70

CHAPTER SEVENTEEN:

Page 157: For a list of Cather's novels published during the 1920's and brief comments on their contents see Hart, James D., with Revisions and Additions by Leininger, Phillip W., *The Oxford Companion to American Literature,* Sixth Edition, (New York, Oxford) Oxford University Press, 1995, p. 114

Page 157: For an account of the popularity of books about World War I and the authors, John Dos Passos, Ernest Hemingway, and Scott Fitzgerald, see Sullivan Mark, *Our Times: Vol. VI, The Twenties,* (New York) Charles Scribner's Sons, 1935, pp. 374-388

Page 158: For the general "disillusion," following the war years see Knoll, Robert E., *prairie university: A History of the University of Nebraska,* (Lincoln) University of Nebraska Press, 1995, p. 69

Page 158: For an account of the regents enforcing the rule against drinking alcohol and their restrictions on the use of cars on campus, see Christianson, Gale E., *Fox At The Woods Edge: A Biography of Loren Eisley,* (New York) Henry Holt & Co, 1990, p. 56

Page 158: For information about "drastic cuts" in the University's budget and the "egalitarian nature of higher education" see Knoll, pp. 69-72

Pages 158-159: For Willa Cather's remarks about changes in national atmosphere that encouraged young people to pursue vocational educations see Knoll, p. 72.

Page 159: For Alexander's views on teaching as an "art" rather than a science see, Knoll, p. 71

Page 159: For Alexander's views on schools serving as community centers see Masters, Margaret Dale, *Hartley Burr Alexander: Writer in Stone,* (Lincoln) Jacob North Printing Company, 1992, p. 90

Page 160: For a description of subject offerings in the 1890s University and for Alexander's student days at the University see Masters, pp. 81-83

Page 160: For Knoll's description of Avery's disgust with Alexander see Knoll, p.71

CHAPTER EIGHTEEN:

Page 162: For an explanation of the University Women's Athletic program under Anne Barr Clapp and her husband Dr. R.E. Clapp and the program's loss of recognition from the American Physical Education Association see Knoll, Robert E., *prairie university: A History of the University of Nebraska,* (Lincoln) University of Nebraska Press, 1995, p. 77

Page 163: For information about the pendulum swinging backward concerning the effect of sports on women's bodies see Roth, Linda Gage, "Are Sports Harmful to Women?" *The Forum,* May 1929, pp. 313-318. (Roth also presented facts proving that sports did not harm women's bodies.)

Pages 163-164: For a record of Lee's childhood sports participation see Lowenthal, Kristi, *Mabel Lee and Louise Pound: The University of Nebraska's Battle Over Women's Intercollegiate Athletics,* Thesis, (Lincoln) July 1999, pp. 17-19

Page 164: For Lee's childhood bouts of illness causing her to lag behind her sisters in athletic accomplishments see Peiper, Don. "Fitness Expert Far From Being a Dud," *Lincoln Sunday Journal Star.* 11 September 1983.

Page 164: For Lee's career history see Lowenthal, pp. 20-28

Pages 164-165: For Lee's clothing choice for her interview with Chancellor Avery see, Lee, Mabel, *Memories Beyond Bloomers,* (Washington D.C.) American Alliance for Health, Physical Education, and Recreation, 1978. p. 6

Page 165: For Lee's opinion of Louise Pound's Basketball rules see Lee, pp. 44-45

Page 165: For Pound's initial endorsement of Lee's appointment see Knoll, p.78

Page 166: For Lee's account of Pound's reaction to the brochure explaining the new organization of University women's athletics see Lee, p. 36

Page 167: For Avery's statement to Lee about Louise Pound trying to "pull you around, too, by the nose," see Lee, pp. 44-45

Page 167: For Knoll's description of Louise Pound as an antagonist who "wanted to defeat the men," and her standing with administrators and deans as "difficult," see Knoll, pp. 78-79

Pages 167-168: For Lee's opinion of Nebraskans see Lee, p. 38

Page 168: For Pound's standing in Lincoln society compared to Lee's, see Knoll p. 78

Page 168: For Lowenthal's statement that the feud between Pound and Lee was not "well-documented," see Lowenthal, p. 10

CHAPTER NINETEEN:

Page 170: For a record of Pound's services as visiting professor in other colleges and universities see NSHS Archives, Louise Pound Papers, Box 18, Scrapbook.

Pages 170-171: For the poem about Louise published in the 15 July 1923 *San Francisco Examiner*, see NSHS Archives, Box 18, Scrapbook

Page 171: For Louise Pound's itinerary as she traveled to England for the International Language Conference see NSHS Archives, Louise Pound Papers, Box 34, Clipping from unidentified Lincoln newspaper

Page 171: For information about Louise staying at the American Club because of her friendship with Ruth Bryan Owen, see NSHS Archives, Louise Pound Papers, Box 34, Folder 5, Clipping "Miss Pound Only Woman at Session."

Page 172: For the contents of Louise's letter to Olivia describing her experience as the only woman delegate to the International Language Conference and her willingness to speak up, see NSHS Archives, Louise Pound Papers, Box 1. Correspondence

Page 172: For Louise's remark that she would like to see national spellings brought into closer accord as well as looking into matters of pronunciation see NSHS Archives, Louise Pound Papers, Box 34, Folder 5, Clipping from the London *Times*, "Pure English. Points of Disputed Usage."

Page 172: For Bernard Shaw's remark that "exactly 42,767,500 dialects are spoken on the British Isles . . ." see NSHS Archives, Louise Pound Papers, Box 34, Folder 5, Clipping titled "Unifying the Language" from unidentified July 12 newspaper

Page 172: For the London newspaper stating that the remedy for unorthodox writing styles "lies beyond the power of committees and councils," see NSHS Archives, Louise Pound Papers, Box 34, File 5, London *Times* clipping, Monday, June 20, 1927, "The English Language."

Page 172: For Louise Pound's report on her activities during her London stay, see NSHS Archives, Louise Pound Papers, Box 1, Correspondence, (Letter to Olivia.)

Page 173: For Louise Pound's remark to a reporter that "'it is of interest to know that a Phi Beta Kappa can be a world's champion of tennis,'" see NSHS Archives, Louise Pound Papers, Box 34, Folder 5

Page 173: For information about Wimbledon winner, Helen Wills see *Encyclopedia Americana*, Vol. 28, pp. 805-06

Page 173: For Louise Pound's itinerary as she returned to the U.S. and her cancellation of further travel plans see NSHS Archives, Louise Pound Papers, Box 34, clipping titled "Louise Pound, Back From Council of English at London Saw Helen Wills in Title Match."

Page 173: For Louise Pound's account of buying her first car see copy of Robert E. Knoll's letter to Ronald R. Butters, editor, *American Speech*, Department of English, Duke University, Durham, North Carolina, 27706, 7 June 1983

Page 174: For Knolls assessment of the Chancellor Burnett as a "man of authority," and also of Mabel Lee's opinion of Burnett see Knoll, Robert E., *prairie university: A History of the University of Nebraska*, (Lincoln) University of Nebraska Press, 1995, p.81

Page 174: For Louise Pound's travel itinerary in November 1927, and her visit at the Charles C. Dawes

Chicago home and attending a Chicago Symphony performance with Carrie Neely see NSHS Archives, Louise Pound Papers, Box 34, File 8, Newspaper clipping of Nov. 27, 1927

Pages 174-175: For a summary of Charles C. Dawes life see Hickey, Donald, R., *Nebraska Moments: Glimpses of Nebraska's Past,* (Lincoln & London) University of Nebraska Press, 1992, pp. 183-89

Page 175: For an account of Grace Gerrard Pound's death see Sayre, Paul, *Roscoe Pound,* (Iowa City) College of Law Committee, State University of Iowa, 1948, pp. 118-119

Page 175: For obituaries of Laura Pound see NSHS Archives, Laura Pound Papers, Box 1, Scrapbook.

Page 176: For Dick Lehmer's letter of condolence on Laura Pound's death see NSHS Archives, Louise Pound Papers, Box 1, Folder 2, Letter dated Dec 22, 1928

Page 176: For Adele Lathrop and Emily Sweet's letters of condolence, see NSHS Archives, Olivia Pound Papers, Box 5.

CHAPTER TWENTY

Page: 178: For Simpson's statement that Louise was willing to put her job on the line when defending colleagues, see Simpson, Evelyn, "Louise Pound, Sports Champion ... and Teacher," *Omaha World-Herald,* Sunday Magazine, Section C, pp. 4-5

Page 178: For Lowenthal's description of Louise Pound's "sportsman's creed," with its emphasis on fairness and clean play" see Lowenthal, Kristi, *Mabel Lee and Louise Pound: The University of Nebraska's Battle Over Women's Intercollegiate Athletics,* A thesis, (Lincoln) July 1999, p. 69

Page 178: For Mamie Meredith's comment that she and others wouldn't have stayed at the University without Louise' support see University of Nebraska Special Collections Archives, Louise Pound Papers, Bio-bib box, 9 May 1938 letter from Meredith to Max J. Herzberg, editor of *Word Study*

Page 179: For Louise Pound's defense of Ruth Odell' study of Helen Hunt Jackson when English department chairman Thomas M. Raysor declared Meredith's work "impermissible and subliterary," see Knoll, Robert E., *prairie university: A History of the University of Nebraska,* (Lincoln) University of Nebraska Press, 1995, pp. 128-29

Page 179 : For Botkin's remarks about Pound's "colonial Quaker heritage" and her family's stress on "integrity, truth, service, and sociability," see Botkin, B.A., "First Lady of Letters: Retrospective-1957," *Nebraska Round-Up,* Faulkner, Virginia, editor (Lincoln). University of Nebraska Press, 1957, pp. 232-36

Page 180: For Stepanek's letter containing W.A. Neilson's recommendation of Louise Pound for the next University English department head, see NSHS Archives, Louise Pound Papers, Box 1, Undated file.

Page 180: For Knoll's account of the Thomas N. Raysor, appointed English department head in 1930, see Knoll, p.128.

Page 180: For Sandoz's evaluation of Louise Pound's attitude toward language as a "growing thing," see Sandoz, Mari, *Love Song to the Plains,* (Lincoln) University of Nebraska Press, 1961, p. 237

Page 180-181: For *Atlantic Monthly* editor, Edward Weeks'letter asking Louise to verify Mari Sandoz's accounts of her father's life, see NSHS Archives, Louise Pound Papers, Box 1, 1935 file, (May 31, 1935.)

Page 181: For Louise Pound staying in Lincoln not because of family and friend, but because she was "a woman of the Plains, not the geographical Plains so much as of the other vast Plains country–language," see Sandoz, p. 236

Pages 181-182: For Louise Pound as one of the American women who pursued careers in male-dominated fields thus violating "the most deeply held conceptions of (their) proper role," see Chafe, William H., *The American Woman: Her Changing Social, Economic and Political Roles 1920-1970,* (Oxford, London) Oxford University Press, 1972, pp. 99-100

Page 182: For Knoll's report on the Nebraska Democratic legislature cutting University funds during the 1930s see Knoll, Robert E., *prairie university: A History of the University of Nebraska,* (Lincoln & London) University of Nebraska Press, 1995, pp. 81, 88

Page 182: For Louise Pound's letter to Olivia written from Chicago's Del Prado Hotel see NSHS Archives, Louise Pound Papers, Correspondence Box, Undated letters file

Page 183: For background material on B.A. Botkin's life and his work in American speech and folklore see Murray, Michael L. "Benjamin Botkin," *Voices: The Journal of New York Folklore,* Vol. 27, Fall-Winter 2001, pp. 3-4.

Louise Pound

Page 183: For Louise Pound's letter advising Botkin to "soft-pedal" his plan to take classes that she teaches, see University of Nebraska Special Collections Archives, (Love Library) B.A. Botkin Papers, Box 432, Letter of 22 April 1930

Page 184: For Louise Pound's letter informing Botkin of faculty salary cuts and a rise in graduate students and references to a ballad paper she wrote see University of Nebraska Special Collections Archives, (Love Library), B.A. Botkin Papers, Box 432, 19 March 1932

Pages 184-185: For Botkin's praise of Pound's continued interest in her students after they leave the University see Botkin, B.A. "Pound Sterling: Letters From a 'Lady Professor,'" *Prairie Schooner*, Vol. 33, No. 1, Spring 1959, pp. 20-31

Page 185: For Dorothy Canfield Fisher's praise of Louise after a 1938 visit see NSHS Archives, Louise Pound Papers, Box 1, Correspondence 1930s.

CHAPTER TWENTY:

Page 188: For Louise Pound's letter of apology to Botkin for visiting his wife and children rather than him, see Botkin, B.A. "Pound Sterling: Letters from a 'Lady Professor,'" *Prairie Schooner*, Vol. 33, No. 1, Spring 1959, pp. 20-31

Page 188: For a list of Louise Pound's 1939 summer speech circuit see NSHS Archives, Louise Pound Papers, Box 33, Clippings file. (List written in Louise Pound's hand.)

Page 188: For Roscoe's advice to Louise when giving public speeches see copy of Knoll's letter to Ronald R. Butters, editor, *American Speech*, Department of English, Duke University, Durham, North Carolina, 27706, 7 June 1983

Pages 188-189: For Louise's participation in planning the *Washington Post* sponsored folklore festival and her comments about its importance see NSHS Archives, Louise Pound Papers, Box 25, Clippings file

Page 189: For a definition of 'Throttlebottom' as used by Louise Pound see Wordsmith.org

Page 189: For information about Louise and four other University of Nebraska graduates cited as "women of distinction" at the Women's Centennial Congress held at the Commodore Hotel November 25-27, 1940, see NSHS Archives, Louise Pound Papers, Box 35, Clipping and brochure

Page 189: For Louise's invitation to attend the Women's Centennial Congress, see NSHS Archives, Louise Pound Papers, Box 34

Pages 190-191: For Louise Pound's list of requirements for those pursuing a Ph.D. in English see NSHS Archives, Louise Pound Papers, Box 1, 1930s correspondence, July 5, 1932 letter to Professor O.J. Campbell

Page 191-192: For Knoll's account of Louise Pound as a teacher during her later years see copy of Knoll's letter to Ronald R. Butters

Page 192: For the statement that "probably no teacher was ever happier than Louise when one of her students received recognition for his or her work," see NSHS Archives, Louise Pound Papers, Box 33, (Anonymous writer.)

Page 192: For Louise Pound's attempt to help Knoll publish a paper see copy of Knoll's letter to Ronald R. Butters

Page 193: For Norman E. Eliason's letter thanking Louise for "help and advice," see NSHS Archives, Louise Pound Papers, undated Correspondence File

Page 193: For letter to Mamie Meredith describing Louise Pound's "lighter" side see University of Nebraska Special Collections Archives, Louise Pound Papers

Page 193: For the letter describing going to a movie and on a picnic etc, see NSHS Archives, Louise Pound Papers, 1940s correspondence file.

Pages 193-194: For Knoll's account of Louise entertaining students see copy of Knoll's letter to Butters

Page 194: For Mari Sandoz's account of Louise taking students into one of Lincoln's "better homes" to read their work, see Christianson, Gale F., *Fox At The Woods Edge: A Biography of Loren Eiseley*, (New York) Henry Holt & Co, 1990, p. 106

Notes and Sources

Pages 194-195: For the article about Chi Delta Phi members of the Lincoln chapter see NSHS Archives, Louise Pound Papers, Box 30, *Lincoln Sunday Journal and Star,* October 3, 1937, "Many Women Writers Connected With Nebraska U. Literary Organization."

Page 195: For the clipping stating that Louise Pound was "one of 28 distinguished linguistic, phonetic, and dictionary making scholars" who worked with Edward L. Thorndike compiling a dictionary for young people see NSHS Archives, Louise Pound Papers, Box 33, Clipping file. (The article also stated that she hadn't "shut herself in an ivory tower.")

Page 196: For the letters from Mencken requesting information from Louise for his *Dictionary of Americanisms* and asking her to recommend someone to write an article or to write is herself see NSHS Archives, Louise Pound Papers, Correspondence Box, 1932 file. This file also contains Mencken's reply stating that her article would "come along in late November."

Page 196: For George Grimes request that Louise attend the World-Herald sponsored Golden Gloves Tourney and write about it see NSHS Archives, Louise Pound Papers, Correspondence Box, 1940s file

Page 196: For Cecily Brownstone's requesting Louise Pouond's help in researching "children's secret languages" and thanking her for the resulting information see NSHS Archives, Louise Pound Papers, Correspondence Box, 1930s File

Page 196: For Mencken's August 21, 1942, letters describing Clinton Sanders' work in collecting words of the fighting forces and shipbuilding terms, see NSHS Archives, Louise Pound Papers, Correspondence Box, 1940s file

Page 196-197: For Clinton Sanders' letters to Louise Pound, see NSHS Archives, Correspondence Box, 1940s file

Page 197: For the 5 August 1951 newspaper article in which Louise Pound recalls Sanders' supplying the definition of "watchstuffing," see NSHS Archives, Louise Pound Papers, Box 33, Clippings file.

PART FIVE

CHAPTER TWENTY-TWO:

Page 199: For Copple's report of newspaper boys cycling through the streets of Lincoln on September 1, 1939, shouting "Extra..." see Copple, Neale, *Tower on the Plains: Lincoln's Centennial History: 1859-1959,* (Lincoln) Lincoln Centennial Publishers, Jacob North Inc., 1959, p. 155

Pages 199-200: For Ani Phister's account of Hitler's rise to power in German and the effect on the population see NSHS Archives, Louise Pound Papers, Correspondence Boxes, 1930s file

Page 200: For Dr. Johannes Hoops' letter stating that he would accept invitations to lecture at universities during his travels in the U.S. in 1937, see NSHS Archives, Louise Pound Papers, Correspondence Boxes, 1930s file

Page 200: For Ani Phister's letter about changes that had taken place in Heidelberg, see NSHS Archives, Louise Pound Papers, Correspondence Boxes, 1930s file

Page 200-201: For Samuel Eliot Morrison's explanation of Hitler's hold over the German people, see Morrison, Samuel Eliot, *The Oxford History of the American People,* (New York) Oxford University Press, 1965, p. 988

Page 201: For Sebastian Hoffner's description of German people who disagreed with Hitler's policies see Haffner, Sebastian, *Defying Hitler: A Memoir,* (Translated by Oliver Pretzel), (New York) Farrar Straus and Giroux, 2000, pp. 69-70

Page 201: For the account of University professors circulation of a petition urging U.S. assistance to England before U.S. participation in World War II, and for Chancellor Boucher's lack of action regarding military use of University facilities see Knoll, Robert E., *prairie university: A History of the University of Nebraska,* (Lincoln and London) University of Nebraska Press and University of Nebraska Alumni Association, 1995, pp. 102-03

Pages 201-202: For Chancellor Boucher's changes at the University of Chicago and his proposed changes at the University of West Virginia as well as Louise Pound's questioning him about his past appointments see Knoll, pp. 95-97

Page 202-203: For University participation in war efforts see Knoll, pp. 102-03

Louise Pound

Page 203: For Lincoln's contributions to U.S. defense during World War II see Copple, pp.155-162

Pages 203-204: For the effect of the war on Nebraska and its citizens and for the transition from economic depression to prosperity, see Creigh, Dorothy-Weyer, *Nebraska, Where Dreams Grow,* (Lincoln) Miller & Paine, Inc., 1980, pp. 136-38

Page 204: For Louise Pound's contributions of "War Words" to Mencken's American Language Studies see NSHS Archives, Louise Pound Papers, Box 11

Page 205: For Louise Pound's recommendation that her former student, Robert Luebs, be graduated "with distinction" or with "high distinction," see NSHS Archives, Louise Pound Papers, 1943 correspondence file

Page 205: For Louise Pound's statement of the obstacles women faced when studying for graduate degrees see, Pound, Louise, "The College Woman and Research," *Selected Writings of Louise Pound,* (Lincoln) University of Nebraska Press, 1949, p.310

Page 206: For a description of the second group of New Woman and their placing more emphasis on self-fulfillment than on social services, see Smith-Rosenberg, Carroll, *Disorderly Conduct: Visions of Gender in Victorian America,* (New York, Oxford) Oxford University Press, 1985, p. 177

Pages 206-207: For Dorothy Jane Hughes letters reporting on her work on an aircraft carrier and thanking Louise for recommending her for a teaching post at the University of Oregon after the war ended, see NSHS Archives, Louise Pound Papers, Correspondence files for 1943, 1944, and 1946

CHAPTER TWENTY-THREE:

Page 208: For Louise Pound's letter to Botkin announcing her retirement see Botkin, B.A., "Pound Sterling: Letters From a Lady Professor," *Prairie Schooner,* Vol. 33, No. 1, Spring 1959, pp. 20-31

Pages 208-209: For Ani Phister's letter hinting that Louise had complained about the declining quality of students who would be attending the University with the aid of the G.I. Bill see NSHSLouise Pound Papers. Correspondence Boxes. Ani Konigsberg Phister letters

Page 209: For Louise Pound's article praising the Victorian period for its "peace and order" see Pound, Louise, "The Class of 1892 ... fifty years after," *Nebraska Alumnus,* May 1942, P. 5

Page 209: For Louise Pound's remarks to Evelyn Simpson concerning the values of the present generation and her criticism of modern-day activities for girls see Simpson, Evelyn, "Louise Pound, Sports Champion ... and Teacher," *Omaha World-Herald* magazine, Section C, June 1945

Pages 209-210: For V. Royce West's letter to Louise offering her employment as a director of an Institute Committee on Flour Milling in Language and Literature, see NSHS Archives, Louise Pound Papers, Box 2, 1945 Correspondence file

Page 210: For Simpson's description of Louise's lifestyle in retirement see Simpson

Page 211: For Isobel McMonies Klopp's letter recalling Pound's statement that she would chose to teach science rather than English if given the opportunity in the present, see NSHS Archives, Louise Pound Papers, Correspondence Box 2, 1945 file

Pages 211-212: For Louise's letter to Botkin stating that she enjoyed keeping up the Pound home, see Botkin, "Pound Sterling....." pp. 20-31.

Pages 212-220, 222-227: For letters that Ani Phister wrote to Louise Pound throughout their long friendship see NSHS Archives, Louise Pound Papers, Correspondence Boxes 1 and 2. (Ani Königsberger Phister Letters.)

Page 213: For Haffner's description of the politically unstable era in Germany following World War I see Haffner, Sebastian, *Defying Hitler: A Memoir,* (Translated by Oliver Pretzel), (New York) Farrar, Straus and Giroux, 2000, pp. 69-70

Pages 213-214: For Cpl. Samuel F. Pughse,'s letter to Louise see NSHS Archives, Louise Pound Papers, Correspondence files Boxes 1 and 2

Pages 220-221: For Louise Pound's letter to the Dean of Student Affairs at Denver University, see NSHS Archives, Louise Pound Papers, Box 2, 1947 Correspondence file

Pages 221-222: For Mrs. Bovell's letter to Louise concerning the sale of Ani's jewels see NSHS Archives, Louise Pound Papers. Box 2, 1947 correspondence file

Pages 223-224: For Johannes Hoops' letter to Louise thanking her for the CARE package see NSHS Archives, Louise Pound Papers, Box 2, 1947 correspondence file

CHAPTER TWENTY-FOUR:

Page 228: For the newspaper report of Louise receiving the Kiwanis Club Distinguished Service Medal see University of Nebraska Special Collection Archives, Louise Pound Papers, Clipping, *The Lincoln Journal Star,*9 November 1947

Page 229: For a copy of the speech honoring Louise Pound at the Kiwanis Award presentation see NSHS Archives, Louise Pound Papers, Box 2, Correspondence file 1945.

Page 229: For the division of topics in Louise Pound's book of selected writings and for Arthur Kennedy's introduction as well Pound's article see Pound, Louise, *Selected Writings of Louise Pound*, (Lincoln) University of Nebraska Press, 1949, pp. ix-xii and Contents

Page 230: For Bruce Nicoll's article about Pound's *Selected Writings* see NSHS Archives, Louise Pound Papers, "Greeks Have a Word For It; We Americans Have 20," *Omaha World-Herald* magazine, 4 December 1949.

Page 230: For Louise Pound's article "American Euphemisms for Dying, Death, and Burial," see Pound, pp. 139-147

Page 230: For George Genzer's review of Pound's *Selected Writings* see NSHS Archives, Louise Pound Papers, Box 32, Clippings file, "Harvest of a Half Century of Scholarship."

Pages 230-231: For *Saturday Review's* comments on Pound's *Selected Writings* see NSHS Archives, Louise Pound Papers, Box 32. Clippings File, Clipping of "Belles-Letters" column in 6 May 1950 *Saturday Review*

Pages 231-232: For congratulatory letters from Dorothy Canfield Fisher, H.M. Beldon, and Melvin Van Den Bark o Pound concerning her *Selected Writings* see NSHS Archives, Louise Pound Papers, Box 2, Correspondence files

Page 232: For Louise Pound's letter to B.A. Botkin informing him of her election to the presidency of MLA and to the Nebraska Sports Hall of fame as well as a letter stating her determination to stop writing articles see Botkin, B.A., "Pound Sterling: Letters From a Lady Professor," *Prairie Schooner,* Vol. 33, No. 1, Spring 1959, pp. 20-31

Pages 232-233: For the MLA resolution congratulating Louise Pound on becoming the first MLA woman president see, NSHS Archives, Louise Pound Papers, Box 20.

Pages 233-234: For Louise Pound's presidential speech, "Then and Now," given at the 1955 MLA convention see NSHS Archives, Louise Pound Papers, Box 29, "Then and Now," PMLA, Vol. LXXI, March 1956, No. 1, pp. 1-13

Page 235: For H.L. Mencken's congratulatory letter to Louise and for Kathryn McHale's congratulatory letter referring to H.L. Mencken's personality and recent death see NSHS Archives, Louise Pound Papers, Box 2, 1950s correspondence file

Page 235: For Edgar Kemplar's comment referring to Louise Pound as a "prime mover" of the movement to emphasize American English see, Kemplar, Edgar, *The Irreverent Mr. Mencken: An Informal History of the Man and His Era,* (Boston) Little Brown & Company, 1950, pp. 128-29

CHAPTER TWENTY-FIVE:

Page 237: For Louise Pound's letter to Margaret Gettys, concerning the former Golden Fleece organization see NSHS Archives, Louise Pound Papers, Box 2.

Pages 237-238: For information about members of the Wooden Spoon presenting a series of skits based on Pound ancestors see Bennet Martin Library, (Lincoln) Pound Family File, Clipping, "Skit Based on Ancestors," *Lincoln Journal,* 10 April 1957

Page 238: For the article stating the Louise Pound was one of several authors honored at a party see NSHS Archives, Louise Pound Papers, Box 33, Clipping, "Author Honors Authors at Party."

Page 238: For Botkin and Alexander's articles about Louise see Faulkner, Virginia, editor, *Nebraska Roundup*, (Lincoln) University of Nebraska Press, 1957, pp. 232-239.

Louise Pound

Pages 238-239: For Roscoe Pound's article about Louise see NSHS Archives, Louise Pound Papers, Pound, Roscoe, "My Sister, Louise," *Omaha World-Herald* Magazine, 27 July 1957, Section C. (Printed originally in the *Boston Globe* 30 June 1957.)

Page 239: For Louise Pound's letter turning down Chancellor Hardin's invitation to speak at the University Honors Convocation see NSHS Archives, Louise Pound Papers, Box 2, 1957-58 correspondence file.

Pages 240: For Louise Pound's letter stating that she would not attend an Omaha golf celebration see Bennett Martin Library, (Lincoln) Pound Family File, Clipping from the *Lincoln Journal Star*, 3 February 1965.

Page 240: For Louise Pound's letter to B.A. Botkin concerning her refusal of the presidency of the American Names Society see Botkin, B.A., "Pound Sterling: Letters From a Lady Professor," *Prairie Schooner*, Vol. 33, No. 1, Spring 1959, pp. 20-31

Pages 240-241: For Ani Phister's letters about modern young women and her opinion on modern writers see NSHS Archives, Louise Pound Papers, Box 2, Ani Phister letters

Page 241: For Louise Pound's remarks to reporter Gretchen Schrag about modern young women see Schrag, Gretchen, "Miss Pound, English Professor, Reveals Tales of Times When She Had Tennis, Bicycle, Golf Titles," *Daily Nebraskan*, Vol. 21, No. 92, 3 February 1932

Page 241: For Ani Phister's letter asking Louise to write her a note, see NSHS Archives, Louise Pound Papers, Box 2, Ani Phister letters

Page 242: For Louise's letter to Botkin inviting him to dinner in January 1958 see Botkin, B.A., "Pound Sterling: Letters from a Lady Professor," *Prairie Schooner*, Spring 1959, pp. 20-31.

CHAPTER TWENTY-SIX:

Pages 243: For details of changes Louise made to her will see University of Nebraska Love Library Special Collections, Louise Pound Papers, Box 1, Clippings, "Authoress Revised Her Will." (Undated.)

Page 244: For Olivia's letter to Mamie Meredith regarding the disposition of Louise Pound's books see NSHS Archives, Louise Pound Papers, Box 5, File 14, Correspondence with Mamie Meredith

Page 244: For Bernard Kreissman's letter requesting that Louise Pound give her papers to the University library see NSHS Archives, Louise Pound Papers, Box 2, 1956 Correspondence file

Page 244: For Louise Pound's letter to Melvin Van den Bark praising Mamie Meredith' accomplishments see NSHS Archives, Olivia Pound Papers, Box 5, File 13

Page 245: For the newspaper clipping in which the Pound siblings commented on the changes taking place around the Pound home see Bennett Martin Library, (Lincoln) Pound Family File, Clipping, "Pound Family Reunion Brings Back Memories," *Lincoln Journal & Star*, October 27, 1949

Page 245: For the article detailing the history and demolition of the Pound home see Bennett Martin Library, (Lincoln) Pound Family File, Clipping, "Pound Home, Early Lincoln Landmark, is Coming Down," *Lincoln Journal*, 21 March 1963

Page 245: For Kathryn A. McEwen's letter to Mamie Meredith referring to Louise Pound's final illness and death see NSHS Archives, Olivia Pound Papers, Box 5, Mamie Meredith Correspondence

Page 245: For Mamie Meredith's letter to Mari Sandoz which gave Olivia's explanation of Louise Pound's mysterious heart lesions see University of Nebraska Library Special Collections and Archives, Mari Sandoz correspondence, Sept 1-10, 1958

Page 246: For the history of Wyuka cemetery and Rudge Chapel see www.wyuka.com

Page 246: For Mamie Meredith's description of the atmosphere of Louise Pound's funeral see NSHS Archives, Olivia Pound Papers, Box 5, Correspondence with Mamie Meredith, 4 July 1958 letter. (Meredith mentions sending copies of Louise's funeral service in letters to others in which she mentions the atmosphere at the service.)

Pages 246-247: For a copy of Dr. Palmer's address at Louise Pound's funeral see Bennett Martin Library, (Lincoln), Pound Family File

Page 247: For Ani Phister's letter of condolence written to Olivia after learning of Louise's death see NSHS Archives, Louise Pound Papers, Box 2

Page 247: For Dorothy Canfield Fisher's letter of condolence written to Olivia on learning of Louise's death see NSHS Archives, Olivia Pound Papers, Box 5

Notes and Sources

Page 247: For obituaries of Louise Pound see Bennett Martin Library, (Lincoln) Pound Family File

Page 247: For B.A. Botkin's article praising Louise for her "dynamic view of modern historical study" see Botkin, B.A. "Louise Pound: 1872-1958," *Western Folklore,* 1959, Vol. 18, No. 3, pp. 201-02

Page 248: For comments in the introduction of *Nebraska Folklore* Pound, Louise. *Nebraska Folklore,* Lincoln, University of Nebraska Press, 1959

Page 248: For W.D. Aeschbacher's foreword to *Nebraska Folklore* see pp. ix-x

Page 248: For Pound's article "Nebraska Cave Lore," see Pound, p.2

Page 248: For further facts about John Brown and Harpers' Ferry see Yanak, Ted, & Cornelison, Pam, *The Great American History Fact-Finder,* (Boston, New York) Houghton Mifflin Company, 1993, p. 57

Page 249:" For Pound's article "Nebraska Snake Lore," see Pound, pp. 25-40

Page 249: For Pound's article "Nebraska Rain Lore and Rain Making" see Pound, pp. 41-60

Pages 249-250: For Pound's article "Nebraska Strongmen," see Pound, pp. 122-134

Page 250: For Pound's article "Some Old Nebraska Folk Customs, see Pound, pp. 184-208

Pages 250-251: For Pound's article "Folklore and Dialect" see Pound, pp.211-243

Page 251: For Meredith's letter to Sandoz discussing the disposition of the "effusive" Cather letter and Louise's clothing see University of Nebraska Special Collections and Archives, Mari Sandoz Correspondence, Sept. 1-10, (Letter of 10 September 1958.)

Page 251: For obituaries of Olivia Pound see NSHS Archives, Olivia Pound Papers, Box 6, Also see Bennett Martin Library. (Lincoln) Pound Family File

Page 252: For Louise Pound's statement "the more you know of anything in all its phases the more interesting it becomes," see Pound, Louise, *The Selected Writings of Louise Pound,* (Lincoln) University of Nebraska Press, 1949, p. 272

Page 252: For Mrs. Robert Lasch's statement about Louise Pound's influence on students, friends, and future generations see Malone, Kemp; Smith, Eldon C.; Meredith, Mamie J. (chairman); Louise Pound Memorial Committee, *Names,* Vol. VII, No. 1, March, 1959, pp 60-62.

INDEX

In the sub-headings of this index, Louise Pound's name is abbreviated to LP

Index

CPSIA information can be obtained at www.ICGtesting.com
Printed in the USA
241334LV00003B/1/A